CAMBRIDGE TEXTS IN THE
HISTORY OF POLITICAL THOUGHT

MARX
Early Political Writings

CAMBRIDGE TEXTS IN THE
HISTORY OF POLITICAL THOUGHT

Series editors

RAYMOND GEUSS
Lecturer in Social and Political Sciences, University of Cambridge

QUENTIN SKINNER
Professor of Political Science in the University of Cambridge

Cambridge Texts in the History of Political Thought is now firmly established as the major student textbook series in political theory. It aims to make available to students all the most important texts in the history of western political thought, from ancient Greece to the early twentieth century. All the familiar classic texts will be included but the series does at the same time seek to enlarge the conventional canon by incorporating an extensive range of less well-known works, many of them never before available in a modern English edition. Wherever possible, texts are published in complete and unabridged form, and translations are specially commissioned for the series. Each volume contains a critical introduction together with chronologies, biographical sketches, a guide to further reading and any necessary glossaries and textual apparatus. When completed, the series will aim to offer an outline of the entire evolution of western political thought.

For a list of titles published in the series, please see end of book.

MARX

Early Political Writings

EDITED AND TRANSLATED BY

JOSEPH O'MALLEY

Professor Emeritus
Marquette University

WITH

RICHARD A. DAVIS

Marquette University

CAMBRIDGE
UNIVERSITY PRESS

CAMBRIDGE UNIVERSITY PRESS
Cambridge, New York, Melbourne, Madrid, Cape Town, Singapore,
São Paulo, Delhi, Dubai, Tokyo

Cambridge University Press
The Edinburgh Building, Cambridge CB2 8RU, UK

Published in the United States of America by Cambridge University Press, New York

www.cambridge.org
Information on this title: www.cambridge.org/9780521349949

First published 1994
Third printing 2007

A catalogue record for this publication is available from the British Library

Library of Congress Cataloguing in Publication data
Marx, Karl, 1818–1883.
[Selections. English. 1994]
Marx: early political writings / edited by Joseph O'Malley.
p.   cm. – (Cambridge texts in the history of political thought)
Translated from the German.
Includes bibliographical references and index.
ISBN 0 521 34241 4 (hardback) – ISBN 0 521 34994 X (paperback).
1. Political science.   2. State. The.
I. O'Malley, Joseph J.   II. Title.   III. Series.
JC233   M29213   1994
306.2– dc20   93–31207 CIP

ISBN 978-0-521-34241-4 Hardback
ISBN 978-0-521-34994-9 Paperback

Transferred to digital printing 2009

Contents

Acknowledgements

The following people contributed to this volume by providing scholarly information or text resources, and I thank them for their help: Curtis Carter and Brigitte Coste (Marquette University) for European press material on the status of the new Marx-Engels critical edition; Terrell Carver (University of Bristol) for providing a copy of W. Hiromatsu's edition of 'The German Ideology. Part One'; Lawrence Stepelevich (Villanova University) for historical information on the careers and writings of the 'Young Hegelians'; Bertell Ollman (New York University), Jürgen Rojahn (International Institute for Social History, Amsterdam), and Maximilien Rubel (Centre National de la Recherche Scientifique, Paris) for detailed information about the status and prospects of the new Marx-Engels critical edition; and Allen Wood (Cornell University) for sharing his and H. B. Nisbet's Glossary from their new translation of Hegel's *Philosophy of Right*. Anne Pasero and Denis Savage (Marquette University), David Duquette (St Norbert College), David McLellan (University of Kent at Canterbury), Fred E. Schrader (Université de Paris-Sorbonne), and Burkhard Tuschling (Phillips-Universität Marburg) read early versions of the Editor's Introduction and offered suggestions for its improvement. Janette Hodge (Marquette University and Belmont Abbey College) prepared the entire first copy for the press, at times working under difficult circumstances, and also contributed editorial help; I am greatly indebted to her. Robin Brunette (Marquette University) prepared the final copy of the revised portions.

In recognition of all that he has done and continues to do to advance serious study of Karl Marx's thought and writings, I dedicate this volume, with deepest regard and respect, to Maximilien Rubel.

Editor's introduction

Karl Marx (1818–1883) wrote no single work in which the essential themes of his political thought are spelled out, no work analogous to, say, Plato's *Republic*, Hobbes' *Leviathan*, or Hegel's *Philosophy of Right*. To get the essentials of his political doctrine, one must read many of Marx's writings, both early and late, including not only things he published but also things left in manuscript form at his death. The editors of this series have decided to offer these writings in two volumes: the present one, which includes texts that pre-date *The Communist Manifesto*, which was published in February 1848, and a second, being edited by Dr Terrell Carver, which will include the *Manifesto* and writings subsequent to it.

Of Marx's writing of 1847 we include here two short pieces: an excerpt from the conclusion of *Poverty of Philosophy*, which was published in the middle of that year, and a speech he gave at the end of the year, shortly before he (and Friedrich Engels) began drafting the *Manifesto*. Our principal texts date from the period spring/summer 1843 to fall 1846. The first of these is Marx's 'Critique of Hegel's Philosophy of Right', excerpts from which are included here, and the last is chapter 1 of 'The German Ideology'. This latter text represents the culmination of a process that began in the earlier 'Critique' of Hegel: Marx's development of a complex insight which he called the 'guideline' (*Leitfaden*) for all of his subsequent theoretical work, and which others have dubbed his 'materialist' theory of history, society and politics (or 'historical materialism' etc.) – about the details of which we will say more below.

Neither the 1843 Hegel Critique nor 'The German Ideology' was published during Marx's lifetime. Moreover, of the six additional texts from the period of 1843–6 which are included here, only three were published by him: two essays that appeared in February 1844 in the *Deutsch-französische Jahrbücher*, which he co-edited with Arnold Ruge in Paris ('On the Jewish Question' and 'A Contribution to the Critique of Hegel's Philosophy of Right: Introduction') and an article published in August 1844 in a radical German-language newspaper in Paris, *Vorwärts!* ('Critical Marginal Notes on "The King of Prussia and Social Reform. By a Prussian" '). These three essays have long been recognised as important documents of Marx's intellectual development and statements of his pre-*Manifesto* political principles, and they are frequently cited in connection with his criticisms of religion, money and the state, and his call for working class ('proletarian') revolution.

Striking as these essays are, however, they do not, in isolation from the unpublished writings of the period, adequately express the complex process of development of Marx's political thought and of his 'materialist' insight, including the extent to which that development was nourished by near-incessant and intensive research, first in political theory and history, then in political economy. The record of these researches lies in Marx's study notebooks of 1843–7. The first five of these notebooks date from the summer of 1843 in Kreuznach, where Marx compiled them while also writing his 'Critique of Hegel's Philosophy of Right'. The results of this research (and to a lesser extent of Marx's earlier historical and legal studies at the University of Berlin) are evident in that Critique, as Marx increasingly used historical data in his criticisms of Hegel's doctrine on the state. The data bear especially on the relationship between property and political institutions, and between property and class divisions (e.g. pp. 17–21 below). The connection between his research in political history and his further research, to which that led, in political economy is plainly reflected in a topic-index he composed in one of his Kreuznach notebooks: In addition to explicitly political topics (e.g. parliament, nobility, bureaucracy, constituent assembly, popular sovereignty, division of powers and so on – all topics touched upon at one or another point in his Hegel Critique), there are 'property and its consequences', including 'the connection of property to lordship and servitude', 'property as condition for voting capacity', 'possession and property'; also 'state property', 'relationship of owner to community', and 'equality and property' (*MEGA²* IV, 2, 116–19). Again, Marx's increased focus on such themes is evident in the Hegel Critique (e.g. pp. 16, 23–5 below).

None the less, that Critique and its accompanying research were just the beginning of the process that would eventually lead to 'The German Ideology' and through that to the *Manifesto*. The Kreuznach research, which culminated in a focus on the French Revolution of 1789 – an event Marx equated with the 'genesis of the modern state' (e.g. p. 115 below) – is also reflected in his essay 'On the Jewish Question' (esp. pp. 43–8 below), which he wrote in large part immediately following his composition of the Hegel Critique and prior to his move from Kreuznach to Paris with his bride in fall 1843. His research was interrupted by the move itself and the task of resettling, then by the work of editing the *Deutsch-französische Jahrbücher* (most of which fell to Marx when his co-editor Ruge became ill) and by the events surrounding the immediate financial failure of the *Jahrbücher*, which was due mainly to censorship (e.g. 800 copies were confiscated by the police at the German border with Switzerland).

Marx resumed his studies in April of 1844, first on the French Revolution (he briefly planned to write a history of the Convention) and then in the literature of political economy. Nine of his 'Paris Notebooks', totalling 300 pages in the new critical edition (*MEGA²*), are filled with excerpts from works in political economy by Say, Skarbek, Smith, Ricardo, James Mill, MacCulloch, Prévost, Destutt de Tracy, Engels, Schütz, List, Osiander, Buret; also included are some excerpts from Hegel's *Phenomenology*. Additionally, there are notebook materials, another 130-odd pages in the same edition, containing excerpts from the political economic sources mentioned, arranged under the headings 'Wages of Labour', 'Profit of Capital', and 'Ground-Rent', together with reflections by Marx on such themes as 'self-estrangement', 'communism', 'money', and human nature as 'species-being' (*Gattungswesen*). These latter are the materials on which the humanistic image of Marx that emerged in the 1930s has been largely based: Editors, beginning with David Rjazanov in 1932, have separated out, rearranged, and presented these materials as the so-called 'Economic and Philosophic Manuscripts of 1844' – a practice which has recently come under sharp scholarly criticism (esp. Rojahn 1983, 1985). From these notebook materials – none of which appeared in print during Marx's lifetime – we include excerpts relevant to his political thought (pp. 71–96 below).

The Paris researches in political economy, as well as the Kreuznach-Paris studies on the French Revolution, are clearly reflected in Marx's 'Critical Marginal Notes on "The King of Prussia and Social Reform" . . . ', where he used his political economic, as well as his historical, sources to expose the shallowness of the social-political analysis of his erstwhile colleague, Ruge (e.g. pp. 100–5 below). Following his composition of this essay, and his and his family's enforced move to Brussels at the beginning of 1845, Marx continued his political economic studies, including a research trip to Manchester with his friend and collaborator Engels in July and August 1845. In the period between February and June alone he compiled notes 'on some sixty books' (Rubel 1981, 123). From his arrival in Brussels through to the end of 1847 he read and excerpted from practically every important political economist whom he had not studied earlier (this in addition to re-reading some authors, e.g. Smith, Ricardo and MacCulloch): Petty, Davenant, Browning, Cooper, Sadler, Tooke, Gilbart, Edmonds, Cobbett, Senior, Thompson, Atkinson, Wade, Eden, Aiken, J.S. Mill *et al.*, and most notably G. von Gülich, from whose five-volume *History of the Commerce, Industry, and Agriculture of the Most Important Commercial States of our Time*, which appeared between 1830 and 1845, Marx compiled over 900 pages (in the *MEGA*² edition) of excerpts during the period September 1846 – December 1847. Nor were Marx's researches limited to political economy, but extended as well to other historical subjects, such as the history of science and technology, all of which contributed to the development of his thought in this period.

Moreover, Marx's extant notebooks are not a complete record of his studies from 1843 onward. Some notebooks have been lost, and even where it is likely that none has been, as with his Kreuznach studies, we know that he read authors who are not included in his notebooks, e.g. A. de Tocqueville and G. de Baumont, who were, along with Thomas Hamilton, early sources for his views on the character of society and politics in the United States (see pp. 32–3, 35, 44, 53 below).

We stress the importance of Marx's researches, and of the notebooks in which they are, albeit incompletely, recorded – and whose contents are at long last becoming generally available, in Sect. IV of the *MEGA*² – because they are evidence of how Marx's so-called 'materialist' theory of history and politics actually took shape. One need only compare the historical matter in his 1843 Hegel Critique with the historical and political-economic material in chapter 1 of 'The German Ideology' (e.g. pp. 149–65 below) to begin to appreciate the role played by his Kreuznach-Paris-Brussels-Manchester researches in Marx's gradual discovery, or formulation, of the 'guideline' for his subsequent life's work. There can be no doubt that Marx had these researches in mind, along with his other writings of 1843–1847, when he later referred to the 'investigation' (*Untersuchung*) that led him to that 'guideline' (*MEGA*² II, 2, 100). In sum, his historical (and political) 'materialism' was a product of lengthy and intense immersion in research and reflection on its data. Before seeing some details of the 'guideline', we should note another, related development in Marx's early thought, which is reflected in the texts presented here: his idea for a major theoretical project encompassing a critical treatise on the state.

As noted above, none of the three largest texts from this period – the 1843 'Critique of Hegel's Philosophy of Right', the 1844 Paris Notebooks (including the so-called 'Economic and Philosophic Manuscripts'), and 'The German Ideology' of 1845–6 – was published in Marx's lifetime. Yet, Marx had plans for publication bearing on all three, and tracing those plans yields an interesting picture of how his theoretical project evolved.

Marx first planned an immediate revision for publication of his 1843 Hegel Critique. But the complexity of themes in the work, he later wrote, made the revision impractical; and so he projected instead a series of brochures, each devoted to a thematic element in the work, to be followed and concluded by a synthesising treatise. While that change of plan was occurring, however, Marx was already becoming absorbed in the literature of political economy and coming to the conclusion that a critique of this subject should precede the projected critique of politics. The critique of political economy was to be based on the materials collected in his Paris Notebooks. Near the end of one these, he jotted down a 'preface' (*Vorrede*) to the projected work. In this 'preface' Marx explained his change of plans and his intentions as follows:

> In the *Deutsch-französische Jahrbücher* I announced my critique of legal theory and the science of politics in the form of a critique

of *Hegel's* Philosophy of Right. However, in preparing that work
[i.e. the revision of the 1843 Critique manuscript] for the press,
it became clear that it was completely inappropriate to mix criticism that is directed strictly against philosophical speculation
together with criticism of the particular subject-matters themselves: it would impede my development of the material and make
comprehension of it difficult. Moreover, if compressed into a
single writing, the wealth and diversity of the subjects to be
treated would have allowed for only an aphoristic treatment, and
for its part such a treatment would have given the appearance of
an arbitrary systematising. Accordingly, I will publish the critique
of law, of morals, politics, etc. in a series of separate and independent brochures or booklets, and then in conclusion attempt
in a special work to show the connectedness of the whole, the
relationship of the individual parts, and finally to provide the
critique of the speculative treatment of that material. Therefore,
the present writing [i.e. the projected revision of the Paris political-economic notebook materials] will deal with the state, law,
morals, civil life, etc. only to the extent that political economy
itself deals expressly with these subjects ... (*MEGA*^{2} I, 2, 314)

The mix of criticisms of 'speculation' and of 'particular subject matters' in his 1843 Hegel Critique, which Marx cited here as an obstacle
to its revision, can be seen in the excerpts from that text presented
in this volume, e.g. the passages on monarchy, sovereignty and property (pp. 20–5 below).

In this 'preface' Marx clearly put his projected critique of political
economy before his critique of law and politics; he intended to do
the former immediately, and then go on to do the latter; and this
order of treatment is precisely in keeping with his developing insight
that legal and political institutions are rooted in 'civil society', which
is the subject matter of political economy. In other words, within a
year of his completion of his Hegel Critique, Marx came to see the
imperative need for a critique of civil society, i.e. of political economy,
something he had mentioned in the Hegel Critique itself only in
passing and as secondary to the critique of the state (e.g. pp. 18, 20
below). Now, however, in fall of 1844, he implies that the critique
of political economy is a systematic prerequisite of the critique of law
and state, in short, of politics.

Yet, some ambiguity on this issue apparently remained in Marx's
thinking, for within five months of writing the 'preface' just quoted,
he signed a contract with a German publisher to produce a two-

volume 'Critique of Politics and Political Economy'. In connection with this project, Marx jotted down in one of his notebooks a list of topics for the critique of politics. The list includes themes treated in his 1843 Hegel Critique and covered in his notebooks, especially those from Kreuznach (see 'Points on the State and Bourgeois Society', p. 115 below). The first of the two projected volumes, then, would presumably be a revised version of the 1843 Critique, and the second a revised version of the Paris Notebook material in political economy. But clearly this new project reversed the order of treatment which Marx had seemingly decided upon only several months earlier and announced in the 'preface' in the Paris Notebooks. In sum, between August 1843 and January 1845 Marx's theoretical project changed from (1) a critique of politics (revision of the Hegel Critique) to (2) a critique of political economy (revision of the Paris Notebook materials) followed by the critique of politics (further revised as a series of short books), and then to (3) a critique of politics in one volume accompanied and followed by a critique of political economy in a second volume.

In the end, however, Marx did not produce the two-volume work, and the publisher eventually cancelled the contract. Instead, after moving to Brussels and continuing his research in political economy as intensively as ever, he resolved to effect a kind of theoretical ground-clearing by doing, in collaboration with Engels and, to a lesser extent, Moses Hess and Joseph Weydemeyer, a criticism of contemporary German (i.e. 'Young Hegelian') philosophy and German socialist doctrines. This work was 'The German Ideology' whose first chapter, entitled 'Feuerbach' (actually among the last parts written of the extant manuscript), Marx apparently had in mind already in early spring of 1845. At that time he wrote down in the same notebook containing his 'Points on the State and Bourgeois Society' a set of eleven notes (or 'theses': a denomination affixed to them by others, and which has become canonical) under the heading '*Ad Feuerbach*' . These notes draw together in a highly condensed, even aphoristic, form elements of Marx's developing 'materialism', 'humanistic' themes from the Paris notebooks, and criticisms of Hegelian philosophy from the same notebooks and other earlier writings (see the notes 'On Feuerbach', pp. 116–18 below).

The synthesis of earlier conceptual elements, informed by his ongoing research, was most fully achieved, however, in the chapter on Feuerbach in 'The German Ideology' (pp. 119–81 below).

Considered by some commentators to mark a 'break' in Marx's intellectual and doctrinal development, involving a rejection of his philosophical and humanist past and his adoption of a new, scientific beginning, chapter 1 of 'The German Ideology' may instead, and more accurately, be seen as a masterpiece of synthesis in which every one of Marx's earlier insights from his 1843 Hegel Critique onward – philosophic, political, historical, economic – is preserved. The notion that modern wage-labour is the antithesis of human 'self-activity' and involves the estrangement of human productive capacities (Paris Notebooks); that human beings will have to 'reappropriate their own forces' (Jewish Question); that the modern working class is revolutionary *par excellence* in its universalistic character (Hegel Critique, and the 'Intro.' to it, also 'King of Prussia and Social Reform'); the idea of universally developed individuals (Paris Notebooks), and of 'communism' as a transitional process and not a future social-economic form (Paris Notebooks); the notion of 'democracy' as something distinct from all forms of political state (Hegel Critique): all of these themes and ideas are present in the chapter on Feuerbach, blended together with the results of Marx's studies to that point in the history and theory of politics and political economy.

Marx, Engels, and Weydemeyer (who acted as intermediary with publishers) failed in their efforts to publish 'The German Ideology'. The version they sent to the press, which was certainly other than the manuscript that has survived, is long lost. Even as the prospects for publication dimmed, Marx continued to work on the chapter on Feuerbach, adding some late thoughts in the form of comments and other additions, some of them highly interesting, into Engels' earlier prepared smooth version. He then composed a 'Preface' to the work (pp. 119–20 below), before finally, as he later put it, consigning the manuscripts 'to the gnawing criticism of the mice', content at having achieved 'self-clarification' (*MEGA*² II, 2, 102).

The self-clarification Marx referred to definitively established, among other things, the order of theoretical treatment of political economy and politics. Treatment of the former (i.e. the 'anatomy of civil society') is more fundamental than and an essential prerequisite for treatment of the latter (i.e. 'law and state'). This conclusion would govern Marx's subsequent plans for his theoretical masterwork, which by the late 1850s would take the form of a six-part treatise: on 'capital, landed property, wage labour; the state, foreign [or international] commerce, world market'. His first public announcement of this large project, in 1859, he used as an occasion also to explain the genesis and features of his particular approach ('guideline') to his subject matter; and he alluded to 'The German Ideology' as the place where it was 'worked out' for the first time (*Preface* to *A Contribution to the Critique of Political Economy: MEGA*^{2} II, 2, 99–102). Let us see some details of that approach.

Marx's 'materialist' guideline includes a general judgement about the relationship between the political and the social-economic processes of life and then a set of judgements about elements and dynamics within the social-economic processes. The general judgement is that the social-economic processes are what is fundamental to human life and that political processes, the institutions, procedures and modes of thinking proper to law and government, are secondary and derivative. Marx stated this general judgement in conscious opposition to Hegel, for whom law (*Recht*) and state (*Staat*) are actualisations of freedom, i.e. actualisations of the human spirit. Against this, Marx asserted

> that legal relationships as well as forms of state are to be understood neither on their own terms nor in terms of the so-called general development of the human spirit, but are rather rooted in the material relations of life, the totality of which Hegel termed '*bürgerliche Gesellschaft*', i.e. 'civil society' ... but that the anatomy of civil society is to be sought in political economy. (*MEGA*^{2} II, 2, 100)

In asserting this general position, Marx claimed no originality. Rather, as we see in 'The German Ideology', he recognised and located himself within an existing historiographic tradition represented by certain of the French and English authors he had studied beginning in 1843 in Kreuznach (p. 127 below; cf. Rubel, in *Œuvres* III, 1722, n.2).

Within the social-economic processes, Marx distinguished two fundamental, interacting elements. These are the 'forces of production' and the 'relations of production'. The forces of production (also called the 'productive forces') are the creative capacities of human beings, which they exercise in order to meet their needs, and which they further develop in the course of that exercise. The relations of production (in 'The German Ideology' also called 'relations' and 'forms of interaction') are the social relationships in and through which human beings exercise and develop their creative capacities, their forces of production.

The interaction between the forces of production and the relations of production is complex. First, the relations of production, whose totality constitutes a social-economic form of society, i.e. a specific form of civil society, foster the exercise and development of the forces of production both of society as a whole and of its members. In fostering this exercise and growth, the social 'mode of cooperation' may itself be seen as a 'productive force' (p. 128 below). More generally, however, the relations of social interaction, on the one hand, and the productive forces, or creative capacities, on the other, are distinguished as correlative elements.

The development of the productive forces, which a set of productive relations fosters, brings about the eventual conflict or 'antagonism' between the set of relations and the now-enhanced forces. Put otherwise, the now-enhanced, actual creative capacities of a society collectively, and of its members individually, come to be constricted by the very social form of interaction which had earlier contributed to their enhancement. The antagonism is between forces that grow and relations that do not change. A point arrives at which the relations, having fostered all the development of the forces of which they are capable, prevent, or in Marx's terms, become 'fetters' upon, the full exercise and fuller development of the productive forces. The antagonism is resolved by a social revolution out of which come new relations of production, a new social-economic form consonant with the enhanced productive forces prepared by the old, now-superseded social form. As a secondary, derivative element in this process political change also occurs; in fact, those caught up in the revolutionary transformation are prone to interpret what is happening to them in purely political or other 'ideological' terms. But what is really happening is that human creative energies and capacities are bursting through, throwing off, 'abolishing' or 'superseding' a totality of outdated, historically and humanly negative, social-economic relations. Such is the complex 'guideline' Marx derived from his process of 'self-clarification', beginning with his 'Critique of Hegel's Philosophy of Right' and culminating in 'The German Ideology' (chapter on Feuerbach), where he used the 'guideline' for the first time to clarify in particular (1) the transition of feudalism into modern 'bourgeois' society, and (2) the developing reality of this bourgeois society, with its capitalist system, as the present 'antagonistic' form of social production.

Marx set all this forth in 'The German Ideology' in a manner less concise but more interestingly nuanced than his 1859 Preface to *A Contribution to the Critique of Political Economy*. Where the *Preface* will appear to imply strict economic determinism in history, 'The German Ideology' recognises 'really significant intrusions of politics into history' (p. 140 below); and where the *Preface* will seem to imply strict determinism of consciousness within past historical revolutions, the earlier text offers a subtle qualification (p. 176 below). In such instances 'The German Ideology' may help us avoid an oversimplified reading of the later text.

Moreover, the core humanistic sense of the 'forces of production', i.e. that they have to do primarily with human creativity and 'self-activity', is more evident in 'The German Ideology' (e.g. pp. 175–6 below) than in the corresponding passages of the 1859 *Preface*. On the other hand, the *Preface* makes explicit that the 'legal expression' for the relations of production is 'property relations', i.e. socially recognised and sanctioned relations of use and disposition of materials and instruments of production. A totality of relations of production, a form of social-economic interaction, is also a system of property relations (*MEGA²* II, 2, 100). But this idea, too, is already present in 'The German Ideology', where the various historical social-economic forms are described as so many different systems of property (e.g. pp. 149–52 below). Overall, one can say that in his presentation and use of it in 'The German Ideology', Marx's materialist guideline reflects its actual genesis as an insight grounded in research, serving as an hypothesis for interpreting data of social, economic, and political history (including contemporary events), and not as a universal law of historical development, as most species of subsequent 'Marxism' have tended to construe it.

One element of his doctrine in 'The German Ideology' is particularly important to the question of whether and how Marx remains relevant as a political thinker, given the recent 'collapse of communism' and the correlative, so-called 'triumph of capitalism'. That element is his concept of the 'world market' as both the culminating framework of capitalism and the matrix within which are prepared the prerequisites and the agencies for capitalism's 'abolition' or supersession.

Under the materialist guideline of 'The German Ideology' (repeated as well in the 1847 *Poverty of Philosophy*, p. 183 below) a social-economic form (a totality of relations of production and a property system) does not give way until it has generated the enhanced productive forces (actualised human creative capacities) of which it is capable. Those forces are what burst through the old relations, which had become their 'fetters', and lay foundations for the new. Capitalism's full development, the form it assumes in order to actualise fully the productive forces latent within it, is the 'world market'. This is 'capital's' development to the status of the world-dominant system. Capitalism, for Marx, was destined from its inception to culminate in a global system which it alone, free of competitive systems, dominates: Capitalism's world triumph is part of its very nature. This conclusion, already reached in 'The German Ideology', is consistently reasserted in Marx's subsequent writings. In the restrained, Hegelian language of the *Grundrisse*:

> The tendency to create the *world market* is directly given in the very concept of capital. Every limit appears as a barrier to be overcome. (*MEGA²* II, 1.2, 320–1)

And in the more colourful language of *The Communist Manifesto* (sect. 1), the bourgeoisie

> compels all nations, on pain of extinction, to adopt its mode of production; it compels them to introduce what it calls civilisation into their midst, that is, to become bourgeois themselves. In a word, it creates a world after its own image. (*MEGA¹* I, 6, 530)

Capitalism's triumph, however, is at once its fulfillment and the beginning of its supersession; for its triumph, as 'The German Ideology' makes clear, includes the generation of the material and spiritual conditions, the instrumentalities and the 'communist' consciousness, required to construct the post-bourgeois order (pp. 178–81 below). This doctrine was to comprise the core of Marx's subsequently projected treatise on the 'world market', where the double outcome of capitalism's fulfillment and incipient supersession is manifested in the 'crises' that plague the world-system of capital: They are the marks of the fatal antagonism within the system, and they are the harbingers of the revolution which will abolish it (*MEGA*² II, 1.1, 43, 151–2, 187: English in *MECW* 28, 45, 160, 194–5).

Against this textual background, we can say, therefore, that the events of the late 1980s and early 1990s neither falsify nor render irrelevant Marx's political thought. The 'communism' which has collapsed resembled in fact nothing so much as the 'crude communism' he himself condemned in 1844 (see pp. 78–9 below). And the 'triumph' of capitalism – if what we are witnessing is indeed a triumph – is an event predicted by the materialist guideline formulated in his early writings, a guideline that continues to provide a powerful analytical perspective from which to interpret presently unfolding events.

Let us turn now to the question of utopian and millennialist elements in Marx's early political thought. Such elements appear to be present throughout his early writings, in his notions of the 'abolition' (or disappearance) of the state, the abolition of the division of labour, of labour itself, and of private property; and the achievement by human beings, for the first time in history, of control over their own, and external, nature, and over the conditions of their lives. All of these developments are to be brought about or prepared for in the process of communism and are to be enduring features of the post-bourgeois order (e.g. pp. 10, 27, 69, 79, 92, 134, 136, 168, 173–4 below).

Nor are such expressions found only in Marx's early writings: In his *Grundrisse* of 1857–8, for example, he reasserted almost verbatim ideas from the 'Paris Notebooks' and 'The German Ideology' affirming the 'universality' of human nature and the full development of human control over both human and external nature (cf. pp. 74–6, 82, below; and *MEGA*² II, 1.2, 392; English in *MECW* 28, 411–12). And in the same text of 1859 in which he announced his materialist guideline, in a book offered to the public as a work of 'science', he described bourgeois (i.e. present-day) society as the final 'antagonistic' form of society, and thus the form with which the 'pre-history of human society draws to a close' (*MEGA*² II. 2, 101). When we ask about utopianism and millennialism in Marx's early writings, therefore, we are asking about features of his thought that persist into his later writings and so cannot be written off as mere expressions of youthful, idealistic enthusiasm.

The key to these features in the early writings lies in Marx's notion of democracy. Regarding the 'abolition of the division of labour', for example, it is clear in chapter 1 of 'The German Ideology' that the issue for Marx is not whether there will be some division of labour within human social-economic production, but whether the division will be 'natural' (*naturwüchsig*), i.e. spontaneously generated and imposed upon those caught up in it – as has been the case, in his view, throughout history – or, alternatively, 'free' (*freiwillig*), i.e. a product of deliberation and choice, of collective self-direction or self-governance by those involved. This contrast between what is 'natural' and what is 'free', and the notion of democracy implicitly connected with it, runs through chapter 1 of 'The German Ideology' as the background of all of Marx's millennialist and utopian sounding expressions (e.g. pp. 132–3, 174). His concept of democracy is the key to the meaning of all of them.*

Three features of Marx's concept of democracy are especially relevant. The first is his idea of 'true', or unqualified, democracy; the second is his idea of what is required for true democracy to exist; and the third is his idea of the character of institutions within true democracy. Let us consider each of these features.

True democracy is defined by contrast with the political form of 'republic'. A republic – of which the United States is for Marx the example *par excellence* – has democratic political arrangements, e.g.

---

* This is perhaps the best point to mention the often-cited passage in chapter 1 of 'The German Ideology' where future 'communistic society' is described as one in which 'society regulates the general production' allowing individuals to move randomly and as they wish through a range of bucolic and abstractly intellectual activities: hunting, fishing, cattle tending, 'critical criticism' (p. 132 below). Oddly out of keeping with the critical thrust of chapter 1 as a whole, and clearly evoking Fourier's model of an agricultural utopia, this passage has been for Marx's severer critics evidence of his naivete or incoherence, and for many more sympathetic critics and commentators a source of embarrassment or perplexity. Some of the latter have pointedly ignored it. Some have suspected it to be a parody or joke. Now, thanks to W. Hiromatsu's 1974 edition of the chapter on Feuerbach, which has been largely ignored in the West, we can see more clearly than before the places where Marx inserted words, comments, etc. into Engels' smooth copy. Hiromatsu's edition (the new *MEGA*[2] version of the text is not yet available) has lead one commentator to conclude that the passage is Engels' (perhaps unconscious) parody of Fourier's utopia, into which Marx sarcastically or humorously inserted the 'critical critics', against whom 'The German Ideology' is largely directed. In this case, the passage should not be taken as a serious expression of Marx's ideas about either 'communism' or the 'abolition' of the division of labour. (See Carver 1988 in the bibliography below.)

elected legislature and executive; i.e. it has a democratic form of government; it is a formal political democracy. But it is not true democracy. The reason is that democratic arrangements do not operate within, do not 'permeate' the 'material state', civil society, the social-economic order of life:

> In all states distinct from democracy the *state*, the law, the *constitution* is what dominates without actually governing, i.e. materially permeating the content of the remaining non-political spheres ... The struggle between monarchy and republic is itself still a struggle within the abstract form of state. The *political* republic is democracy within the abstract form of state. Hence the abstract state-form of democracy is the republic; but here [i.e. in true democracy] it [democracy] ceases to be *mere political* constitution ... Property etc., in brief the entire content of law and the state is, with small modification, the same in North America as in Prussia. There accordingly, the *republic* is a mere state *form* just as monarchy is here. The content of the state lies outside these constitutions. (p. 10 below)

Democracy 'ceases to be *mere political* constitution' when democratic procedures cease to operate at the level of political formality alone and operate instead, or as well, within the social-economic sphere of civil society. In short, Marx's 'true democracy' is 'economic democracy': determination of social-economic processes and relationships by democratic procedure in lieu of their determination by the 'natural spontaneity' (*Naturwüchsigkeit*) of the 'hidden hand' or uncontrolled, supposedly 'free', market mechanisms. These, for Marx, are euphemisms for and rationalisations of the generalised egoism and particularistic self-seeking characteristic of the modern (bourgeois) form of civil society, which he describes in 'On the Jewish Question' and elsewhere as a Hobbesian *bellum omnium contra omnes* (esp. pp. 36–7, 46 below). His call in that essay for people to reappropriate their 'own forces' (p. 50 below) exactly prefigures the vision in 'The German Ideology' of collective, democratically exercised control by people over their conditions of existence, over their social-economic processes and relationships (pp. 174, 178–80 below).

For true democracy to exist, however, people must recognise that they share a common interest, namely, preservation of the social whole as a common good on which they depend for their particular well-being. This recognition carries with it the task of continually reconciling and balancing the 'common' and the 'particular' interests, the continuous effort to effect the synthesis of universal and particular. It is the total lack of such recognition and effort, the lack of 'even the *semblance* of a universal content' (p. 49 below) that makes modern civil society a 'war of all against all', the atomistic correlate of the political state and its illusory universality.

Marx took this point up again in 'The German Ideology'. He and Engels first identified 'the common interest of all individuals who associate with one another' as grounded in 'the mutual dependence of the individuals'. They noted that within their mutual dependence, the division of labour has historically generated conflict between individuals' particular interest and their common interest:

> Precisely because of this conflict of particular and common interests, the common interest takes on as the *state* an independent shape, separate from the genuine individual and collective interests, and simultaneously presents itself as an illusory community ... (p. 131 below)

Not satisfied with this formulation, Marx expanded on the point in a long note added alongside of Engels' smooth copy:

> It is precisely because individuals seek *only* their own particular interests, taking these to coincide in no way with their common interest, that this common interest asserts itself as a particular, peculiar 'universal' interest, 'alien' to and 'independent' of them; an alternative is to operate, necessarily, within this discord [of their particular and their genuine common interests], as is the case in democracy. On the other hand, when the *practical* struggle of these particular interests is in constant opposition to both the *genuine* and the illusory common interests, it makes necessary the *practical* intervention and the exercise of restraint by the illusory 'universal' interest, in the form of the state. (p. 132 below)

Democracy, therefore, requires that individuals recognise a 'genuine' common interest and make an ongoing effort to resolve the 'conflict' between that common interest and their particular interests. In this, democracy is the antithesis of all forms of political state (including the 'republic'), which exist because individuals either refuse or are unable to recognise their genuine common interest and serve it along with their particular interests. Were they to do so, the political state and all of its organs would 'disappear' (p. 10 below). A society of individuals capable of defining their particular interests in light of the common interest or of seeking the common interest while pursuing their particular interests would have no need, Marx thought, for a professional governing class. Hence his assertion in the Hegel Critique that

> the abolition of the bureaucracy can consist only in the universal interest becoming *actually* ... a particular interest; and this is possible only through the *particular* interest actually becoming universal. (p. 14 below)

Even before seeing the third feature of Marx's concept of democracy, we can already draw the following conclusions. Marx's notions of the 'abolition' or 'supersession' (*Aufhebung*) of the division of labour, of labour itself, and of the political state and its constituent organs do not envisage an absence of all organised division of social-economic functions, an absence of all differentiation in talent and capacities among people (see pp. 95–6 below, where such differentiation is for him a clear prerequisite of truly human social production), an absence of the productive 'species-activity' itself of human beings, and an absence of regularised procedures for identifying and effecting common ends and the means to them. Rather, 'abolition' ('supersession') for Marx means transforming the extant, 'natural' and spontaneously generated bourgeois form of the division of labour, of wage-labour, and of 'political state' into forms consonant with 'true democracy'. It means replacing these historical products of 'natural spontaneity' with a democratic organisation of social-economic life and of humankind's collective creative forces, an exercise by individuals of their creative capacities that is truly human 'self-activity', and (what is implicit in the democratisation of social-economic life) the fullest popular participation in determining humankind's collective social-economic ends and means.

Were such democracy to exist (here now the third feature of Marx's concept), the social 'relations of production' in and through which individuals exercise and develop their creative capacities (productive forces) would themselves cease to be products of 'natural spontaneity', marked by 'fixity and independence' from human control (p. 171). Instead, they would be products of the deliberate self-determining activity of those whose relations they are.

As such they would be marked by openness and responsiveness to change in keeping with the continually developing social 'forces of production'. In 'The German Ideology', Marx states this in terms of associated individuals creating their form of interaction (e.g. pp. 173–5). But this is an idea already asserted in the Hegel Critique, with reference to a people's 'constitution':

> To be sure, entire state constitutions have changed such that as new requirements gradually arose, the old [order] broke down; but for the *new* constitution a real revolution was always necessary ... [Hegel's] category of *gradual* transition is, first of all, historically false, and second, it explains nothing. In order that the constitution be altered, and thus that this illusory appearance [of its permanence] not be in the end forcefully shattered; in order, moreover, that man do consciously what he is otherwise forced to do unconsciously by the essence or nature of the thing, it is necessary that the movement of the constitution, that *progress*, be made the principle of the constitution, thus that the real cornerstone of the constitution, the people, be made the principle of the constitution. Progress itself is then the constitution. (p. 16 below)

Although the word is not mentioned, there can be no doubt that Marx is speaking here about democracy. Now we need only substitute 'relations of production' or 'form of interaction' for 'constitution' to see the doctrine of 'The German Ideology' (and the Preface of 1859) prefigured here: In true democracy, the relations of production will not ossify into 'fetters' on the productive forces exercised and enhanced by means of them; hence, they need never 'be forcefully shattered'. Evidently Marx envisaged the post-bourgeois form of society, unique in history in being devoid of antagonism between the forces and relations of production, as the first historical actualisation of true or unqualified democracy, and as such the first fully 'human' society.

We conclude then by stating once more that Marx's social and political doctrine in his writings up to 1848 was the product of intense intellectual effort at research and reflection, and by observing that its central concepts remain relevant today and are as much or as little utopian as is the concept of democracy itself.

Chronology of Marx's life and career, 1818–48

1818 15 May: Birth in Trier (Trèves).
1819 Sept.–Oct.: The 'Carlsbad Decrees' institute censorship of university teaching and scholarly publication; in Prussia, censorship is extended to newspapers.
1820 Jan.: Publication of Hegel's *Philosophy of Right*.
1830 July: 'July Revolution' in France.
      Oct.: Enters Friedrich Wilhelm Gymnasium in Trier.
1831 Nov.: Death of Hegel in Berlin.
1835 Sept.–Oct.: Graduates from Gymnasium and enters University of Bonn to study law. 'September Laws' promulgated in France, restricting freedom of press and banning criticism of existing property relations and political institutions.
1836 Founding in Paris of 'The League of the Just' (formerly 'League of the Banished'), first German workers' organisation.
      Oct.: Transfers to University of Berlin.
1838 May: Death of Marx's father in Trier.
1840 May–June: Death of Friedrich Wilhelm III and succession of Friedrich Wilhelm IV to throne of Prussia.
1841 Feb.: Publication of Feuerbach's *The Essence of Christianity*.
      March–Apr.: Finishes studies in Berlin; submits doctoral dissertation ('The Difference Between the Natural Philosophies of Democritus and Epicurus') to University of Jena, which awards the degree.
1842 April: Fails to gain an academic position; writes articles for *German Yearbooks* and *Rhenish Gazette*.

Oct.: Moves to Cologne and is appointed editor-in-chief of *Rhenish Gazette*.

Nov.: First meeting with Friedrich Engels. Publication of L. Stein's *Socialism and Communism in Contemporary France*.

Dec.: Publication of W. Weitling's *Guarantees of Harmony and Freedom*.

1843 Feb.: Publication of Feuerbach's 'Preliminary Theses for the Reform of Philosophy'.

Mar.: Under pressure of censorship, resigns from *Rhenish Gazette*, which is subsequently suppressed.

June: Marries Jenny von Westphalen; refuses post of editor-in-chief of *Prussian State Newspaper*.

Summer–autumn: Drafts 'Critique of Hegel's Philosophy of Right' and compiles 'Kreuznach Notebooks' on political history and theory. Begins drafting 'On the Jewish Question'.

Oct.: Moves to Paris to co-edit with A. Ruge the *German-French Yearbooks*.

(?) Dec.: Reads M. Hess' 'On Money'; continues research on French Revolution.

1844 Feb.: Publication of the *German-French Yearbooks*, including Marx's 'Contribution to the Critique of Hegel's Philosophy of Right: Introduction' and 'On the Jewish Question'.

Spring–summer: First studies in political economy; compiles Paris Notebooks.

Apr.: Reacquaintance with Engels, beginning lifelong friendship and collaboration.

June: Uprising of weavers in Silesia.

Aug.: Publishes 'Critical Marginal Notes on "The King of Prussia and Social Reform. By a Prussian" ', in *Forward!* (Paris).

Nov.: Publication of M. Stirner's *The Ego and Its Property*.

1845 Jan.: Drafts 'Points on the State and Bourgeois Society'.

Feb.: Expelled from Paris by request of Prussian Government; moves to Brussels. Publishes *The Holy Family*, a polemic against B. Bauer, M. Stirner *et al.*; continues studies of political economists, compiling additional notebooks.

Mar.: Drafts notes 'On Feuerbach'.

July–Aug.: Travels with Engels to London and Manchester for political economic research.

Autumn: Begins drafting 'The German Ideology', a critique of recent German philosophy and socialist theory.

Dec.: Formally renounces his Prussian citizenship.

1846 Feb.: Sets up, with Engels, the 'Communist Correspondence Committee' in Brussels.

Spring–autumn: Continued drafting of 'The German Ideology'; efforts to publish it fail.

Dec.: Reads J.-P. Proudhon's *System of Economic Contradictions or Philosophy of Poverty.*

1847 Jan.: Joins 'The League of the Just'.

June: First congress, in London, of 'The Communist League', successor to 'The League of the Just'.

July: Publishes *Poverty of Philosophy*, a response to Proudhon's *System.* . . .

Aug.: Helps organise 'Brussels German Workers' Association'.

Sept.: Begins collaboration with the *German Brussels Gazette.*

Nov.: Elected vice-president of the 'Brussels Democratic Association'.

Nov.–Dec.: With Engels attends second congress of 'The Communist League' in London; agrees to draft a programme for the League; addresses London meeting of the 'Fraternal Democrats' on the subject of Poland; begins drafting a 'Manifesto of the Communist Party'.

1848 Feb.: Publication in London of the 'Manifesto of the Communist Party'.

Bibliography

The intent here is to provide students with information about primary text editions in German, French, and English that are especially important in Marx-scholarship past and present. Attention to secondary sources is limited to selected titles, including biographies, that students may find helpful for further study either of Marx's thought overall or of his political thought in particular.

Primary Sources

MEGA[1] Karl Marx/Friedrich Engels/*Historisch-kritische Gesamtausgabe* (Marx-Engels-Institut, Moscow), ed. D. Rjazanov (1927–30/1) and V. Adoratski (1931–2). Frankfurt-on-Main and Berlin: Marx-Engels-Verlag, 1927–32, 1935. The first attempt to produce a critical edition through collaboration of the German Social Democratic Party (Berlin), the Institute of Sociology (Frankfurt-on-Main) and the Marx-Engels-Institute (Moscow). Projected to include forty in-octavo vols. divided into three sections: I. philosophic, historical, political and economic writings, with the exception of *Capital* (17 vols.); II. *Capital*, including the unpublished mss. of Marx and vols. I, II, III and IV ('Theories of Surplus Value') of *Capital* (13 vols.); III. complete correspondence of Marx and Engels (10 vols.); there was to have been a supplementary sect. IV with indexes of names, subjects, texts and works cited, and a detailed chronology of Marx's life and work. Publication broke off without explanation in 1932 with 10 vols. published (six in sect. I, four in sect. III). Two additional vols. appeared in 1935, one containing Engels' scientific writings to commemorate the 40th anniversary of his death. This edition has been reprinted: Glaschutten im Taunus, Verlag Detlev-Auvermann EG, 1970.

MEW Karl Marx/Friedrich Engels/*Werke* (Institut für Marxismus-Leninismus beim Zentralkomitee der Sozialistischen Einheitspartei Deutschlands). Berlin: Dietz Verlag, 1957–68. 41 vols. This edition was produced by the Institute for Marxism-Leninism in Berlin (German Democratic Republic) with collaboration of the Institute for Marxism-Leninism, Moscow. It was intended to be a 'working' not a 'critical' edition, and was not intended to be complete. All texts, including those originally written in languages other than German (e.g. 'The Civil War in France, 1871', *Misère de la Philosophie*) are presented in German.

Grundrisse Karl Marx, *Grundrisse der Kritik der politischen Ökonomie* (*Rohentwurf*) 1857–8. First published in two vols. and without critical apparatus in Moscow: Verlag für fremdsprachige Literatur, 1939 and 1941; photomechanically reproduced in one vol. Berlin: Dietz Verlag, 1953. The title is not Marx's but was assigned by the first editors. The text was re-edited and published as a supplementary vol. 42 (1983) in the *MEW* edn under the title 'Karl Marx. Ökonomische Manuskripte 1857/1858'. An edition bearing this same title and with full critical apparatus is in *MEGA*² (details below), sect. II, vol. I (in two parts). An English version of the text in one vol. is Karl Marx, *Grundrisse*, trans. with fwd. by M. Nicolaus, N.Y.: Random House, 1973. A second English version is in vols. 28 (1986) and 29 (1987) of *MECW* (details below).

Hiromatsu Karl Marx/Friedrich Engels/*Die deutsche Ideologie. Kritik der neuesten deutschen Philosophie in ihren Repräsentanten, Feuerbach, B. Bauer und Stirner, und des deutschen Sozialismus in seinen verschiedenen Propheten.* I. Band 1. Abschnitt. Neuveröffentlichung mit text-kritischen Anmerkungen. Hrsg. von Wataru Hiromatsu. Tokyo: Kawadeshobo-Shinsha Verlag, 1974. This is the best scholarly edition now available of the first part ('On Feuerbach') of 'The German Ideology'.

*MEGA*² Karl Marx/Friedrich Engels/*Gesamtausgabe (MEGA)* (Institut für Marxismus-Leninismus beim Zentralkomitee der

Kommunistischen Partei der Sowjetunion und vom Institut für Marxismus-Leninismus beim Zentralkomitee der Sozialistischen Einheitspartei Deutschlands). Berlin: Dietz Verlag, 1974– . Intended to be the definitive, complete and critical original-language edition, totalling 142 vols. of writings with accompanying vols. of critical apparatus, divided into four sections: I. works, articles, drafts (33 vols.); II. *Capital* and writings preparatory to it (24 vols.); III. correspondence (45 vols.); IV. excerpts, notes, marginalia (7 vols.). To date 45 vols. are published (14 in sect. I, 16 in sect. II, 8 in sect. III, 7 in sect. IV) with another 35 in various stages of production. Publication was interrupted in 1989/90 by the political changes in the Soviet Union and the German Democratic Republic. Completion of the edition is now in the hands of an International Marx-Engels Foundation – *Internationale Marx-Engels-Stiftung (IMES)* – created in Oct. 1990 through the cooperation of the Institute for Marxism-Leninism (Moscow), the Academy of Sciences (Berlin), the Karl-Marx-House (Trier), and the International Institute for Social History (Amsterdam), where the Foundation's Secretariat is located (Cruquiusweg 31, NL-1019 AT Amsterdam). An international editorial commission and a distinguished body of scholar-advisors have been established, as has a set of eight scholarly work-centres in Germany, France, and Russia. Relative to this new *MEGA*, see Rojahn (1991) and Rubel (1991) below.

Œuvres Karl Marx *Œuvres*, édition établie par Maximilien Rubel. Paris: Éditions Gallimard ('Bibliothèque de la Pléiade'), vol. I ('Économie I'), 1963; vol. II ('Économie II'), 1968; vol. III ('Philosophie'), 1982; vol. IV ('Politique'), in press. In its text arrangements, translations, annotations, overall scholarly quality, this French edition is outstanding.

MECW Karl Marx/Frederick Engels/*Collected Works*. Moscow: Progress Publishers/London: Lawrence and Wishart/NY: International Publishers, 1975– . Intended to be the most complete English edition, in 50 vols., to include the writings published by the authors during their lifetime as well as much of the unpublished manuscript material and their correspondence: 27 vols. of writings, excluding *Capital* and other economic works of Marx; 10 vols. of *Capital* etc.; 13 vols. of correspondence

To date 42 vols. have appeared, and another four are ready for publication. The editing is uniformly careful and the translations dependable.

Selected secondary sources

Biographies

McLellan, David. *Karl Marx. His Life and Thought.* London and Basingstoke: Macmillan, 1973.
Rubel, Maximilien. *Marx: Life and Works*, trans. Mary Bottomore. London and Basingstoke: Macmillan, 1980.
Rubel, Maximilien and Manale, Margaret. *Marx without Myth. A Chronological Study of His life and Work.* New York, Evanston and San Francisco: Harper and Row, 1975.

Introductory and general studies

Adams, H.L. *Karl Marx in His Earlier Writings.* 2nd edn. New York: Russell & Russell, 1965.
Dupré, Louis. *The Philosophical Foundations of Marxism.* New York: Harcourt, Brace & World, 1966.
Ollman, Bertell. *Alienation. Marx's Conception of Man in Capitalist Society.* 2nd edn. Cambridge: Cambridge University Press, 1976.
Prawer, S.S. *Karl Marx and World Literature.* Oxford: Oxford University Press, 1976.
Rubel, Maximilien. *Rubel on Karl Marx. Five Essays,* ed. and trans. J. O'Malley and K. Algozin. Cambridge: Cambridge University Press, 1981.
Wood, Allen W. *Karl Marx.* London, Boston and Henley: Routledge & Kegan Paul, 1981.

Socio-political studies

Avineri, Shlomo. *The Social and Political Thought of Karl Marx.* Cambridge: Cambridge University Press, 1968.
Carver, Terrell. *Marx's Social Theory.* Oxford: Oxford University Press, 1982.

Evans, Michael. *Karl Marx*. Bloomington and London: Indiana University Press, 1975.

Hunt, Richard N. *The Political Ideas of Marx and Engels*. Vol. I: *Marxism and Totalitarian Democracy, 1818–1850*. Pittsburgh: The University of Pittsburgh Press, 1974.

McGovern, Arthur. 'Marx's First Political Writings: The *Rheinische Zeitung*-1842–43', in *Demythologising Marxism*, ed. F. Adelman. The Hague: Nijhoff, 1969.

McGovern, Arthur. 'The Young Marx on the State', *Science and Society*, 34, no. 4 (Winter, 1970), 430–66.

Bibliographic and text-editing information.

Andréas, Bert. 'Marx et Engels et la gauche hégélienne', *Annali*. Instituto Giangiacomo Feltrinelli. Milan, 1964/5, vol. 7 (1965), 353–517.

Carver, Terrell. 'Communism for Critical Critics? *The German Ideology* and the Problem of Technology', *History of Political Thought*, 11, no. 1 (Spring 1988), 129–36.

Rojahn, Jürgen. 'Marxismus-Marx-Geschichtswissenschaft: Der Fall der sogenannten"Ökonomisch-philosophischen Manuskripte aus dem Jahre 1844" ', *International Review of Social History*, 28, pt. 1 (1983), 2–49.

'Die Marxschen Manuskripte aus dem Jahre 1844 in der neuen Marx-Engels-Gesamtausgabe (MEGA)', *Archiv für Sozialgeschichte* (Herausgegeben von der Friedrich-Ebert-Stiftung in Verbindung mit dem Institüt für Sozialgeschichte Braunschweig-Bonn), 25 (1985), 647–63.

'Die Marx-Engels-Gesamtausgabe (MEGA): Stand der Arbeit und geplante Fortführung', *Internationale wissenschaftliche Korrespondenz zur Geschichte der deutschen Arbeiterbewegung*. 27. Jahrgang, Heft 4 (Dez. 1991), 470–82.

Rubel, Maximilien. 'Les infortunes de la MEGA', *Économie et Société*, 'Études de Marxologie', S, nos. 28–9 (1991), 207–19.

Editor's and Translator's Note

In Marx's texts all materials in square brackets are the editor's; in 'The German Ideology. Chapter One' the bracketed headings reproduce those of M. Rubel in his French edition of that text (Karl Marx, *Œuvres*, vol. III (1982), pp. 1049–123), the arrangement of which we follow. Additionally, in 'The German Ideology. Chapter One', we follow W. Hiromatsu's German edition in indicating with editorial marks (< >) the material that Marx wrote in over Engels' smooth copy.

The excerpts from the 'Critique of Hegel's Philosophy of Right' follow the order of the material in the manuscript. For that reason the material under the editor's heading 'Sovereignty, Private Property, and State' differs from other editions, which relocate part of that material.

The excerpts from the Paris Notebooks also follow the order of the material in the manuscripts. We offer a possible reading of a passage where a piece of manuscript is missing (p. 86 below).

Most of our translation is based on the new Marx-Engels critical edition (*MEGA²*); section, volume and page numbers as follows:

> From the 'Critique of Hegel's Philosophy of Right': I, 2, 7–131 (selections).
> 'On the Jewish Question': I, 2, 141–69.
> 'Contribution to the Critique of Hegel's Philosophy of Right. Introduction': I, 2, 170–83.
> From the Paris Notebooks: I, 2, 235–309 (selections); and IV, 2, 447–66 (selections).

'Critical Marginal Notes on "The King of Prussia and Social Reform. By a Prussian" ': I, 2, 445–63.

'The German Ideology. Chapter One': *Probeband*, 33–117 (with close consultation of Hiromatsu's edition).

We used the 1927–32 *MEGA* (or *MEGA¹*) with its section, vol., and page numbers for the following:

'Points on the State and Bourgeois Society': I, 5, 532.

Notes 'On Feuerbach': I, 5, 533–5.

The *MEW* edition, vol. and page numbers given, was the basis for:

Address 'On Poland': 4, 416–17.

For the *Poverty of Philosophy* (excerpt) we used Karl Marx, *Œuvres* vol. 1 (1963), pp. 134–6.

The excerpts from the 'Critique of Hegel's Philosophy of Right' and the entire 'Contribution to the Critique of Hegel's Philosophy of Right Introduction' are revised versions of material first published in Karl Marx, *Critique of Hegel's Philosophy of Right*, ed. J. O'Malley, Cambridge: Cambridge University Press, 1970.

In doing our translation we consulted at times English versions of David McLellan, Martin Milligan, and W. Lough, and throughout we consulted the French versions of Maximilien Rubel.

From the Critique of Hegel's Philosophy of Right (1843)

[Hegel's Mystification of the State]

[In §262 of *The Philosophy of Right* Hegel says that] the manner and means of the state's mediation with the family and civil society are 'circumstances, arbitrary will, and personal choice of vocation'. Accordingly, the rationality of the state has nothing to do with the division of the material of the state into family and civil society. The state results from them in an unconscious and arbitrary way. Family and civil society appear as the dark natural ground from which the light of the state emerges. 'Material of the state' here means the *business* of the state, i.e. family and civil society, in so far as they constitute components of the state and, as such, participate in the state.

This development is remarkable in two respects.

(1) Family and civil society are conceived of as *spheres of the concept* of the state, specifically as spheres of its *finiteness*, as *its finiteness*. It is the state which *divides* itself, which *presupposes* them, and indeed *does* this only in order to emerge from its ideality and become *infinite* and actual spirit for itself ... The so-called 'actual Idea' (spirit as infinite, actual) is described as though it acted according to a determinate principle and toward a determinate end. It divides itself into finite spheres, and it does this 'in order to return to itself, to be for itself', and it does this such that things turn out exactly as they are.

Here [Hegel's] logical, pantheistic mysticism is clearly evident.

The *actual* situation is this: 'the allocation' of the material of the state 'to the individual is mediated by circumstances, arbitrary will, and personal choice of vocation'. This fact, this *actual situation* is expressed by speculative philosophy as *appearance*, as *phenomenon*.

I

These circumstances, this arbitrary will, this choice of vocation, this *actual mediation* are merely the *phenomenal* side of a *mediation* which the actual Idea undertakes with itself and which goes on behind the scenes. Actuality is not expressed as itself but rather as another reality. Ordinary empirical existence does not have its own spirit but something alien for its spirit, while on the other hand the actual Idea does not have an actuality developed out of itself, but rather has as its existence what is ordinary and empirical.

The Idea is made into a subject and the *actual* relationship of family and civil society is conceived to be its *inner imaginary* activity. Family and civil society are the presuppositions of the state; they are what is really active; but in speculative philosophy it is reversed. But if the Idea is made subject, then the actual subjects – civil society, family, 'circumstances, arbitrary will, etc.' – become *unreal* and take on another meaning, that of objective moments of the Idea.

[(2)] The 'circumstances, arbitrary will, and personal choice of vocation', through which the material of the state is assigned 'to the individual', are not clearly said to be things that are genuine, necessary, and justified in and for themselves; they are *as such* not declared rational; but then again they are so declared, but only in so far as they are presented as the phenomena of a mediation which leaves them as they are but allows them to acquire the meaning of a determination of the Idea, a result and product of the Idea. The difference lies not in the content, but in the way of considering it, or in the *manner of speaking*. There is a two-fold history, one esoteric and one exoteric. The content lies in the exoteric side. On the esoteric side the interest is always recovering the history of the logical concept in the state. But it is on the exoteric side that the real development goes forward.

Taken rationally, Hegel's sentences mean only the following:

The family and civil society are components of the state. The material of the state is divided amongst them 'through circumstances, arbitrary will, and personal choice of vocation'. The citizens of the state are members of families and members of civil society ... Family and civil society are actual components of the state, actual spiritual existences of the will; they are the state's modes of existence; family and civil society make *themselves* into the state. They are the active force. According to Hegel they are, on the contrary, *made* by the actual Idea; it is not their own life's course that unites them into the state, but rather the life's course of the Idea, which has distinguished them from itself; and they are precisely the finiteness of this Idea; they owe their existence to a spirit other than their own; they are determinations established by a third party, not self-determinations ... [But] the political state cannot exist without the natural basis of the family and the artificial basis of civil society; they are the state's *conditio sine qua non*; but [with Hegel] the conditions are put forward as what is conditioned, what determines as what is determined, the producer as the product of its product. The actual Idea reduces itself into the 'finiteness' of family and civil society in order to enjoy and to bring forth its infinity through their supersession ... The state is composed of [the mass of human beings], and this, its composition is expressed here as an action of the Idea, as an 'allocation' which it undertakes with its own material. The fact is that the state issues from the mass of human beings existing as members of families and members of civil society; but speculative philosophy expresses this fact as an achievement of the Idea, not the idea of the mass of human beings, but as the deed of an Idea-Subject different from the fact itself ... Thus empirical actuality is admitted just as it is and is also said to be rational, but not rational because of its own reason, but because the empirical fact in its empirical existence has a significance other than itself. The fact, which is the starting-point, is not conceived to be such but rather to be the mystical result. The actual becomes phenomenon; but the Idea has no other content than this phenomenon. And the Idea has no other than the logical aim, namely 'to become infinite and actual spirit for itself'. In this [§262] is contained the entire mystery of the Philosophy of Right and of Hegelian philosophy in general.

[On Sovereignty, Monarchy, and Democracy]

The activities and functions of the state are attached to individuals (it is only through individuals that the state acts), but not to the individual as *physical* but as *political*; they are attached to the *political quality* of the individual. So it is ludicrous to say, as Hegel does [in §277] that it is in an 'external and contingent' way that these offices are linked with 'particular personalities'. On the contrary, they are linked with them by a *vinculum substantiale*, by reason of an essential quality of particular personalities. These offices are the natural action

3

of this essential quality. Hence the absurdity of Hegel's conceiving the activities and agencies of the state in the abstract, and particular individuality in opposition to it. He forgets that particular individuality is a human individual and that the activities and functions of the state are human activities. He forgets that the nature of the 'particular personality' is not his beard, his blood, his abstract *Physis*, but rather his *social quality* and that the activities etc. of the state are nothing but the modes of existence and operation of the social qualities of men. It is evident, therefore, that individuals, in so far as they are the bearers of the state's activities and functions, are to be considered according to their social and not their private quality.

[...]

[In §278 and Hegel's Remark thereto, sovereignty as 'the ideality of the state's particular spheres and functions'] is not developed into a comprehended, rational system. In times of *peace* it appears to be either a mere external constraint effected by the ruling power on private life through 'direct influence of higher authority', or a blind uncomprehended result of self-seeking. This ideality has its 'proper actuality' only in the state's 'situation of war or exigency', such that here its essence is expressed as the actually existing state's 'situation of war and exigency', while its *'peaceful'* situation is precisely the war and exigency of self-seeking.

Accordingly, sovereignty, the ideality of the state, exists merely as *internal* necessity, as *idea*. And Hegel is satisfied with that because it is only a question of the *Idea*.

[...]

Had Hegel started with the actual subjects as the basis of the state, it would not have been necessary for him to let the state become subjectified in a mystical way. 'But subjectivity', says Hegel [in §279], 'attains its truth only as a *subject*, and personality only as a *person*'. This too is a mystification. Subjectivity is a characteristic of the subject and personality a characteristic of the person. Instead of considering them to be predicates of their subjects Hegel makes the predicates independent and then lets them be subsequently and mysteriously converted into their subjects.

The existence of the predicate is the subject; thus the subject is the existence of subjectivity, etc. Hegel makes the predicates, the

4

objects, independent, but independent as separated from their actual independence, their subject. Subsequently, and because of this, the actual subject appears to be the result, whereas one ought to start with the actual subject and examine its objectification. The mystical substance becomes the actual subject and the actual subject appears to be something else, namely a moment of the mystical substance. Precisely because Hegel starts with the predicates, with the universal characteristic, instead of with the real *Ens* (υποκείμενον subject), and because there must be a bearer of this characteristic, the mystical Idea becomes this bearer. This is the dualism: Hegel does not consider the universal to be the actual essence of the actual finite, i.e. existing determinate thing, nor the actual *Ens* to be the *true subject* of the infinite.

Accordingly, sovereignty, the essence of the state is here first conceived to be an independent being; it is objectified. Then of course this object must again become a subject. But then this subject appears as a self-incarnation of sovereignty, while sovereignty is really nothing but the objectified spirit of the state's subjects ... [S]overeignty, the ideality of the state as person, as subject, obviously exists as many persons, many subjects, because no single person absorbs in himself the sphere of personality, nor any single subject the sphere of subjectivity. What kind of ideality of the state would it have to be which, instead of being the actual self-consciousness of the citizens, the communal soul of the state, were *one* person, *one* subject[?] ... What Hegel wants to do is represent the monarch as the actual God-man, the *actual incarnation* of the Idea.

[...]

But even while conceiving of sovereignty as the ideality of the state, as the actual determination of the parts through the idea of the whole, Hegel now makes it 'the will's *abstract* – and to that extent *ungrounded* – self-determination in which the ultimate decision is vested. This is the *individual aspect* of the state as such'. Before, the discussion was about subjectivity, now it is about individuality. The state as sovereign must be *one*, *one individual*, it must possess individuality. The state is one 'not only' in this individuality; individuality is but the *natural* moment of its oneness, the state's *natural characteristic*. 'This absolutely decisive moment of the whole, *therefore*, is not individuality in general, but one individual, the *monarch*'. How so?

Because 'each of the three moments of the concept [i.e. individuality, particularity, and universality] has its distinctive shape which is *actual for itself*'. One moment of the concept is 'individuality'; by itself this is not yet *one individual*. And what kind of constitution would it have to be in which universality, particularity, and individuality each had 'its distinctive shape which is *actual* for itself'? Because we are not dealing here with some abstraction, but with the state, with society, we can adopt Hegel's classification. And what follows from that? The citizen of the state as determining the universal is lawgiver, and as the one deciding, as *actually* willing, is sovereign. Is that supposed to mean that the *individuality of the state's will* is 'one individual', a particular individual distinct from all others? *Universality*, legislation, also has 'its distinctive shape which is *actual*'. Could one conclude from that that 'legislation' is these particular individuals [?]

[...]

Hegel makes all the attributes of the contemporary European constitutional monarch into absolute self-determination of the *will*. He does not say the will of the monarch is the final decision, but rather the final decision of the will is – the monarch. The first statement is empirical. The second twists the empirical fact into a metaphysical axiom. Hegel joins together the two subjects, sovereignty as 'subjectivity which is certain of itself' and sovereignty as *'ungrounded* self-determination of the will,' as the individual will, in order to construct out of that the 'Idea' as *'one* individual'.

It is obvious that self-certain subjectivity must also *actually* will, must will as unity, as an individual. But who ever doubted that the state acts through individuals? Hegel wanted to develop the idea that the state must have one individual as representative of its individual unity, so he did not establish the *monarch*. The only certain *positive* result of this §[279] is this:

In the state *the monarch* is the moment of *individual will*, of ungrounded self-determination, of caprice or arbitrariness.

[...]

[In Hegel's Remark to this § we see that] no *advance* has taken place. *Abstract personality* was the subject of abstract right; there has been no progress; the *personality of the state* remains *abstract personality*. Hegel should not have been surprised that the *actual person* – and persons make the state – reappears everywhere as the being of the state. He should have been surprised at the opposite, and still more surprised that the person as person of the state reappears in the same impoverished abstraction as the person of private right.

Hegel here defines the monarch as 'the personality of the state, its certainty of itself'. The monarch is 'personified sovereignty', 'sovereignty-become-man', incarnate political-consciousness, whereby all other persons are thus excluded from this sovereignty, from personality, and from political-consciousness. Yet at the same time Hegel can give this *'Souveraineté-Personne'* no more content than 'I will', the moment of arbitrariness in the will. The 'rationality of the state' and the 'consciousness of the state' is a 'unique' empirical person to the exclusion of all others, but this personified Reason has no more content than the abstraction 'I will'. *L'État c'est moi.*

[...]

[Hegel further states] 'The term *"popular sovereignty"* may be used to indicate that a people is self-sufficient for all *external* purposes, and constitutes a state of its own etc.'. That is a triviality. If the sovereign is the 'actual sovereignty of the state', then 'the sovereign' could necessarily be considered a 'self-sufficient state' for all external purposes, even without the people. But he is sovereign in so far as he represents the unity of the people, and so he himself is just a representative, a symbol of the sovereignty of the people. The sovereignty of the people does not derive from him, but he from it.

[...]

[Hegel speaks] as though the people were not the actual state. The state is an *Abstractum.* The people alone is the *Concretum.* And it is remarkable that Hegel without hesitation ascribes to the *Abstractum* what he ascribes only with hesitation and conditions to the *Concretum* – a living quality like that of sovereignty.

[He says that] the 'popular sovereignty [as] *the opposite of that sovereignty which exists in the monarch* ... is one of those confused thoughts which are based on a *garbled* notion of the *people*'. The 'confused thoughts' and the *'garbled* notion' are only here on Hegel's pages. Certainly if sovereignty *exists* in the monarch then it is foolishness to speak of an opposite sovereignty in the people, for it lies in the concept of sovereignty that it can have no double and absolutely opposite existence. But:

7

(1) the question is precisely: Is not the sovereignty absorbed in the monarch an illusion? Sovereignty of the monarch or of the people, that is the question;

(2) one can speak of a sovereignty of the people *in opposition to the sovereignty existing in the monarch*. But then it is not a question of *one and the same sovereignty* taking shape on two sides but rather of *two wholly opposed concepts of sovereignty*, one such that it can come to existence in a *monarch*, the other such that it can come to existence only in a *people*. This is like asking, is God the sovereign or is man the sovereign[?] One of the two is a fiction, even though an existing fiction.

[...]

[Hegel says that] 'if "popular sovereignty" is taken to mean a *republican* form [of government], or more specifically democracy . . . then . . . there can be no further discussion of such a notion in face of the developed Idea'.

That is certainly correct if one has only 'such a notion' and no 'developed idea' of democracy.

Democracy is the truth of monarchy, monarchy is not the truth of democracy. Monarchy is necessarily democracy in contradiction with itself, whereas the monarchical moment is no contradiction within democracy. Monarchy cannot, while democracy can be understood in its own terms. In democracy none of the elements [*Momente*] takes on a significance other than what befits it. Each is actually just an element of the whole *Demos*. In monarchy one part determines the character of the whole. The entire constitution must be modified in accord with the fixed point. Democracy is the generic constitution. Monarchy is a species, and indeed a poor one. Democracy is content and form. Monarchy *should* be form only, but it adulterates the content.

In monarchy the whole, the people, is subsumed under one of its modes of existence, the political constitution; in democracy the *constitution itself* appears as only *one* determination, and indeed as a self-determination of the people. In monarchy we have the people of the constitution, in democracy the constitution of the people. Democracy is the resolved *mystery* of all constitutions. Here the constitution not only *in itself*, with regard to its essence, but with regard to its *existence*, its actuality, is returned to its actual ground, to *actual man*,

8

the *actual people*, and established as the people's *own* work. The constitution looks like just what it is, the free product of man. One could say that this also applies in a certain respect to constitutional monarchy; only the specific difference of democracy is that here the constitution is in general but one aspect of the people's existence, that is to say the political constitution does not form the state for itself.

Hegel proceeds from the state and makes man into the subjectified state; democracy starts with man and makes the state objectified man. Just as it is not religion that creates man but man who creates religion, so it is not the constitution that creates the people but the people which creates the constitution. In a certain respect democracy is to all other forms of state what Christianity is to all other religions. Christianity is the religion κατέξοχήν, the *essence of religion*, deified man as a *particular* religion. In the same way democracy is the *essence of every political constitution*, socialised man as a *particular* constitution of the state. It relates to other constitutions as the genus to its species; only here the genus itself appears as an existent and is therefore opposed as a *particular* species to those existents that do not conform to the essence. Relative to democracy all other forms of state are its Old Testament. Man does not exist for the law but rather the law for the good of man; it is *human existence*, while in the others man has only *legal existence*. That is the fundamental difference of democracy.

All remaining *forms of state* are a certain, determinate, *particular form* of state. In democracy the *formal* principle is simultaneously the *material* principle. For that reason it is the first true unity of the universal and the particular. In monarchy for example, [or] in the republic as a merely particular form of state, political man has his particular and separate existence alongside the unpolitical, private man. Property, contract, marriage, civil society appear here (as Hegel quite rightly develops them for these *abstract* forms of state, except that he *means* to develop the Idea of the state) to be *particular* modes of existence alongside the *political* state, i.e. to be the *content* to which the *political state* relates as the *organising form*, or really only as the determining, limiting intelligence which says now 'yes' now 'no' without any content of its own. In democracy the political state, to the extent that it is placed alongside this content and differentiated from it, is itself just a *particular* content, like a particular *form* of the people's *existence*. In monarchy, for example, this particular entity, the political

9

constitution, has the meaning of the *universal* which is governing and determining all the particulars. In democracy the state as particular is *only* particular, and as universal is the actual universal, i.e. not a determinate thing in distinction from other content. The modern French have conceived it thus: in true democracy the *political state disappears* [*untergehe*]. This is correct inasmuch as *qua* constitution it is no longer equivalent to the whole.

In all states distinct from democracy the *state*, the *law*, the *constitution* is what dominates without actually governing, i.e. materially permeating the content of the remaining non-political spheres. In democracy the constitution, the law, the state is itself only a self-determination of the people and a determinate content of the people, in so far as it is political constitution.

Furthermore it is self-evident that all forms of state have democracy as their truth and for that reason are untrue to the extent that they are not democracy.

In the ancient states the political state constituted the content of the state with the exclusion of other spheres; the modern state is an accommodation between the political and the non-political state.

In democracy the *abstract* state has ceased to be the dominating element. The struggle between monarchy and republic is itself still a struggle within the abstract form of state. The *political* republic is democracy within the abstract form of state. Hence the abstract state-form of democracy is the republic; but here [in true democracy] it [democracy] ceases to be *mere political* constitution.

[Genesis of the modern state]

Property etc., in brief the entire content of law and the state is, with small modification, the same in North America as in Prussia. There, accordingly, the *republic* is a mere state *form* just as monarchy is here. The content of the state lies outside these constitutions. Hence Hegel is right when he says that the political state is the constitution, i.e. that the material state is not political. What obtains is merely an external identity, a mutual determination. Only with great difficulty did the political state, the constitution, take shape out of the various moments of the life of the people. It was developed as the universal reason in opposition to the other spheres, as something opposite to them. The historical task then consisted in its revindication; but *in doing that* the particular spheres are not conscious of the fact that their private being declines relative to the opposed being of the constitution, or of the political state, and that its opposed existence is nothing but the affirmation of their own estrangement. The *political constitution* was until now the *religious sphere*, the *religion* of popular life, the heaven of its universality in opposition to the *earthly existence* of its actuality. The political sphere was the sole sphere of the state within the state, the sole sphere in which the content, like the form, was species-content, the authentic universal, but at the same time in such a way that, because this sphere opposed the others, its content too became formal and particular. *Political life* in the modern sense is the *Scholasticism* of popular life. *Monarchy* is the fullest expression of this estrangement. The *republic* is the negation of this estrangement within its own sphere. Clearly, the political constitution as such is perfected only when the private spheres have attained independent existence. Where commerce and landed property are not free, not yet autonomous, there is also not yet the political constitution. The Middle Ages was the *democracy of unfreedom.*

The abstraction of the *state as such* belongs only to modern times because the abstraction of private life belongs only to modern times. The abstraction of the *political state* is a modern product.

In the Middle Ages there was serf, feudal property, trade corporation, corporation of scholars, etc.; that is, in the Middle Ages property, trade, society, man was *political*; the material content of the state is fixed by reason of its form; every private sphere has a political character or is a political sphere; or, politics is also the character of the private spheres. In the Middle Ages the political constitution is the constitution of private property, but only because the constitution of private property is a political one. In the Middle Ages popular life and political life are identical. Man is the actual principle of the state, but he is *unfree* man. Hence it is the *democracy of unfreedom*, fulfilled estrangement. The abstract, reflected opposition [between popular and political life] belongs only to modern times. The Middle Ages is the *actual* and modern times the *abstract* dualism.

[...]

In unmediated monarchy, democracy, aristocracy, there is yet no political constitution distinct from the actual material state or from the remaining content of popular life. The political state does not yet appear as the *form* of the material state. Either, as in Greece, the *res publica* is the actual private concern, the actual content of the citizen, and the private man is slave, that is the political state as political is the true and sole content of the citizen's life and will; or, as in Asiatic despotism, the political state is nothing but the private will of a single individual, or the political state, like the material state, is slave. What distinguishes the modern state from the states in which there is substantial unity of people and state is not that the various moments of the constitution take the form of *particular* actuality, as Hegel would have it, but rather that the constitution itself has taken the form of a *particular* actuality alongside the actual life of the people, that the political state has become the *constitution* of the rest of the state.

[…]

[Bureaucracy]

[In §§288–97] Hegel proceeds from the *separation* of the 'state' and 'civil' society, the separation of the 'particular interests' and the 'universal interest which has being in and for itself', and the bureaucracy is certainly based on this *separation*. Hegel proceeds from the presupposition of the 'corporations' [of civil society], and the bureaucracy certainly presupposes the '*corporations*', or at least the 'corporation spirit'. Hegel develops no *content* of the bureaucracy, but merely some general indications of its 'formal' organisation, and the bureaucracy certainly is merely the 'formalism' of a content that lies outside the bureaucracy itself.

[…]

The 'state formalism', which the bureaucracy is, is the 'state as formalism', and Hegel has described it precisely as such a formalism. Because this 'state formalism' constitutes itself as an actual power and becomes its own *material* content, it is evident that the 'bureaucracy' is a tissue of *practical* illusion, or the 'illusion of the state'. The bureaucratic spirit is through and through a Jesuitical, theological spirit. The bureaucrats are the Jesuits and theologians of the state. The bureaucracy is *la république prêtre*.

Because the bureaucracy is in its *essence* the state as formalism, so it is also in its *end*. The actual end of the state, therefore, seems to the bureaucracy to be an end *opposed to* the state. The spirit of the bureaucracy is the 'formal spirit' of the state. It therefore makes the 'formal spirit' of the state, or the *actual* spiritlessness of the state, a categorical imperative. The bureaucracy asserts itself to be the final end of the state. Because the bureaucracy makes its 'formal' aims its content, it comes into conflict everywhere with the 'real' aims. Hence it is obliged to present what is formal for the content and the content for what is formal. The aims of the state are transformed into aims of bureaux, or the aims of bureaux into the aims of the state. The bureaucracy is a circle from which no one can escape. The hierarchy is a *hierarchy of knowledge.* The highest point entrusts to the lower echelons insight into individual matters, whereas the lower echelons credit the highest with insight into the universal; and thus they deceive one another.

The bureaucracy is the imaginary state alongside the real state; it is the spiritualism of the state. Consequently everything has a double meaning, a real one and a bureaucratic one, just as knowledge is double, one real and one bureaucratic (and the same with the will). A real thing, however, is treated according to its bureaucratic being, according to its otherworldly, spiritual being. The bureaucracy has the being of the state, the spiritual being of society, in its possession; it is its *private property.*

The general spirit of bureaucracy is the *secret*, the mystery, preserved inwardly by means of the hierarchy and outwardly as a closed corporation. Manifested political spirit and disposition seem therefore to the bureaucracy to be a *betrayal* of its mystery. Accordingly *authority* is the principle of its knowledge and the deification of authority is its *disposition.* But at the very heart of the bureaucracy this *spiritualism* turns into a *crass materialism*, the materialism of passive obedience, of trust in authority, the *mechanism* of an ossified and formalistic behaviour, of fixed principles, conceptions, and traditions. As for the individual bureaucrat, the state's end becomes his private end: a *pursuit of higher posts*, the *building of a career.* In the first place he considers actual life to be purely *material* because *the spirit of this life has its separate existence* in the bureaucracy. Thus the bureaucrat has to make life as materialistic as possible. Secondly, real life is material for the bureaucrat, i.e. in so far as it becomes an object of bureaucratic action, because its spirit is prescribed for it, its end lies outside of it, its existence is the existence of the bureau. The state, then, exists only as various determinate bureau-minds whose connection consists of subordination and dumb obedience. Real science seems devoid of content just as actual life appears dead because this imaginary knowledge and life pass for what is real and essential. Thus the bureaucrat has to use the actual state Jesuitically, no matter whether his Jesuitism be conscious or unconscious. But given that his antithesis is knowledge, he will inevitably attain self-consciousness and, at that moment, deliberate Jesuitism.

While the bureaucracy is on one hand this crass materialism, it shows its crass spiritualism in its will *to do everything*, i.e. in its making the *will* the *causa prima*, because it is a pure *active* existence which receives its content from without and thus can manifest its existence only by forming and restricting this content. The bureaucrat has the world as a mere object for his action.

When Hegel [in §293] calls the Executive Power the *objective* aspect of sovereignty residing in the crown, it is precisely in the same sense that the Catholic Church was the *real existence* of the sovereignty, content, and spirit of the Blessed Trinity. In the bureaucracy the identity of the state's interest and the particular private aim is established such that the *state's* interest becomes a *particular* private aim opposed to the other private aims.

The abolition [*Aufhebung*] of the bureaucracy can consist only in the universal interest becoming *actually* – and not, as with Hegel, becoming purely in thought, in *abstraction* – a particular interest; and this is possible only through the *particular* interest actually becoming *universal*. Hegel starts from an unreal contradiction and therefore brings it to a merely imaginary identity which, in fact, is itself all the more contradictory. Such an identity is the bureaucracy.

[...]

[In §289] Hegel has the 'state', the 'executive', 'perform the task of upholding legality and the universal interest of the state, etc.' within civil society through 'delegates of the executive power'; and according to him these 'executive office holders', the 'executive civil servants' are the *true 'political representation'*, not 'of' but 'against' 'civil society'. The opposition of state and civil society is therefore fixed; the state resides not within but outside of civil society; it affects civil society merely through '*office holders*' to whom is entrusted the '*upholding of the state*' within these spheres. The opposition is not overcome through these 'office holders' but has become a 'legal', 'fixed' opposition. The 'state' is made something alien and external to the *nature* of civil society, and this nature's deputies are invoked against civil society. 'Public authority' [*Polizei*] and the 'judiciary' and the 'administration' are not deputies of civil society itself, which manages its *own* general interest in and through them, but rather state office holders whose purpose is to manage the state against civil society.

[...]

[On constitutional change]

[In the 'Addition' (*Zusatz*) to §298] Hegel says: 'The constitution must be in and for itself the firm and recognised ground on which the legislative power is based, so that it does not first have to be constructed. Thus, the constitution *is*, but it just as essentially *becomes*, i.e. it undergoes progressive development. This progression is a change which takes place imperceptibly and without possessing the form of change.'

This is to say that according to law (illusion) the constitution *is*, but in actuality (truth) it *becomes*. By its definition it is unalterable, but it is actually altered, only this alteration is unconscious and lacks the form of alteration. The *appearance* contradicts the *essence*. The appearance is the *conscious* law of the constitution, and the essence is its *unconscious* law which contradicts the other. What is in the essence or nature of the thing is not in the law. Rather, the opposite is in the law.

Is it not true, then, that in the state – the highest existence of *freedom*, according to Hegel, the existence of self-conscious freedom – not law, the existence of freedom, but rather blind natural necessity governs? And if now the law of the thing is recognised as contradicting the legal definition, why not also recognise the law of the thing, the law of reason, as the law of the state, [but] how now consciously retain the dualism? Hegel wants above all to present the state as the actualisation of free spirit, but *re vera* he resolves all difficult conflicts by appeal to natural necessity, which is the opposite of freedom. Thus [for him], the transition of particular interest into the universal or general interest is not a conscious law of the state, but is mediated through chance and ratified *contrary* to consciousness;

and in the state Hegel wants everywhere the realisation of free will! (Here we see Hegel's *substantial* standpoint.)

Hegel uses as examples to illustrate the *gradual* alteration of the constitution the conversion of the private property of the German princes and their families into state domains, and the conversion of the German emperors' personal administration of justice into an administration through delegates. His choice of examples is unfortunate. In the first case, for instance, the transition happened only in such a way that all state property was transformed into royal private property.

Besides, these changes are particular. To be sure, entire state constitutions have changed such that as new requirements gradually arose, the old [order] broke down; but for the new constitution a real revolution was always necessary.

'Thus [Hegel continues], conditions evolve in an apparently peaceful and imperceptible manner, with the result that a constitution changes its character completely over a long period of time.' The category of *gradual* transition is, first of all, historically false, and second, it explains nothing. In order that the constitution be altered, and thus that this illusory appearance [of its permanence] not be in the end forcefully shattered, in order, moreover, that man do consciously what he is otherwise forced to do unconsciously by the essence or nature of the thing, it is necessary that the movement of the constitution, that *progress*, be made the principle of the constitution, thus that the real cornerstone of the constitution, the people, be made the principle of the constitution. Progress itself is then the constitution.

[...]

Posed correctly, the question is simply this: does a people have the right to give itself a new constitution? The answer must be an unqualified yes, because the constitution becomes a practical illusion the moment it ceases to be a true expression of the people's will.

[The individual in modern society]

Civil society and the state are separated. Consequently the citizen of the state [*der Staatsbürger*] and the citizen as member of civil society are also separated. Thus the individual has to effect an *essential schism* within himself. As *actual citizen* [*Bürger*] he finds himself in a two-fold organisation: the *bureaucratic*, which is an external formal determination of the other-worldly state, of the executive power, which does not touch him and his independent actuality; and the *social*, the organisation of civil society, within which he stands as *private man* outside the state, and which does not touch the political state as such. The former [the bureaucratic] is an organisation of the state to which he continually contributes the *material*. The latter is a *civil organisation* whose material is not the state. In the former the state relates to him as formal opposition; in the latter he relates himself to the state as material opposition. Thus, in order to behave as *actual citizen of the state*, to acquire political significance and efficacy, he must abandon his civil actuality, abstract from it, withdraw himself from this whole organisation into his individuality, because the only existence he finds for his state-citizenship is his pure, blank *individuality*, for the existence of the state as executive is complete without him, and his existence in civil society is complete without the state. Only in opposition to these *exclusively existing communities*, only as an *individual* can he be *citizen of the state*. His existence as citizen of the state is an existence that lies outside of his *communal* existences, and is therefore purely *individual*. [...] The separation of civil society and the political state appears necessarily to be a separation of the *political* citizen, the citizen of the state, from civil society, from his own actual, empirical actuality; for as a state-idealist he is something *completely other*, distinct, different from and opposed to his own actuality. Here civil society effects within itself the relationship of the state and civil society, which already exists on the other side [i.e. within the political state] as the bureaucracy. [...] The citizen [Bürger] must renounce his estate, civil society, the private estate, in order to achieve political significance and efficacy; for it is precisely this *estate* which stands between the *individual* and the *political state*.

[The character of modern society]

It is a development of history that has transformed the *political estates* into *social* estates such that, just as Christians are equal in Heaven yet unequal on earth, so the individual members of the people are *equal* in the heaven of their political world yet unequal in the earthly existence of *society*. The real transformation of the *political estates* into

17

civil estates occurred under the *absolute monarchy*. The bureaucracy asserted the idea of unity over and against the various states within the state. Still, even alongside the bureaucracy of the absolute governing power, the *social difference* of the estates remained a political difference, *political within* and alongside the bureaucracy of the absolute governing power. Only the French Revolution completed the transformation of the *political* estates into social estates, or in other words, made the *estate-distinctions* of civil society into merely *social* distinctions, distinctions of private life, which are meaningless in political life. With that, the separation of political life and civil society was completed.

At the same time the estates of civil society were likewise transformed: civil society underwent a change by reason of its separation from political society. *Estate* in the medieval sense remained only within the bureaucracy itself, where the civil and the political position are immediately identical. Over against this stands civil society as *private estate*. Here estate distinction is no longer one of *need* and of *labour* as autonomous bodies. The sole general, *superficial* and *formal* distinction remaining is that of *town* and *country*. But within civil society itself the distinction takes shape in changeable, unfixed circles whose principle is *arbitrariness*. *Money* and *education* are the prevalent criteria. Yet it is not here, but in the critique of Hegel's treatment of civil society that this should be developed. It is enough to say here that the estate in civil society has neither need – and therefore a natural impulse – nor politics for its principle. It is a division of the masses whose development is unstable and whose structure is arbitrary and *in no sense* an organisation.

The sole characteristic thing is that the *lack of property* and the *estate of immediate* labour, of concrete labour, form less an estate of civil society than the basis upon which the circles of civil society rest and move. The only estate in which political and civil positions coincide is that of the *members of the executive power*. The present-day social estate already manifests a difference from the earlier estate of civil society by the fact that it does not, as was earlier the case, regard the individual as a communal individual, as a communal being; rather, it is partly chance, partly labour etc. of the individual that determines whether he remains in his estate or not, an *estate* which is, furthermore, only an *external* determination of this individual, for he neither inheres in his labour nor does the estate relate to him as an objective community organised according to firm laws and related firmly to him. Rather, he stands in no *actual* relationship at all to his substantial activity, to his *actual estate*. The medical man, for instance, forms no particular estate in civil society. One businessman belongs to an estate different than that of another businessman, i.e. he belongs to another *social position*. Just as civil society is separated from political society, so within itself civil society is divided into *estate* and *social* position, even though some relations obtain between the two. The principle of the civil estate or of civil society is *enjoyment* and the *capacity to enjoy*.

In his political role the member of civil society rids himself of his estate, of his actual private position; by this alone does he acquire significance as *man*, i.e. his vocation as member of the state, as social being, appear to be his *human* vocation. For all of his other characteristics in civil society *seem unessential* to the man, to the individual, i.e. they seem to be *external* features that, while indeed necessary to his existence within the whole, i.e. as a bond with the whole, are none the less a bond that he can just as well throw off. (Present civil society is the accomplished principle of *individualism*: individual existence is the final end, while activity, labour, content etc. are *mere* means.)

[...]

The *actual man* is the *private man* of the present-day political constitution.

In general, the significance of the estate is that it makes the *existence* [*Bestehen*] of the individual one of *difference, separation*. The manner of his life, his activity etc. is his privilege, and instead of making him a member and function of society, it makes him an *exception* from society. The fact that this *difference* is not only an *individual* but takes the shape of *community*, estate, corporation, not only fails to abolish the exclusivity of its nature but is rather the expression of it. Instead of being a function of society, the individual function becomes a society for itself.

Not only is the *estate* based on the *separation* of society as the ruling law, but it separates man from his universal nature; it makes him an animal whose being coincides directly with its determinate character. The Middle Ages constitutes the *animal history* of humankind, its zoology.

Modern times, *civilisation*, makes the opposite mistake. It separates man's *objective* being from him, as something merely *external* and material. It does not consider the content of man to be his true actuality.

Anything further regarding this is to be developed in the section on 'Civil Society'.

[Sovereignty, private property, and state]

In the constitution [endorsed by Hegel], in which *primogeniture** is a guarantee [of political inclination], *private property* is the guarantee of the political constitution. In primogeniture, it appears that a *particular* form of private property is this guarantee. But *primogeniture* is merely a particular existence of the universal relationship of *private property and political state*. Primogeniture is the *political* sense of private property, private property in its political significance, i.e. in its universal significance. Thus the constitution is here the *constitution of private property*.

With the Germanic peoples, where we encounter primogeniture in its *classical* formation, we also find the constitution of *private property*. *Private property* is the universal category, the universal bond of the state. Even the universal functions appear as the private property sometimes of a corporation, sometimes of an estate.

Trade and business in their particular nuances are the private property of particular corporations. Royal offices, jurisdiction etc. are the private property of particular estates. The various provinces are the private property of individual princes etc. Service for the realm is the private property of the ruler. The spirit is the private property of the spiritual authority. One's loyal activity is the private property of another, just as one's right is, once again, a particular private property. Sovereignty, here *nationality*, is the private property of the Emperor.

It has often been said that in the Middle Ages every form of right, of freedom, of social existence, appears to be a *privilege*, an *exception* from the rule. The empirical fact that all these privileges have the apparent form of *private property* could not therefore have been overlooked. What is the universal reason for this coincidence? *Private property* is the *species-existence* of *privilege*, of right as an *exception*.

---

* The institution of entailed landed property, which cannot be divided or sold but must be passed on to the eldest son, whose ownership is subject to the same conditions. Hegel (§306) saw in it a possible basis for disinterested political spirit.

Where the sovereigns, as in France for instance, attacked the *independence* of private property, they directed their attention more to the property of the *corporations* than to that of *individuals*. But in attacking the private property of the corporations they attacked private property as corporation, as the *social* bond.

In the *feudal reign* it is apparent that the power of the crown is the power of private property, and that in the power of the crown is deposited the mystery of *universal power*, the *power of all spheres of the state*.

(The *powerfulness* of the state is expressed in the sovereign as the representative of the state's power. The *constitutional* sovereign, therefore, expresses the idea of the constitutional state in its sharpest abstraction. On one hand he is the *idea* of the state, the sanctified majesty of the state, and precisely as *this* person. At the same time he is a *pure* imagination: as person and as sovereign he has neither actual power nor actual function. Here the separation of the political and the actual, the formal and the material, the universal and the particular person, of man and social man, is expressed in its highest contradiction.)

Private property is [a product] of *Roman* intellect and *Germanic* heart. At this point it will be valuable to undertake a comparison of these two extreme developments. This will help solve the political problem as discussed.

(ad XII)* 'A so-called *moral* person', says [Hegel's] Remark [to §279], 'a society, community, or family, however concrete it may be in itself, contains personality only abstractly as one of its moments. In such a person, personality has not yet reached the truth of its existence. The state, however, is precisely this totality in which the moments of the concept attain actuality in accordance with their distinctive truth.'

The moral person, society, family, etc. has personality within it only abstractly; against that, in the monarch, the *person* has the *state* within him.

In fact, the *abstract person* has brought his *personality* to a true existence only in the *moral* person, society, family, etc. But Hegel conceives of society, family, etc. in general the moral person, not as

---

* A notation by Marx, referring to the discussion of 'sovereignty' earlier in the manuscript.

the actualisation of the real empirical person, but as the real person which, however, has the moment of personality in it only abstractly. Whence also comes his notion that it is not actual persons who come to be a state, but that the state must first come to be an actual person. Instead of the state being brought forth, therefore, as the ultimate actuality of the person, as the ultimate social actuality of man, *one single* empirical man, an empirical person, is brought forth as the ultimate actuality of the state. This inversion of subject into object and object into subject is a consequence of Hegel's wanting to write the biography of the abstract Substance, of the Idea, with human activity, etc. having consequently to appear to be the activity and result of something other than man; it is a consequence of Hegel's wanting to have man's essence act for itself as an imaginary individual instead of acting in its *actual human* existence, and this necessarily has as its result that an *empirical existent* is taken in an *uncritical way* to be the real truth of the Idea; because it is not a question of bringing empirical existence to its truth, but of bringing the truth to empirical existence with some obvious thing developed as a real moment of the Idea. (More later concerning this inevitable change of the empirical into speculation and of speculation into the empirical.)

In this way the impression of something *mystical* and *profound* is also created. That man must be born is quite vulgar, so too that this existence through physical birth comes to be social man, etc. and citizen of the state; everything man becomes is through his birth. But it is very profound and striking that the Idea of the state is directly born, that it brought itself forth into empirical existence in the birth of the sovereign. In this way no new content is gained, only the *form* of the old content altered. It has received a philosophical *form*, a philosophical certification.

Another consequence of this mystical speculation is that a *particular* empirical existent, a single empirical existent in distinction from the others is conceived to be the *existence of the Idea*. Once again it makes a deep mystical impression to see a particular empirical existent posited by the Idea, and thus to encounter at all levels an incarnation of God.

If we take the modes of man's social existence, for example in the development of the family, civil society, state, etc., to be the actualisation and objectification of his essence, then family etc. resemble qualities inhering in a subject. Man remains always what is essential to all these realities, while they then appear to be his *actual* universality, and hence the *commonality*. But if, on the contrary, family, civil society, state, etc. are specifications of the Idea, of Substance as Subject, then they must receive an empirical actuality, and the mass of men in which the idea of civil society is developed takes on the identity of *burgher*, the other of state citizen. For it is a matter only of *allegory*, of ascribing to any empirical existent the *meaning* of actualised Idea; and so it is evident that these receptacles have fulfilled their destiny once they have become a determinate incarnation of a life-moment of the Idea. Consequently, the universal appears everywhere as a determinate particular, and the individual nowhere attains his true universality.

At the deepest, most speculative level it therefore appears necessary when the most abstract determinations which in no way really ripen to true social actuality, the natural bases of the state like birth (in the case of the prince) or private property (in primogeniture), appear as the highest Ideas-directly-become-man.

And it is evident that the true method is turned upside down. What is simplest is made most complex and vice versa. What should be the point of departure becomes the mystical result, and what should be the rational result becomes the mystical point of departure.

If, however, the prince is the abstract *person* who has the *state within* him, this can only mean that the essence of the state is the abstract *private person*. It utters its secret only at its peak of development. The prince is the sole private person in whom the relation of the private person in general to the state is actualised.

The Romans were the first to have formulated the *right of private property*, abstract right, private right [*Privatrecht*], the right of the abstract person. The *Roman* conception of *private right* is *civil law* [*Privatrecht*] in its *classical formulation*. Yet nowhere with the Romans do we find that the right of private property was mystified, as is the case with the Germans. Nowhere does it become *right of the state* [or *constitutional law: Staatsrecht*].

The right of private property is *jus utendi et abutendi*, the right of *wilfulness* over the thing. The main interest of the Romans consisted in working out the *relationships* and in determining which ones resulted in *abstract* relations of private property. The actual basis of private property, *possession*, is a *factum*, an *unexplainable factum*, and *no right*. Only through legal determinations, which the society attributes to the factual possession, does it receive the quality of rightful possession, of *private property*.

Regarding the connection between the political constitution and private property with the Romans, it appears that:

(1) *Man* (as slave), as with ancient peoples in general, [is] object of private property.

There is nothing specific in that.

(2) Conquered countries are treated as private property, *jus utendi et abutendi* is asserted over them.

(3) Within their history itself appears the struggle between poor and rich, patricians and plebians etc.

In other respects, private property as a whole, as with the ancient classical peoples in general, is asserted to be *public property*, either as the republic's expenditure, in good times, or as *luxurious and universal benefaction* (baths, etc.) towards the mob.

Slavery is explained by the *rights of war*, the right of occupation; they are slaves because their political existence is destroyed.

We especially stress two [sic] relationships in distinction from the Germans.

(1) The *imperial* power was not the power of private property, but rather the *sovereignty* of the *empirical will* as such, which was far from regarding *private property* as the bond between itself and its subjects; on the contrary, it dealt with private property as it did with all other social goods. The imperial power, therefore, was nothing other than *factually hereditary*. The highest formation of the right of private property, of private right, indeed belongs to the imperial epoch; but it is a consequence of the political dissolution rather than the political dissolution being a consequence of private property. Furthermore, when private right achieved full development in Rome, state right [or constitutional law] was abolished, was in the process of its dissolution, while in Germany it is the opposite.

(2) In Rome state honours are never hereditary; i.e. private property is not the dominant category of the state.

(3) Contrary to German primogeniture etc., in Rome the *wilfulness of the testator* appears to be the derivative of private property. In

this latter antithesis lies the *entire* difference between the German and the Roman development of private property.

(In primogeniture it appears that private property is the relationship to the function of the state of a sort that the existence of the state is something inhering in, is an accident of, *immediate* private property, i.e. *possession of land.* At its highest levels the state appears to be private property, whereas here private property should appear as property of the state. Instead of making private property a quality of citizenship, Hegel makes political citizenship, existence, and disposition a quality of private property.)

[On universal suffrage]

[In his Remark to §308] Hegel calls 'membership of the state' an *'abstract* determination', although according to the *Idea,* [and therefore] the intention of his own doctrinal development, it is the highest, *most concrete* determination of the ethical-political person [*Rechtsperson*], the member of the state. To stop at the determination of 'membership of the state' and to conceive of individuals in such terms does not therefore seem to be merely 'superficial thinking' which 'sticks to abstractions' [as Hegel claims]. That the determination 'membership of the state' is an *'abstract'* determination is not, however, the fault of this thinking but of Hegel's line of argument and of actual modern conditions which presuppose the separation of actual life from political life and make the political quality an 'abstract determination' of actual political participation, of actual participation in the state.

According to Hegel, the direct participation of all in deliberations and decisions on the universal concerns of the state admits 'in the organism of the state a *democratic* element *devoid of rational form,* although it is only by virtue of its rational form that the state is an organism'. That is to say, the democratic element can be admitted only as a *formal* element within a state organism that is merely a formalism of the state. 'The democratic element' should be, rather, the actual element that acquires its *rational* form in the *whole* of the state organism. If it enters the state organism or state formalism as a *'particular'* element, then the 'rational form' of its existence means only a drill [*Dressur*], an accommodation, a form in which it does not exhibit what is characteristic of its essence; in other words, it enters the state organism merely *as a formal* principle.

We have already pointed out that Hegel develops merely a *state formalism*. For him, the actual *material* principle is the *Idea*, the abstract thought-*form* of the state as a subject, the absolute Idea which has in it no passive or *material* moment. In contrast to the abstraction of this Idea the determinations of the actual, empirical state formalism appear as the *content*; and hence the *actual* content (in this case actual man, actual society etc.) appears as formless inorganic matter.

[...]

As we have seen, the state exists *merely* as *political* state. The totality of the state [in Hegel's account] is the *legislature* [*gesetzgebende Gewalt*].* To participate in the legislature is thus to participate in the political state and to prove and actualise one's existence as *member of the political state*, as *member of the state*. That *all as individuals* want to participate integrally in the legislature is nothing but the will *of all* to be actual (active) members of the state, or to give themselves a *political existence*, or to prove their existence as *political* and to effect it as such. We have further seen that the Assembly of Estates [*das ständische Element*] is the civil society of the legislature,† civil society's *political existence*. The fact, therefore, that civil society invades the sphere of *legislative* power *en masse*, and where possible *totally*, that actual civil society wants to substitute itself for the *fictional* civil society of the legislature, is nothing but the drive of civil society to give itself *political* existence, or to make *political existence* its actual existence. The drive of civil society to transform itself into *political* society, or to make *political* society and *actual* society one and the same manifests itself as the drive for the fullest possible *universal* participation in legislative power.

---

* In the *Philosophy of Right*, Hegel's account of the content and interrelationship of the three 'powers' in the state's 'internal constitution' – the crown [*fürstliche Gewalt*], the executive [*Regierungsgewalt*], and the legislature – is completed in his treatment of the latter, within which the other two powers operate along with representatives of the landed gentry and deputies from the 'corporations' of civil society, who sit in an Assembly of Estates. In this sense the legislature can be said to be 'the totality of the (political) state'.

† I.e. is the represented presence of civil society in the legislative power.

[...]

Within the representative constitution ... it is not a question of whether civil society should exercise legislative power through deputies or though all [of its members] as individuals. Rather, it is a question of the extension and greatest possible *universalisation* of *voting*, of *active* as well as *passive* suffrage. That is the real point of dispute in political *reform*, in France as well as England.

Voting is not considered philosophically, that is not in terms of its proper nature, if it is conceived only in relation to the *crown* or the *executive*. The *vote* is the *actual relation* of *actual civil society* to the *civil society* of the *legislature*, to the *representative element*. In other words, the *vote* is the *immediate*, *direct*, existing and not *simply imagined* relation of civil society to the political state. It therefore goes without saying that the *vote* is the chief political interest of actual civil society. In *unrestricted suffrage*, both active and passive, civil society has *actually* raised itself for the first time to an abstraction of itself, to *political* existence as its true universal and essential existence. But the full achievement of this abstraction is at once also the supersession [*Aufhebung*] of the abstraction. In actually establishing its *political existence* as its *true* existence civil society has simultaneously established its civil existence, in distinction from its political existence, as unessential; and with the one separated, the other, its opposite, falls. The *reform of voting* is therefore, within the *abstract political state*, the demand for the *dissolution* [*Auflösung*] of this state, but also the *dissolution of civil society*.

'On the Jewish Question'

I

Bruno Bauer, *The Jewish Question*
Braunschweig, 1843

The German Jews desire emancipation. Which emancipation do they want? *Civic,* that is, *political* emancipation.

Bruno Bauer replies to them: nobody in Germany is politically emancipated. We ourselves are not free. How are we supposed to liberate you? You Jews are *egoists* if you demand a special emancipation for yourselves as Jews. You have to participate as Germans in the political emancipation of Germany, as human beings in the emancipation of humanity, and not perceive the special form of your oppression and your humiliation as an exception to the rule, but rather as confirmation of the rule.

Or do the Jews demand equality with the *Christian subjects*? In that case they recognise the *Christian state* to be justified, they acknowledge the regime of general subjugation. Why should your special yoke displease you when you are satisfied with the general yoke? Why should the Germans take an interest in the liberation of the Jews when the Jews take no interest in the liberation of the Germans?

The *Christian* state knows only *privileges.* In this state the Jews have the privilege of being Jews. As Jews they have rights which the Christians do not have. Why do they desire rights which they do not have and which the Christians enjoy?

If the Jew wishes to be emancipated from the Christian state, he demands that the Christian state renounce its *religious* prejudice. Does the Jew renounce his religious prejudice? Does he, then, have the right to demand of another that he abjure religion in this way?

By *its essence* the Christian state cannot emancipate the Jews; but, Bauer adds, by their essence the Jews cannot be emancipated. As

28

long as the state is Christian and the Jews are Jewish, one is just as incapable of granting emancipation as the other is of receiving it.

The Christian state can only relate to the Jew in the manner of a Christian state, that is by way of privilege, in that it permits the separation of the Jew from its other subjects while allowing him to feel the pressure of the other separated spheres, with him feeling this pressure all the more as he stands in a *religious* opposition to the dominant religion. But the Jew can only relate to the state in the manner of a Jew, that is, relate to the state as to a foreign entity, in that he contrasts his chimerical nationality with the true nationality, his illusory law with the true law; in that he deems himself justified in separating himself from humanity, in taking no part in historical development as a matter of principle, in cherishing a future which has nothing to do with the general future of mankind, in considering himself a part of the Jewish people and considering the Jewish people the chosen people.

How do you Jews justify your demand for emancipation? On account of your religion? It is the arch enemy of the state religion. As citizens of the state? In Germany there are no citizens of the state. As human beings? You are no more human beings than those to whom you direct your appeal.

Bauer has raised the question of Jewish emancipation anew, following his criticism of previous positions and solutions to the question. How, he asks, are they both *constituted*, the Jews who are to be emancipated and the state which is to do the emancipating? He answers by means of a critique of the Jewish religion; he analyses the *religious* contrast between Judaism and Christianity; he enlightens [his reader] on the essence of the Christian state; and he does all this with a boldness, rigour, liveliness, and thoroughness, in a precise, pithy, and energetic writing style.

How then does Bauer resolve the Jewish question? What is his result? The formulation of a question is its solution. The critique of the Jewish question is the answer to the Jewish question. The resumé is as follows:

We have to emancipate ourselves before we can emancipate others.

The most rigid form of the opposition between Jews and Christians is the *religious* opposition. How does one dissolve an opposition? By making it impossible. How does one make a *religious* opposition impossible? By *annulling [aufheben] religion.* As soon as Jews and

Christians recognise their opposing religions as only *various stages of development of the human spirit*, as 'snake skins' sloughed off by *history*, and recognise themselves as the 'snakes', then they will no longer exist in a religious relationship but rather in a critical, *scientific* one, in a human relationship. *Science* then constitutes their unity. But oppositions in science are resolved through science itself.

Opposing the *German* Jews is the lack of political emancipation in general and the pronounced Christianness of the state. In Bauer's sense, however, the Jewish question has a universal meaning, independent of the specifically German relationships. It is the question of the relation of religion to the state, of the *contradiction between religious constraints and political emancipation*. The emancipation from religion confronts, as a condition, both the Jews, who want to be politically emancipated, and the state, which is supposed to emancipate and to be itself emancipated.

'All right, it is said – and the Jew himself says it – the Jew should not be emancipated because he is a Jew, not because he has such a fine, universal human principle of morality; the *Jew* should give primacy to *citizenship within the state* and be a *citizen of the state* despite the fact that he is and should remain a Jew: i.e. he is and remains a *Jew*, despite being a *citizen of the state* and living in universal, human relationships; his limited and Jewish essence is ever and always victorious over his human and political obligations. The prejudice remains despite its being overshadowed by *universal* principles. But if it does remain, much more does it overshadow everything else'. 'Only seemingly, as a piece of sophistry, would the Jew be able to remain a Jew in the life of the state; the mere semblance would therefore, if he wanted to remain a Jew, be the essential thing and would prevail, i.e. his *life in the state* would be mere semblance or just a momentary exception to the essence and the rule.' ('The Capacity of Contemporary Jews and Christians to Become Free', Twenty-One Folios, p. 57)

Let us see on the other hand how Bauer represents the function of the state:

'With respect to the Jewish Question – as in all other political questions –', it is stated, 'France has recently (Proceedings of the Chamber of Deputies, 26 December 1840) given us a view of a life which is free but whose freedom is revoked in the law: it makes freedom a mere appearance and on the other hand refutes its free law by its deeds'. ('Jewish Question', p. 64)

'Universal freedom is not yet the law in France, and the *Jewish question* is *also not* resolved, because legal freedom – that all citizens are equal – is restricted in a life still governed and divided by religious privileges; and this unfreedom of life affects the law, constraining it to sanction the division of the citizens, who are free in themselves, into oppressor and oppressed' (p. 65).

When then would the Jewish question be resolved in France?

'The Jew, for example, must have ceased to be Jew, if he does not allow himself to be obstructed by his law in fulfilling his obligations to the state and his fellow citizens, for example if on the sabbath he attends the Chamber of Deputies and takes part in the public sessions. Every *religious privilege* in general, and so also the monopoly of a privileged church, must be abolished, and if a few or many or *even the overwhelming majority still believe they have to fulfill their religious duties*, then this would have to *their own purely private concern*' (p. 65). 'There is no more religion if there is no more privileged religion. Take away from religion its power of exclusion and it will exist no longer' (p. 66). 'Just as Herr Martin du Nord saw, in the suggestion that any mention of Sunday be eliminated from the law, a proposal for a proclamation that Christianity has ceased to exist, so too declaring that the law of the sabbath no longer obliges the Jew would be with equal justification (and justification well founded) tantamount to proclaiming the end of Judaism' (p. 71).

Thus, Bauer demands on the one hand that Jews give up Judaism – in fact, that man give up religion in general – in order to be emancipated as *citizens of the state.* On the other hand he takes the *political* abolition of religion to be logically equivalent to the abolition of religion *in toto.* The state which presupposes religion is not yet a true, an actual state. 'To be sure, the religious concept [*Vorstellung*] gives guarantees to the state. But to which state? *To which sort of state?*' (p. 97).

It is on this point that the *one-sided* formulation of the Jewish question stands out.

It is by no means sufficient to ask: who should do the emancipating? who should be emancipated? There is a third thing that criticism has to do. It has to ask: what *sort of emancipation* is at issue? What conditions flow from the nature of the desired emancipation? Only the critique of *political emancipation* itself was the definitive critique of the Jewish question and its true dissolution into the *'general question of the times'*.

Because Bauer does not raise the question to this level, he falls into contradictions. He poses conditions that are not founded in the nature of *political* emancipation itself. He raises questions that are not part of his task, and he resolves issues that leave his question unanswered. When Bauer says of the opponents of Jewish emancipation, 'their only error was that they presupposed the Christian state as the only true one and did not subject it to the same criticism with which they treated Judaism' (p. 3), then we find Bauer's error in the fact that he subjects to criticism only the 'Christian state' and not the 'state simply', that he does not examine the *relationship of political emancipation to human emancipation*, and therefore poses conditions whose sole explanation lies in an uncritical confusion of political emancipation with general human emancipation. If Bauer asks the Jews: from your standpoint do you have the right to desire *political emancipation?* then we ask in return: does the standpoint of *political* emancipation have the right to demand of the Jews the abolition of Judaism, and of mankind in general the abolition of religion?

The Jewish question has a different formulation according to which state the Jews happen to be in. In Germany, where no political state, no state as state, exists, the Jewish question is a purely *theological* question. The Jew finds himself in *religious* opposition to a state which recognises Christianity as its basis. This state is a theologian *ex professo*. The critique here is a critique of theology, a two-edged critique, a critique of the Christian and of the Jewish theology. But in this fashion we are still involved in theology, however *critically* we may be involved in it.

In France, in a *constitutional* state, the Jewish question is a question of constitutionalism, a question of the *half-heartedness of the political emancipation*. Because the *semblance* of a state religion, even if in a mute and self-contradictory formulation, is maintained here in the shape of a *religion of the majority*, the relationship of the Jews to the state maintains the *semblance* of a religious, theological opposition.

Only in the North American free states – at least in a part of them – does the Jewish question lose its *theological* significance and become a truly *secular* question. Only where the political state exists

32

in its complete development can the relationship of the Jews, and in general of religious persons, to the political state – that is, the relationship of religion to the state – step forth in its proper characteristics and its pure form.

The critique of this relationship ceases to be a theological critique as soon as the state ceases to relate to religion in a *theological* manner, as soon as it relates as a state, i.e. relates *politically* to religion. The critique then becomes a *critique of the political state.* At this point, where the question ceases to be *theological,* Bauer's critique ceases to be critical. 'There exists in the United States neither a state religion nor a religion declared to be that of the majority, nor is there preeminence of one cult over another. The state stands apart from all cults.' (*Marie ou l'esclavage aux états-unis etc.,* par G. de Beaumont, Paris, 1835, p. 214) Indeed, there are several North American states in which 'the constitution does not impose any religious belief or any religious practice as a condition of political privilege' (*ibid.* p.224). Nevertheless, 'in the United States people do not believe that a man without religion can be an honest man' (*ibid.,* p. 224). Nevertheless, North America is the preeminent land of religiosity, as Beaumont, Tocqueville, and the Englishman, Hamilton, tell us with one voice. However the North American states only serve as an example. The question is: how does *accomplished* political emancipation relate to religion? If we find not only the existence, but the *vigorous* and *flourishing* existence, of religion in the very land of accomplished political emancipation, then we have proof that the existence of religion does not contradict the accomplishment of the state. But since the existence of religion is the existence of a defect, the source of this defect can only be sought in the *nature* of the state itself. We then no longer regard religion as the *basis,* but rather only as the *phenomenon* of a secular limitedness. We therefore explain the religious bias of free citizens of a state as resulting from their secular bias. We do not insist that they must abolish their religious limitation in order to abolish their secular limitations. We contend that they will abolish their religious limitation as soon as they abolish their secular limitations. We do not turn secular questions into theological ones; we turn theological questions into secular ones. After history has long enough been reduced to superstition, we are going to reduce superstition to history. The question of *the relationship of political emancipation to religion* becomes for us the question of the *relationship of political emancipation to human emancipation.* We criticise the religious weakness of the political state by criticising the political state in its *secular* construction, *apart* from its religious weaknesses. We humanise this issue by making the contradiction of the state with a *specific religion*, say, *Judaism*, into a contradiction of the state with *specific secular* elements, and the contradiction of the state with *religion in general* into a contradiction of the state with its *presuppositions* in general.

The *political* emancipation of the Jews, of the Christians, of *religious* persons in general, is the *emancipation of the state* from Judaism, from Christianity, from *religion* in general. In its form, in a fashion proper to its nature, the state as *state* emancipates itself from religion in that it emancipates itself from *state religion*, i.e. in that the state as state acknowledges no religion, in that the state rather acknowledges itself as state. *Political* emancipation from religion is not the completed, contradiction-free emancipation from religion, because political emancipation is not the completed, contradiction-free form of *human* emancipation.

The restricted character of political emancipation immediately appears in the fact that the *state* can free itself of a limitation without the human being *truly* being free of it, in the fact that the state can be a *free state* without the man being *a free man*. Bauer himself silently admits this when he postulates the following condition of political emancipation: 'Every religious privilege at all, and so also the monopoly of a privileged church, has to be abolished, and if a few or many or even the *vast majority still believe they have to fulfil their religious duties*, then this would have to be their own *purely private concern*'. The *state*, therefore, can have emancipated itself from religion even if the *vast majority* is still religious. And the *vast majority* does not cease being religious by being *privately* religious.

But the attitude of the state, namely the *free state*, towards religion is, still, only the attitude towards religion of the *people* who form the state. It follows from this that man frees himself from a barrier *politically*, via the *medium of the state*, in that, in contradiction with himself, he raises himself above it partially, in an *abstract* and *limited* fashion. Further, it follows that in freeing himself *politically* he frees himself in a round-about way, through a *medium*, even if a *necessary medium*. Finally, it follows that even if the person proclaims himself an atheist through the mediation of the state, i.e. if he proclaims the state to be atheistic, he still remains locked in a religious frame of reference, precisely because he recognises himself only in this round-about way, through a medium. Religion is precisely the recognition of the human being in a round-about fashion, through a *mediator*. The state is the mediator between man and human freedom. Just as Christ is the mediator whom the human being burdens with all of his divinity, all of his *religious constraint*, so too is the state the mediator into which he places all of his non-divinity, all of his *human spontaneity*.

The *political* elevation of the person over religion shares all the advantages and disadvantages of political elevation in general. The state *qua* state annuls, for example, *private property*; in a *political* fashion the person declares private property to be *superseded* as soon as he supersedes the *census* in favour of active and passive eligibility for elections, as this has been done in many North American states. From a political standpoint, *Hamilton* interprets this quite correctly thus: '*The masses have been victorious over the property owners and the moneyed classes.*' Is not private property ideally superseded when individuals without property become the legislators for those with property? The census is the final *political* form of recognition of private property.

Nevertheless, the political annulment of private property does not supersede private property, but on the contrary presupposes it. The state dissolves distinctions of *birth*, of *social rank*, of *education*, and of *occupation* if it declares birth, social rank, education, and occupation to be *non-political* distinctions; if without consideration of these distinctions it calls on every member of the nation to be an *equal* participant in the national sovereignty; if it treats all elements of the actual life of the nation from the point of view of the state. Nevertheless the state allows private property, education, occupation to *function* and affirm their *particular* nature in *their own* way, i.e. as private property, education, and occupation. Far from superseding these factual distinctions, the state's existence presupposes them: it feels itself to be *political state* and can affirm its *universality* only in opposition to these factors. *Hegel* thus quite correctly defines the relationship of the *political state* to religion when he says: 'If the state is to attain existence as the *self-knowing ethical actuality* of spirit, its form must become *distinct* from that of authority and faith. But this distinction emerges only in so far as the Church for its part becomes *divided* within itself. *Only* then, *above* the *particular* Churches, can the state attain *universality* of thought as its formal principle and bring it into existence' (Hegel's *Philosophy of Right*, 2nd edn, p. 346). To be sure! Only *above* the *particular* elements does the state constitute itself as universality.

The perfected political state is essentially the *species life* of man in opposition to his material life. All presuppositions of this *egoistic* life are retained *outside* the sphere of the state in *civil society*, but as attributes of civil society. Where the political state has attained its true development, man leads – and not only in thought, in consciousness, but also in *reality*, in *life* – a double life, a heavenly one and an earthly one, a life in the *political community*, in which he counts as a *communal being*, and a life in *civil society*, in which he acts as a *private individual*, views other people as means, debases himself to the status of a means, and becomes the plaything of alien forces. The political state relates just as spiritually to civil society as heaven does to earth. It stands in the same opposition, and overcomes it in the same way as religion overcomes the limitedness of the secular world, i.e. by recognising, restoring, and allowing itself to be governed by civil society. Man in his *immediate* reality, in civil society, is a secular being. Here, where he counts for himself and others as a real individual, he is a *false* semblance. In the state, on the other hand, where man counts as a species-being, he is an imaginary member of an illusory sovereignty, is robbed of his actual individual life, and is filled with an unreal universality.

The conflict in which the human being finds himself as an adherent of a *particular* religion, with his citizenship in a state, with other men as members of a community, reduces itself to the *secular* diremption between the *political* state and *civil society*. For the individual as *bourgeois*, 'life in the state is mere semblance or a momentary exception to the essence and the rule'. To be sure, the *bourgeois*, like the Jew, remains in the state only sophistically, just as the *citoyen* only sophistically remains a Jew or *bourgeois*; but this sophistry is not personal. It's the *sophistry of the political state* itself. The difference between the religious individual and the citizen of the state is the difference between the businessman and the citizen of the state, between the day-labourer and the citizen of the state, between the land owner and the citizen of the state, between the *living individual* and the *citizen of the state*. The contradiction in which the religious individual finds himself with the political individual, is the same contradiction

36

in which the *bourgeois* finds himself with the *citoyen,* or the member of civil society with his *political lion-skin.*

This secular antagonism to which the Jewish question reduces, this relationship of the political state to its presuppositions, whether these be material features such as private property, etc., or spiritual ones like education or religion, the conflict between the *universal* interest and *private interests,* the division between the *political state* and *civil society* – all these secular oppositions Bauer allows to remain, while polemicising against their *religious* expression. 'Precisely its basis, need, which secures for *civil society* its existence and *guarantees its necessity,* places its existence in constant danger, maintains within it an element of uncertainty, and brings forth that constantly changing mixture of poverty and wealth, want and plenty, in a word fluctuation.' (p. 8)

Look at the entire section, 'Civil Society' (pp. 8–9), which is composed according to the principles of the Hegelian Philosophy of Right. Civil society is recognised as necessary in its contrast to the political state, because the political state is recognised as necessary.

Political emancipation is to be sure a great advance, but it is certainly not the final form of human emancipation in general. Rather it is the final form of human emancipation *within* the previous order of things: Obviously we are speaking here of actual, practical emancipation.

Man emancipates himself *politically* from religion in that he banishes it from public right to the realm of private right. Religion is no longer the spirit of the *state,* in which man functions as a species-being – even if in a limited fashion, in a particular form and in a particular sphere – in society with other men; it becomes the spirit of *civil society,* of the sphere of egoism, of the *bellum omnium contra omnes.* It is no longer the essence of the *community,* but rather the essence of the *separation.* It has become the expression of the *diremption* of man from his *communal being,* from himself and other men – as it *originally* was. It is but the abstract acknowledgement of a particular folly, of a *private whim,* of caprice. The infinite splintering of religion in North America, for example, has already given it the *external* form of a purely individual matter. It has been relegated to the numerous private interests and, as the communal essence, exiled from the community. But let no one delude himself about the boundaries of political emancipation. The diremption of man into a *public* and a *private* man, the *dislocation* of religion out of the state into civil society, is not just a state, but rather the *completion* of political emancipation, which neither does nor tries to supersede the *actual* religiosity of man.

The *disintegration* of man into Jew and citizen of a state, into Protestant and citizen of a state, into religious person and citizen of a state, this disintegration is no lie *about* citizenship, it is not a circumvention of political emancipation, it *is political emancipation itself*, the *political* manner of emancipating oneself from religion. To be sure: in times when the political state is forcibly born as a political state out of civil society, when human self-liberation strives to complete itself in the form of political self-liberation, the state can and must continue to the point of *supersession of religion*, to the *destruction* of religion, although only in the same way as it moves to the supersession of private property, to declaration of the maximum, to confiscation, to progressive taxation, and even to the supersession of life, to the *guillotine*. In the moments of its special feeling of self, political life seeks to suppress its presuppositions, civil society and its elements, and to constitute itself as the actual, consistent species-life of man. It is able to do this only by *forcibly* contradicting its own conditions of life, only by declaring the revolution to be *permanent*, and therefore the political drama ends with the resurrection of religion, of private property, of all the elements of civil society, just as necessarily as war ends with peace.

Indeed, it is not the so-called *Christian* state, which recognises Christianity as its basis, its state religion, and which therefore has an exclusive relationship to other religions, that is the perfected Christian state, but rather the *atheistic* state, the *democratic* state, the state that relegates religion to the ranks of the other elements of civil society. The state which is still theological and which testifies officially to its adherence to Christianity, which does not yet dare to proclaim itself a *state*, does not succeed in expressing in its *reality* as a state, in *secular, human* form, the *human* basis whose rapturous expression is Christianity. The so-called Christian state is simply the *non-state*, because it is not Christianity as religion, but only the *human background* of the Christian religion that can fulfill itself in real human creations.

The so-called Christian state is the Christian denial of the state and in no way the political realisation of Christianity. The state which still professes Christianity in the form of religion does not yet profess it in the form of the state, for it relates religiously to religion, that is, it is not the *actual fulfillment* of the human basis of religion, because it still evokes the *unreality*, the *imaginary* form of this human core. The so-called Christian state is the *incomplete* state and the Christian religion serves as its *complement* and as the sanctification of its lack of completion. Religion therefore necessarily becomes a *means* for the state and it is a state of *hypocrisy*. It makes a considerable difference whether the *completed* state counts religion among its *presuppositions* because of the lack which lies in the general *nature* of the state, or whether the uncompleted state declares religion to be its *basis* because of the lack which lies in its *particular existence* as a deficient state. In the latter case religion becomes *unfinished politics*. In the former the incompletion of even completed *politics* is manifested in religion. The so-called Christian state requires the Christian religion in order to complete itself *as a state*. The democratic state, the real state, does not require religion for its political completion. It can abstract much more easily from religion because in this sort of a state the human basis of religion is carried out in a secular way. The so-called Christian state relates politically to religion and religiously to politics. In degrading the forms of state to a mere semblance, it just as much degrades religion to a mere semblance.

To make this contrast clear, let us examine Bauer's construction of the Christian state, a construction which stems from his observation of the Christian-Germanic state.

'Recently', says Bauer, 'in order to prove the *impossibility* or *nonexistence* of a Christian state, reference has often been made to those claims in the New Testament which the state *not only does not* follow but *cannot* follow *if it does not wish to disintegrate completely*'. 'But the matter is not as easy as all that. What do those claims of the New Testament demand? A supernatural self-denial, submission to the authority of revelation, a turning away from the state, the supersession of worldly relationships. Now the Christian state demands and fulfills all that. It appropriates the *spirit of the New Testament,* and if it does not repeat the spirit in the same words used in the New Testament, that is only because it expresses this spirit in political forms, i.e. in forms which are borrowed from the secular state, but which are degraded to mere semblances because of the religious metamorphosis they have to undergo. It is a turning away from the state that is achieved by using forms of the state' (p. 55).

Bauer then shows how the people of a Christian state is not a people, has no will of its own, has its true existence in the sovereign who rules over it although foreign to it by origin and nature, i.e., is given to it by God without the people's doing; how its laws are not of its own making but rather are positive revelations; how its master requires privileged intermediaries with his own people, with the mass; how this mass itself is divided into a conglomeration of particular spheres, constituted and determined by accident, which differ in their interests and their particular passions and prejudices, and which receive as their privilege the permission to segregate themselves from one another, etc. (p. 56).

But Bauer himself says: 'If politics is supposed to be nothing but religion, then it cannot be considered politics any more than cleaning the kitchen utensils, if supposed to be a religious affair, would be considered a household matter' (p. 108). But in the Christian-Germanic state religion is a 'household matter' just as the 'household matter' is religion. In the Christian-Germanic state the dominance of religion is the religion of dominance.

The separation of the 'spirit of the gospel' from the 'letter of the gospel' is an *irreligious* act. The state which allows the gospel to speak in the words of politics, in words other than those of the Holy Spirit, commits a sacrilegious act, if not in human eyes, then in its own religious eyes. The *words* of Holy Scripture must be used against the state which recognises Christianity as its highest norm, which accepts the *Bible* as its *charter*, for every word of Scripture is holy. This state, as well as the *human refuse* on which it bases itself, lands in a contradiction that is painful and, from the standpoint of religious consciousness, insurmountable if reference is made to those claims of the New Testament which it 'not only does not follow but *cannot follow if it does not want to disintegrate completely as a state*'. And why does it not want to disintegrate completely? On this it can answer neither itself nor others. In its *own consciousness* the official Christian state is a ' *supposed to be*' whose realisation is unachievable. This state can confirm the reality of its existence to itself only through lies, and therefore it remains for itself always an object of doubt, an unreliable, problematic object. Criticism, then, is fully justified if it forces the state which evokes the Bible to a point of mental derangement, where it no longer knows itself whether it is *imaginary or real*, where the infamy of its *secular* goals, for which religion serves as a cover, lands in insoluble conflict with the honesty of its *religious* consciousness, for which religion seems the goal of the world. This state can only resolve its inner torment if it becomes the *myrmidon* of the Catholic Church. Against this church, which declares secular power to be in its service, the state is powerless, a powerless *secular* power which claims to be the supremacy of the religious spirit.

In the so-called Christian state *estrangement*, to be sure, has worth, but not *man*. The only man of worth is the *king*, the one being who is specifically different from all others, himself a religious creature directly connected with heaven, with God. The connections that prevail here are still connections of *faith*. Thus the religious spirit is not yet really secularised.

But the religious spirit also cannot be *actually* secularised, for what is it but the *unsecular* form of a state of development of the human spirit? The religious spirit can only be secularised insofar as the stage of development of the human spirit whose religious expression it is steps forth and constitutes itself in its *secular* form. This occurs in the *democratic* state. Not Christianity, but rather the *human ground* of Christianity is the basis of this state. Religion remains the ideal, unworldly consciousness of its members because it is the ideal form of the *human stage of development* which is achieved in it [i.e. in the democratic state].

The members of the political state are religious through the dualism between individual life and species-life, between the life of civil society and political life; religious in that man relates to the life of the state, which is foreign to his actual individuality, as though it were his true life; religious in so far as religion here is the spirit of civil society, the expression of the separation and the distancing of man from man. Political democracy is Christian in that in it man – not only one man, but every man – has value as a *sovereign* being, the highest being, but this is man in his uncultivated, unsocial aspect, man in his accidental existence, man just as he is, corrupted by the entire organisation of our society, lost to himself, alienated, under the domination of inhuman relationships and elements – in a word, man who is not yet an actual species-being. The fantasy, the dream, the postulate of Christianity, namely the sovereignty of man – but man as an alien being, different from actual man – is in democracy a sensuous reality, presence, secular maxim.

In perfected democracy, religious and theological consciousness takes itself to be all the more religious and theological in having no political significance or earthly purposes, a matter of an unworldly disposition, expressive of a restricted spirit, a product of caprice and fantasy, a really other-worldly life. Christianity attains here the *practical* expression of its universally religious significance, in that the most diverse world views are grouped together in the form of Christianity, and even more through the fact that not once did it demand Christianity of others, but only religion in general, any religion (cf. the work of Beaumont cited above). Religious consciousness revels in the wealth of religious opposition and variety.

We have therefore shown that the political emancipation from religion allows the continued existence of religion, even if not a privileged religion. The contradiction in which the adherent of a particular religion finds himself with his state citizenship is only a *part* of the universal *secular contradiction between the political state and civil society*. The completion of the Christian state is the state which acknowledges itself to be a state and abstracts from the religion of its members. The emancipation of the state from religion is not the emancipation of actual man from religion.

Therefore we do not, with Bauer, say to the Jews: you cannot be politically emancipated without radically emancipating yourselves from Judaism. Rather we tell them: because you can be politically emancipated without fully and definitively withdrawing from Judaism, *political emancipation* itself is not *human* emancipation. If you Jews want to be politically emancipated without emancipating yourselves humanly, the imperfection and contradiction lies not only in you, it lies in the *essence* and the *category* of political emancipation. If you are caught in this category, then you share a general constraint. Just as the state *evangelises* if it, despite being a state, relates in a Christian manner to the Jews, so also the Jew *politicises* if, despite being a Jew, he demands the rights of citizenship.

But if the man, even though he is a Jew, can be politically emancipated and receive the rights of citizenship, can he claim and receive the so-called *human rights*? Bauer denies it. 'The question is whether the Jew as such, i.e. the Jew who admits to himself that by his true essence he is forced to live in eternal separation from others, is capable of receiving *universal human rights* and granting those rights to others.'

'The idea of human rights was first discovered in the Christian world in the previous century. It is not inherent in man, but is won in the struggle against the historic tradition in which man was previously raised. So human rights are not a gift of nature, nor a dowry of previous history, but rather the prize of the struggle against the accident of birth and privilege, which until now history has bequeathed from generation to generation. They are the results of a formative process, and only those can possess them who have gained them and earned them.'

'Can the Jew now really take possession of them? As long as he is a Jew, the restricted nature that makes him a Jew and separates him from non-Jews must triumph over the human nature that should bind him as a man to other men. Through this separation he declares that the particular nature that makes him a Jew is his true and highest nature, before which the nature of man must give way.'

'In the same fashion the Christian as Christian can grant no human rights' (pp. 19, 20).

According to Bauer, man must sacrifice the *'privilege of belief'* to be able to receive universal human rights. Let us look for a moment at the so-called human rights, and indeed human rights in their authentic form, the form in which they are found among their *discoverers,* the North Americans and the French! In part these human rights are *political* rights, rights which are exercised only in community with others. *Participation* in the *community* and specifically in the *political* community, in the state, constitutes their content. They fall under the category of *political freedom,* under the category of the *rights of citizenship,* which, as we have seen, in no way presupposes an unconditional and positive supersession of religion, nor therefore of Judaism. The other part of the rights of man remain to be considered, the *rights of man* in so far as they differ from the rights of citizen.

Among these rights we find the freedom of conscience, the right to exercise the cult of one's choice. The *privilege of belief* is expressly recognised, either as a *human right* or as the consequence of a human right, of freedom.

Declaration of the Rights of Man and of the Citizen, 1791, Art. 10: 'No one is to be disturbed because of his opinions, even religious opinions'. Title 1 of the Constitution of 1791 guarantees as a human right: 'The freedom of every man to practice the *particular religion* to which he belongs'.

Declaration of the Rights of Man etc. 1793 numbers among the rights of man, Art. 7: 'The free exercise of religion'. Indeed, with respect to the right of publicly expressing one's thoughts and opinions, of assembly, of practising one's religion, it is even stated: 'The need to enunciate these rights supposes either the presence or the recent memory of despotism'. See also the Constitution of 1795, title XIV, Art. 354.

Constitution of Pennsylvania, Art. 9 §3: 'All men have received from nature the imprescriptable *right* to adore the Almighty as their conscience inspires them, and none may be legally constrained to follow, institute, or support against his wish any cult or religious ministry. No human authority may, in any case, intrude into matters of conscience and control the powers of the soul.'

Constitution of New Hampshire, Art. 5 and 6: 'Among the natural rights some are inalienable by their nature because nothing can be their equivalent. Among these are the rights of conscience' (Beaumont, l.c. pp. 213, 214).

The incompatibility of religion with human rights is so little grounded in the concept of human rights that the right to be *religious*, and to be religious in the way one chooses, to practice one's particular religion, is in fact to be numbered expressly among human rights. The *privilege of belief* is a *universal human right*.

The *droits de l'homme*, the rights of man, human rights, as *such* are different from the *droits du citoyen*, from the rights of the citizen. Who is the *homme* who differs from the *citizen*? None other than the *member of civil society*. Why is the member of civil society called 'man', man pure and simple, and why are his rights called *human rights*? How are we to explain this fact? From the relationship of the political state to civil society, from the nature of political emancipation.

Above all we confirm the fact that the so-called *human rights*, the *droits de l'homme* in contrast to the *droits du citoyen*, are nothing but the rights of the *member of civil society*, i.e. of egoistic man, of the man who is separated from other men and from the community. Let the most radical constitution, that of 1793 speak:

Declaration of the Rights of Man and of the Citizen.

Art. 2. These rights etc. (the natural and imprescriptable rights) are: *equality, liberty, security, property*.

In what does *liberty* consist?

Art. 6. 'Liberty is the power belonging to man to do everything that does not harm the rights of another', or according to the Declaration of Human Rights of 1791: 'Liberty consists in being able to do everything that does not harm another'.

Freedom, then, is the right to do and to pursue what does not harm another. The limit within which everyone can operate in a way not harmful to others is determined by law, like the boundary between two fields is determined by the fencepost. This is the freedom of man as a monad isolated and withdrawn into himself. Why, according to Bauer, is the Jew incapable of having human rights. 'As long as he is a Jew, the restricted nature that makes him a Jew and separates him from non-Jews, must triumph over the human nature that should bind him as a man to other men.' But the human right of freedom is not based on the connection of man with man, but much more on the separation of man from man. It is the *right* of this separation, the right of the individual who is *limited*, enclosed within himself.

The practical application of the human right of freedom is the right of *private property*.

In what consists the right of private property?

Art. 16 (Constitution of 1793). 'The right of *property* is that which belongs to each citizen to enjoy and to dispose *as he pleases* of his goods, of his revenues, of the fruit of his labour and of his industry'.

The human right of private property is thus the right to enjoy and dispose of one's wealth arbitrarily (as one pleases), without relation to other men, independently of society, the right of personal use. That individual freedom together with this application of it constitutes the basis of civil society. It allows each man to find in the others not the *actualisation*, but much more the *limit*, of his freedom. But above all it proclaims the human right to 'enjoy and to dispose *as he pleases* of his goods, of his revenues, of the fruit of his labour and of his industry'.

There still remain the other human rights, equality and security.

Equality here, in its non-political significance, is nothing but the parity of the *liberté* described above, namely: that every human as such is equally considered to be a self-based monad. The Constitution of 1795 defines the concept of this parity, in keeping with its meaning, thus:

Art. 3 (Constitution of 1795). 'Equality consists in the fact that the law is the same for all, whether it protects or punishes'.

And security?

Art. 8 (Constitution of 1793). 'Security consists in the protection accorded by society to each of its members for the conservation of his person, of his rights, and of his properties'.

Security is the highest social concept of civil society, the concept of the *police*, the concept that the entire society exists only to guarantee each of its members the preservation of his person, of his rights, and of his property. In this sense Hegel calls civil society 'the state of necessity and of the understanding' [*Philosophy of Right* §183].

Civil society does not by the concept of security transcend its egoism. Much more so is security the *insuring* of its egoism.

None of the so-called human rights then goes beyond the egoistic man, beyond man as member of civil society, namely withdrawn into his private interests and his private will, separated from the community. Not only is man not considered in these human rights to be a species-being, but also species-life itself, society, appears to be a context external to the individuals, and a restriction of their original independence. The one tie that holds them together is natural necessity, need and private interest, the conservation of their property and their egoistic person.

It is curious that a nation that begins to liberate itself, to tear down all barriers between the various national groupings and to found a political community, that such a nation solemnly proclaims (Declaration of 1791) the privileges of egoistic man, separated from his fellow man and from the community, indeed even repeats this proclamation at a moment when only heroic sacrifice can save the nation and is therefore imperative, at an instant when relinquishing every interest of civil society has to be the order of the day and egoism must be punished as a crime. (Declaration of the Rights of Man, etc. of 1793.) This fact becomes even more curious if we consider that citizenship in the state, that the *political community*, is even reduced by the political emancipators to the status of a mere *means* for the preservation of these so-called human rights, in other words that the citizen is declared to be the servant of the egoistic man and the sphere in which man functions as a communal being is degraded and subordinated to the sphere in which he functions as a partial being; finally, that it is not man as citizen but man as bourgeois who is taken to be the *real* and *true* human being.

'The *aim* of all *political associations* is the *preservation* of the natural and imprescriptible rights of man'. (Declaration of the Rights etc. of

1791, Art. 2) '*Government* is instituted to guarantee to man the enjoyment of his natural and imprescriptable rights'. (Declaration etc. of 1793 Art. 1) Thus, in the very moments of its youthful enthusiasm, to the extreme of which it is driven by the force of circumstances, political life is declared to be a mere *means* whose purpose is the life of civil society. Surely its revolutionary practice stands in flagrant contradiction to its theory. For example, while security is declared to be a human right, the violation of the secrecy of the mail is publicly made the order of the day. While the '*unlimited* freedom of the press' (Constitution of 1793, Art. 122) is guaranteed as a consequence of the rights of man, a consequence of individual freedom, the freedom of the press is completely destroyed, for 'freedom of the press should not be permitted when it compromises public freedom' (Robespierre jeune, *Histoire parlementaire de la Révolution française,* par Buchez et Roux, T. 28, p. 59); that is to say, the human right of freedom ceases to be a right as soon as it conflicts with *political* life, while according to the theory, political life is only the guarantee of human rights, the rights of the individual man, and thus must be relinquished as soon as it contradicts its *purpose,* these human rights. But practice is only the exception and theory is the rule. Should one wish, however, to consider revolutionary practice itself as the correct position of the relationship, then there still remains a puzzle to be solved: why in the consciousness of the political emancipators the relationship is turned on its head and the end appears as the means and the means as the end. This optical illusion of their consciousness would still be the same puzzle, but then a psychological, a theoretical puzzle.

The puzzle is easily solved.

Political emancipation is also the *dissolution* of the old society, on which rests the state which is estranged from the people – the sovereign power. Political revolution is the revolution of civil society. What was the character of the old society? One word characterises it: *feudalism.* The old civil society had *immediately* a *political* character, i.e. the elements of civil life, e.g. property or the family, or the form and manner of labour, were raised in the form of estate ownership, of the social orders and corporations, to elements in the life of the state. In these forms they determined the relationship of the single individual to the *whole of the state,* i.e. his *political* relationship, i.e. his relationship of division and exclusion from the other component parts of society. For that organisation of the life of the people did not elevate property or labour to the status of social elements, but rather completed their *separation* from the state as a whole and constituted them as *special* particular societies within society. Thus the functions and conditions of the life of civil society were still political, although political in the feudal sense, i.e. they separated the individual from the whole of the state, they transformed the *particular* relationship of his guild to the whole of the state into his own general relationship to the life of the people, just as his specific civil activity and situation were transformed into his general activity and situation. As a consequence of this organisation, the unity of the state, along with its consciousness, will, and activity, the universal power of the state, likewise necessarily appears to be a *particular* concern of a ruler separated from his people and surrounded by his servants.

The political revolution that toppled this sovereign power and raised state matters to the status of concerns of the people, which constituted the political state as a *universal* concern, i.e. as an actual state, necessarily destroyed all social orders, corporations, guilds, and privileges, which were just so many expressions of the separation of the people from their community. With that the political revolution *abolished* the *political character of civil society*. It broke civil society down into its simple components, on the one hand the *individuals*, on the other the *material* and *spiritual elements* that constituted the content of life, the civil situation of these individuals. It released the political spirit which had been, as it were, divided, dispersed, and decomposed in the various cul-de-sacs of feudal society; it collected this spirit out of this helter-skelter dispersion, freed it from its confusion with civil life, and constituted it as the sphere of the community, of the *universal* concern of the people in an ideal independence from those *particular* elements of civil life. The *specific* activity and *specific* situation of life were debased to merely individual significance. They no longer formed the universal relationship of the individual to the whole of the state. Public affairs as such became the universal affair of each individual and the political function became his universal function.

But the completion of the state's idealism was at the same time the completion of civil society's materialism. The shedding of the political yoke was at the same time the shedding of the ties that restrained the egoistic spirit of civil society. Political emancipation was at the same time the emancipation of civil society from politics, from even the *semblance* of a universal content.

Feudal society was dissolved into its basis, into man, but into man as he was truly its basis, into *egoistic* man.

This man, the member of civil society, is now the basis, the presupposition, of the *political* state. He is recognised as such by the state in the rights of man.

But the freedom of egoistic man and the recognition of this freedom is really the recognition of the *unbridled* movement of the spiritual and material elements which form the content of his life.

Man, therefore, was not freed from religion, he received the freedom of religion. He was not freed from property. He received the freedom of property. He was not freed from the egoism of trade, he received the freedom of trade.

The *constitution of the political state* and the dissolution of civil society into independent *individuals* – whose relationship is Right, just as men's relationship within the estate and guild was *privilege* – is completed in *one and the same act.* But man as a member of civil society, *unpolitical* man, necessarily appears to be the *natural* man. The rights of man appear to be natural rights, for *self-conscious activity* is concentrated on the *political act.* Egoistic man is the *passive* and merely *discovered* result of the dissolved society, an object of *immediate certainty,* and thus a *natural* object. The *political revolution* dissolves civil life into its components, without *revolutionising* these components themselves and subjecting them to criticism. It relates to civil society, to the world of need, of labour, of private interests, and of private right as to the *basis of its existence, its fundamental premise,* hence its *natural basis.* Finally, man in his capacity as member of civil society counts as the *genuine* man, as the *homme* in contrast to the *citoyen,* because he is man in his sensuous, individual, and *immediate* existence, while *political* man is only abstract, artificial man, man as an *allegorical, moral* person. Actual man is recognised only in the form of the *egoistic* individual, and true man only in the form of the *abstract citoyen.*

Rousseau correctly describes the abstraction of political man thus: 'whoever undertakes to create a people must consider himself capable of changing, so to speak, *human nature;* of *transforming* each individual, who by himself is a perfect and solitary whole, into a *part* of a larger whole from which this individual in some way receives his life and his being; of substituting a *partial* and *moral* existence for physical and independent existence. He must take from *man his own forces* so as to give him others that are foreign to him and that he can use only with the help of another' (Contrat Social, Bk liv. II. London, 1782, pp. 67, 68.).

Every emancipation *leads* the human world and its relationships *back* to *man himself.*

Political emancipation is the reduction of man on the one hand to the member of civil society, to the *egoistic, independent* individual, and on the other to the *citizen of the state*, to the moral person.

Only when the actual individual man absorbs the abstract citizen of the state into himself and has become in his empirical life, in his individual labour, in his individual relationships a *species-being*, only when he has recognised and organised his 'own forces' as *social* forces and therefore no longer separates the social force from himself in the form of *political* force; only then is human emancipation completed.

II
'The Capacity of Contemporary Jews and Christians to Become Free'
by Bruno Bauer
(*Twenty-One Folios*, pp. 56–71)

In this form Bauer treats the relationship between the *Jewish and Christian religions* as well as their relationship to criticism. Their relationship to criticism is their relationship 'to the capacity to become free'.

The result: 'The Christian has to surmount only one stage, namely his religion, in order to supersede religion altogether', and thus to become free; 'the Jew on the contrary has to break not only with his Jewish nature, but also with the development of his religion's fulfillment, a development that has remained foreign to him' (p. 71).

Here, therefore, Bauer transforms the question of the emancipation of the Jews into a purely religious question. The theological scruple of who has the better prospect of achieving blessedness, the Jew or the Christian, is repeated in enlightened form: which of the two is *more capable of emancipation?* It is no longer a question of whether Judaism or Christianity is liberating, but rather the reverse: which is more liberating, the negation of Judaism or the negation of Christianity?

'If they want to become free, the Jews must not acknowledge Christianity, but rather a dissolved Christianity, dissolved religion in general, i.e. enlightenment, criticism and its result, free humanity' (p. 70).

It is still a matter of the Jews acknowledging a *creed*, no longer the creed of Christianity but of a dissolved Christianity.

Bauer exhorts the Jews to break with the essence of the Christian religion, a demand which, as he himself says, does not flow from the developed essence of Judaism.

After Bauer, at the conclusion of *The Jewish Question*, had conceived of Judaism as only the crude religious critique of Christianity, and thus had ascribed to it 'only' a religious significance, it was to be expected that the emancipation of the Jews would also be transformed into a philosophical-theological act.

Bauer considers the *ideal*, abstract essence of the Jew, his *religion*, to be his *entire* essence. He therefore rightly concludes: 'The Jew gives humanity nothing, if he disregards for himself his limited law', if he supersedes all of his Jewishness (p. 65).

Accordingly, the relationship of Jews and Christians becomes as follows: the sole interest of the Christian in the emancipation of the Jew is a universal human one, a *theoretical* interest. Judaism is an affront in the religious eye of the Christian. As soon as his eye ceases to be religious, this fact ceases to be offensive. The emancipation of the Jew is neither implicitly nor explicitly a task for the Christian.

On the contrary, for the Jew to liberate himself, he has to carry out not only his own task, but at the same time the task of the Christian, the *Critique of the Synoptic Gospels* and *The Life of Jesus*, etc.

'They themselves must deal with it: they themselves will determine their fate: but history is not to be scoffed at' (p. 71).

We are trying to break through the theological formulation of the question. The question about the capacity of the Jew to be emancipated is for us transformed into the question of which particular *social* element is to be overcome in order to supersede Judaism? For the capacity of the contemporary Jew to be emancipated is the relationship of Judaism to the emancipation of the contemporary world. This relationship results necessarily from the particular position of Judaism in the contemporary servile world.

Let us consider the actual secular Jew, not the *Sabbath Jew*, as Bauer does, but rather the *everyday Jew*.

Let us not look for the secret of the Jew in his religion, but rather for the secret of the religion in the actual Jew.

What is the secular basis of Jewry? *Practical* need, *self-interest*.

What is the secular cult of the Jew? *Haggling* [*Der Schacher*]. What is his secular God? *Money*.

Now then! Emancipation from *haggling* and from *money*, thus from practical, real Jewishness would be the self-emancipation of our times.

An organisation of society which would abolish the presuppositions, and thus the possibility of haggling, would make the Jew impossible. His religious consciousness would dissolve like a stale vapour in the actually living atmosphere of society. On the other hand: if the Jew recognises his *practical* essence to be nullified and works toward its supersession, he will overcome his previous development, will contribute to *human emancipation* in general and will turn against the *supreme practical* expression of human self-estrangement. We thus recognise in Judaism a universal *contemporary anti-social* element, which through an historical development, to which Jews in this negative sense have industriously contributed, has been brought to its present peak, a peak at which it must necessarily be dissolved.

In its final significance the *emancipation of the Jews* is the emancipation of humanity from *Jewishness*.

The Jew has already emancipated himself in the Jewish manner. 'The Jew who is only tolerated in Vienna, for example, determines through his financial power the fate of the entire empire. The Jew who may be without rights in the smallest of the German states decides the fate of Europe. While the corporations and guilds are closed to the Jews, or are not yet sympathetic to them, the boldness of industry mocks at the obstinacy of these medieval institutions' (B. Bauer, *The Jewish Question*, p. 114).

This is not an isolated fact. The Jew has emancipated himself in a Jewish fashion not only in that he has acquired financial power, but also in that with and without him, *money* has become a world power and the practical Jewish spirit has become the practical spirit of the

Christian peoples. Jews have emancipated themselves in so far as Christians have become Jews.

'The pious and politically free inhabitant of New England', reports, for example, Captain Hamilton, 'is a kind of *Laocoon* who makes not the least effort to escape from the serpents which are crushing him. *Mammon* is his idol which he adores not only with his lips but with the whole force of his body and mind. In his view the world is no more than a Stock Exchange, and he is convinced that he has no other destiny here below than to become richer than his neighbor. Trade has seized upon all his thoughts, and he has no other recreation than to exchange objects. When he travels he carries, so to speak, his goods and his counter on his back and talks only of interest and profit. If he loses sight of his own business for an instant it is only in order to pry into the business of his competitors.' [Thomas Hamilton, *Men and Manners in America*]

Indeed, the practical domination of Judaism over the Christian world has achieved in North America the unequivocal, normal expression: the very *preaching of the Gospels*, the Christian Ministry, has become an article of commerce, and the bankrupt merchant does business with the Gospels just like the newly rich evangelist engages in small business.

'The man who you see at the head of a respectable congregation began as a trader; his business having failed, he became a minister. The other began as a priest, but as soon as he had some money at his disposal he left the pulpit to go into business. In the eyes of a great many, the religious ministry is a veritable industrial career' (Beaumont, op. cit., pp. 185, 186).

According to Bauer, it is 'hypocrisy' if in theory the Jew is denied political rights while in practice he has great power and exercises *en gros* a political influence that is *en detail* restricted! (*The Jewish Question*, p. 114).

The contradiction between the practical political power of the Jew and his political rights is the contradiction between politics and the power of money in general. While the former ideally takes precedence over the latter, in fact politics has become the servant of this power.

Judaism has maintained itself *next* to Christianity not only as a religious critique of Christianity, not only as incorporated doubt about the religious origin of Christianity, but every bit as much because the practical Jewish spirit, because Jewishness has been preserved in

Christian society itself, and has there even found its highest development. The Jew, who is otherwise a particular member of civil society, is but the particular manifestation of the Jewishness of civil society.

Judaism has preserved itself not despite history but by means of history.

Out of its own entrails civil society continuously brings forth the Jew.

What was implicitly and explicitly the fundament of the Jewish religion? Practical need, egoism.

The monotheism of the Jews, therefore, is in reality the polytheism of the multiplicity of needs, a polytheism which even makes the latrine into an object of divine law. *Practical need, egoism*, is the principle of *civil society* and shows itself as such in all its purity as soon as civil society gives complete birth out of itself to the political state. The god of *practical need and personal self-interest* is *money*.

Money is the jealous god of Israel, before which no other god can exist. Money humbles all of man's gods – and turns them into a commodity. Money is the universal *value* of all things, constituted for itself. It has therefore robbed the entire world, the world of man as well as nature, of their own value. Money is the estranged essence of man's labour and existence, and this estranged essence dominates him, and he worships it.

The god of the Jews has been secularised; he has become a worldly god. The bill of exchange is the real god of the Jews. Their god is just an illusory bill of exchange.

The idea of nature to which one comes under the domination of private property and of money is the actual contempt, the practical degradation, of nature, which certainly exists in the Jewish religion, but exists only in the imagination.

In this sense Thomas Münzer declares it intolerable 'that all creatures have been made into property, the fish in the water, *the birds in the air*, the plants on the earth – the creatures, too, must be free'.

What the Jewish religion contains abstractly, the contempt of theory, of art, of history, of humanity as an end in itself, is the *actual, conscious* standpoint, the virtue of the man of money. The species-relationship itself, the relationship of man and woman, etc. becomes an object of trade. Women are bartered off.

The *chimerical* nationality of the Jew is the nationality of the businessman, of the financial man in general.

The law of the Jew, devoid of any basis, is but the religious carica-
ture of the baseless morality and Right in general, the merely *formal*
rites with which the world of self-interest surrounds itself.

Here, too, the highest relationship of man is the *legal* relationship,
the relationship to laws which are not important to him because they
are laws of his own will and being, but rather because they *dominate*
and because their violation brings *punishment*.

Jewish Jesuitism, the same practical Jesuitism that Bauer detects
in the Talmud, is the relationship of the world of self-interest to the
governing laws, whose artful circumvention is the principal skill of
this world.

Indeed, the movement of this world within its laws is necessarily
a constant abolishing of the law.

Judaism could not evolve further as a *religion*, could not develop
itself further theoretically, because the world view of practical need
is by its nature restricted and is totally exhausted in a few traits.

By its very nature the religion of practical need cannot find its
completion in theory but rather in *praxis* only, precisely because its
truth is praxis.

Judaism could not create a new world; it could only draw the new
creations and relationships of the world into its sphere of activity,
because practical need, whose understanding is self-interest, remains
passive and does not expand as it desires, but rather *finds* itself
expanded with the on-going development of social circumstances.

Judaism reaches its high point with the completion of civil society;
but civil society first completes itself in the *Christian* world. Only
under the authority of Christianity, which makes *all* national, natural,
ethical, theoretical relationships *external* to man, can civil society fully
separate itself from the life of the state, sunder all species-bonds of
man and replace them with egoism, self-seeking need, and dissolve
the world of man into a world of atomic, mutually hostile individuals.

Christianity derives from Judaism. It has once again been dissolved
back into Judaism.

From the very beginning the Christian was the theorising Jew, the
Jew therefore is the practical Christian, and the practical Christian
has again become a Jew.

Christianity has surpassed real Judaism only in appearance. It was
too *refined*, too spiritual, to dispose of the crudity of practical need
other than by dissolving it in thin air.

Christianity is the sublime thought of Judaism, Judaism is the vulgar application of Christianity, but this application became universal only after Christianity as the perfected religion had *theoretically* completed the self-estrangement of man from himself and from nature.

Only then could Judaism attain universal dominion and make *alienated* man and nature into *alienable* objects, to be bought and sold, in the service of egoistic need, into objects of trade.

Buying and selling is the praxis of alienation. Just as man, so long as he remains the captive of religion, can objectify his being only by making it into an *alien*, phantasy being, so too, under the dominion of egoistic need, he can be active practically, produce practical objects, only by placing his products and his activity under the domination of an alien being and bestowing on them the significance of an alien being – of money.

In its completed praxis the Christian egoism of happiness is necessarily transformed into the material egoism of the Jew, heavenly need into worldly need, subjectivism into self-interest. The tenacity of the Jew is not to be explained by his religion, but much rather by the human basis of his religion, by practical need and egoism.

Because the real essence of the Jew has been universally realised and secularised in civil society, civil society could not convince the Jew of the *unreality* of his *religious* essence, which is just the ideal view of practical need. Thus, not just in the Pentateuch or in the Talmud [but] in contemporary society do we find the essence of the contemporary Jew, not as an abstract but rather as a highly empirical being, not just as a limitation of the Jew but as the Jewish limitation of society.

As soon as society succeeds in abolishing the *empirical* essence of Judaism, i.e. haggling and its presuppositions, the Jew will become *impossible*, because his consciousness will no longer have an object, because the subjective basis of Judaism, practical need, will be humanised, because the conflict of individual sensuous existence with the species-existence of man will be superseded.

The *social* emancipation of the Jew is the *emancipation of society from Judaism*.

'A Contribution to the Critique of Hegel's Philosophy of Right: Introduction'

For Germany, the *critique* of *religion* is essentially completed; and the critique of religion is the prerequisite of every critique.

Error in its *profane* form of existence is compromised once its *celestial oratio pro aris et focis* has been refuted. Man, who has found only his own *reflection* in the fantastic reality of heaven, where he sought a supernatural being, will no longer be disposed to find only the *semblance* of himself, only a non-human being, here where he seeks and must seek his true actuality.

The foundation of irreligious criticism is this: *man makes religion*; religion does not make man. Religion is, in fact, the self-consciousness and self-esteem of man who either has not yet gained himself or has lost himself again. But *man* is no abstract being squatting outside the world. Man is *the world of man*, the state, society. This state, this society, produce religion, which is an *inverted world-consciousness*, because they are an *inverted world*. Religion is the general theory of this world, its encyclopedic compendium, its logic in popular form, its spiritualistic *point d'honneur*, its enthusiasm, its moral sanction, its solemn complement, its universal basis of consolation and justification. It is the *fantastic realisation* of the human being because the *human being* has attained no true actuality. Thus, the struggle against religion is indirectly the struggle against *that world* of which religion is the spiritual *aroma*.

The wretchedness of *religion* is at once an *expression* of and a *protest* against real wretchedness. Religion is the sigh of the oppressed creature, the heart of a heartless world and the soul of soulless conditions. It is the *opium* of the people.

The abolition of religion as the *illusory* happiness of the people is a demand for their *true* happiness. The call to abandon illusions about their condition is the *call to abandon a condition that requires illusions.* Thus, the critique of religion is the *critique in embryo of the vale of tears* of which religion is the *halo.*

Criticism has plucked the imaginary flowers from the chain, not so that man shall never bear the chain without fantasy or consolation, but so that he shall cast off the chain and gather the living flower. The critique of religion disillusions man so that he will think, act, and fashion his reality as a man who has lost his illusions and regained his reason, so that he will revolve about himself as his own true sun. Religion is only the illusory sun about which man revolves so long as he does not revolve about himself.

It is the *task of history*, therefore, once the *other-world of truth* has vanished, to establish the *truth of this world.* It is above all the *task of philosophy*, which is in the service of history, to unmask human self-estrangement [*Selbstentfremdung*] in its *secular forms*, once its *sacred form* has been unmasked. Thus, the critique of heaven is transformed into the critique of the earth, the *critique of religion* into the *critique of law* [*Recht*], the *critique of theology* into the *critique of politics.*

The following exposition – which is a contribution to this task – does not deal directly with the original, but with a copy, i.e., with the German *philosophy* of the state and of right, simply because it deals with *Germany.*

Were we to begin with the German status quo itself, even in the only appropriate way, which is negatively, the result would still be an *anachronism.* For even the negation of our political present is already a dusty fact in the historical junkroom of modern nations. If I negate powdered wigs, I still have unpowdered wigs. If I negate the German conditions of 1843, I am according to French chronology barely in the year 1789, and still less at the centre of the present day.

Indeed, German history prides itself on a development which no other nation has previously achieved or will ever imitate in the historical firmament. We have shared in the restorations of modern nations without ever having shared in their revolutions. We have been restored, first because other nations ventured a revolution, and second because other nations endured a counter-revolution; in the first case because our leaders were afraid, and in the second case because they were not. Led by our shepherds, we have only once been in the company of freedom, and that was on the *day of its interment*.

One school of thought, which justifies the infamy of today by the infamy of yesterday, a school which interprets every cry of the serf under the knout as a cry of rebellion once the knout is time-honoured, ancestral, and historical, a school to which history shows only its *a posteriori* as did the God of Israel to his servant Moses – the *Historical School of Law* – might well have invented German history were it not itself an invention of German history. A Shylock, but a servile Shylock, it swears by its bond, its historical bond, its Christian–Germanic bond, for every pound of flesh cut from the heart of the people.

On the other hand, good-natured enthusiasts, German nationalists by sentiment and enlightened radicals by reflection, seek our history of freedom beyond our history in the primeval Teutonic forests. But then how does our history of freedom differ from that of the wild boar, if it is only to be found in the forests? Besides, as the saying goes: What is shouted in the forest echoes back from the forest. So peace to the primeval Teutonic forests!

But *war* upon the conditions in Germany! By all means! They are *beneath the level of history, beneath all criticism*; yet they remain an object of criticism just as the criminal who is beneath the level of humanity remains an object of the *executioner*. In its struggle against them criticism is no passion of the brain, but is rather the brain of passion. It is not a scalpel but a weapon. Its object is its *enemy*, which it wants not to refute but to *destroy*. For the spirit of these conditions is already refuted. They are not, in themselves, objects *worthy of thought*, but rather *existences* equally despicable and despised. Criticism itself needs no further self-clarification regarding this object, for criticism already understands it. Criticism is no longer an *end in itself*, but now simply a *means*. *Indignation* is its essential pathos, *denunciation* its principal task.

It is a matter of describing the stifling pressure of all the social spheres on one another, the universal, passive ill-feeling, the recognised yet misunderstood narrow-mindedness, all framed in a system of government which, living by the conservation of all this wretchedness, is itself *wretchedness in government*.

What a spectacle! The infinite division of society into the most diverse races confronting one another with their petty antipathies, bad conscience and crude mediocrity, and which, precisely because of their mutually ambiguous and suspicious disposition, are treated by their *masters* without distinction, though with differing formalities, as *merely tolerated existences*. And they are to recognise and acknowledge the very fact that they are *dominated, ruled* and *possessed* as a *concession from Heaven*! On the other hand, there are the masters themselves, whose greatness is in inverse proportion to their number!

Criticism dealing with this situation is criticism in *hand-to-hand combat*; and in this kind of combat one does not bother about whether the opponent is noble, or of equal rank, or *interesting*; all that matters is to *strike* him. It is a question of permitting the Germans not a single moment of illusion or resignation. The burden must be made still more oppressive by adding to it a consciousness of it, and the shame made still more shameful by making it public. Every sphere of German society must be described as the *partie honteuse* of German society, and these petrified conditions must be made to dance by singing to them their own melody! The nation must be taught to be *terrified* of itself in order to give it *courage*. In this way an imperative need of the German nation will be fulfilled, and the needs of nations are themselves the final causes of their satisfaction.

This struggle against the limited content of the German status quo is not without interest even for the *modern* nations; for the German status quo is the *overt perfection of the ancien régime*, and the *ancien régime* is the *hidden defect of the modern state*. The struggle against the political present in Germany is the struggle against the past of the modern nations, who are still continually troubled by the reminiscences of this past. It is instructive for them to see the *ancien régime*, which experienced its moment of *tragedy* in their history, play its *comic* role as a German ghost. Its history was *tragic* so long as it was the privileged power in the world and freedom was a personal fancy; in short, so long as it believed, and necessarily so, in its own justification. So long as the *ancien régime*, as the existing world-order, struggled against a new world coming into existence, it was guilty of a world-historical, but not a personal, error. Its decline was, therefore, tragic.

The present German regime, on the other hand – an anachronism, a flagrant contradiction of universally recognised axioms, the nullity of the *ancien régime* revealed to the whole world – only imagines that it believes in itself, and asks that the world imagine this also. If it believed in its own *nature*, would it hide that nature under the *appear-*

ance of an alien nature, and seek its preservation in hypocrisy and sophistry? The modern *ancien régime* is nothing but the *humbug* of a world order whose *real heroes* are dead. History is thorough, and passes through many phases when it conveys an old form to the grave. The final phase of a world-historical form is its *comedy*. The Greek gods, already once mortally wounded, tragically, in Aeschylus' *Prometheus Bound*, had to die once more, comically, in the dialogues of Lucian. Why does history proceed in this way? So that mankind will separate itself *happily* from its past. We claim this *happy* historical destiny for the political powers of Germany.

Meanwhile, the moment *modern* political and social actuality is subjected to criticism, the moment, therefore, criticism focuses on genuine human problems, either it finds itself outside the German status quo or it must treat its object *under* a different form. For example, the relationship of industry, of the world of wealth in general, to the political world is a major problem of modern times. Under what form does this problem begin to occupy the Germans? Under the form of *protective tariffs*, the *system of prohibitions, national economy*. German chauvinism has passed from men to matter, and so one fine morning our cavaliers of cotton and heroes of iron found themselves metamorphosed into patriots. Thus, in Germany the sovereignty of monopoly within the nation has begun to be recognised through its being invested with *sovereignty vis-à-vis other nations*. In Germany, therefore, we now begin with what in France and England is the end of a development. The old decayed state of affairs against which these nations are in theoretical revolt, and which they still bear only as chains are borne, is welcomed in Germany as the dawning of a glorious future as yet hardly daring to proceed from a *cunning [listigen]** theory to a pitiless practice. While in France and England the problem reads: *political economy* or the *mastery of society over wealth*; in Germany it reads: *national economy* or the *mastery of private property over nationality*. Thus, in France and England it is a question of abolishing monopoly, which has progressed to its final consequences, while in Germany it is a question of proceeding on to the final consequences of monopoly. There it is a question of the solution, here only a question of the collision. This is an adequate example of the

---

* A punning reference to Friedrich List (1789–1846) whose economic theory was published under the title *Das nationale System der politische Œkonomie* (1840).

German form of modern problems, an example of how our history, like a raw recruit, has until now only done extra drill on old historical matters.

If the *whole* of German development were at the level of German *political* development, a German could participate in contemporary problems no more than can a *Russian*. But if the single individual is not limited by the boundaries of the nation, still less is the nation as a whole liberated by the liberation of one individual. That a Scythian [Anarchasis] was numbered among the Greek philosophers did not enable the Scythians to advance a step toward Greek culture.

Fortunately, we Germans are not Scythians.

Just as ancient peoples lived their past history in their imagination, in *mythology*, so we Germans have lived our future history in thought, in *philosophy*. We are *philosophical* contemporaries of the present day without being its *historical* contemporaries. German philosophy is the *ideal prolongation* of German history. If, then, we criticise the *oeuvres posthumes* of our ideal history, *philosophy*, instead of the *oeuvres incomplètes* of our actual history, our criticism centres on the very questions of which the present age says: *that is the question*. What for advanced nations is a *practical* break with modern political conditions is in Germany, where these conditions themselves do not yet exist, essentially a *critical* break with their philosophical reflection.

German *philosophy of right and the state* is the only *German history* that is *al pari* with *official* modern times. Thus, the German nation is obliged to connect its dream history with its present circumstances, and subject to criticism not only these circumstances but also their abstract continuation. Its future can be *restricted* neither to the direct negation of its real, nor to the direct fulfillment of its ideal, political and juridical circumstances; for the direct negation of its real circumstances is already there in its ideal circumstances, and it has almost *outlived* the direct fulfillment of these in its contemplation of neighbouring nations. The *practical* political party in Germany is right, therefore, in demanding the *negation of philosophy*. Its error lies not in the demand, but in limiting itself to the demand which it neither does nor can fulfill. It believes that it can achieve this negation by turning its back on philosophy, averting its gaze, and murmuring a few irritable and trite phrases about it. In its narrow outlook it does not even count philosophy a part of *German* actuality, or it considers philosophy to be *beneath* the level of German practical life and its attendant theories. You [of the practical party] demand that *actual germs of life* be the point of departure, but you forget that the German nation's actual germs of life have until now sprouted only in its *cranium.* In short, *you cannot supersede philosophy without actualising it.**

The same error, but with the elements *reversed*, was committed by the *theoretical* political party, which originated in philosophy.†

This party saw in the present struggle *only* the *critical struggle of philosophy against the German world.* It failed to note that *previous philosophy* itself belongs to this world and is its *complement*, even if only an ideal complement. Critical of its counterpart, it remained uncritical of itself: it took its point of departure from the *presuppositions* of philosophy, and either accepted the conclusions reached by philosophy or else presented as directly philosophical demands and results drawn from elsewhere; even though these – assuming their validity – are obtainable only through the *negation of previous philosophy*, i.e., of philosophy as philosophy. We reserve until later a fuller account of this party. Its basic defect reduces to this: *It believed that it could actualise philosophy without superseding it.*

The criticism of *German philosophy of right and of the state*, which was given its most logical, profound and complete expression by *Hegel*, is at once the critical analysis of the modern state and of the reality connected with it, and the definite negation of all the past *forms* of *consciousness in German jurisprudence and politics*, whose most distinguished and most general expression, raised to the level of a *science*, is precisely the *speculative philosophy of right*. If it was only in Germany that the speculative philosophy of right was possible – this abstract and extravagant thought about the modern state, whose reality remains in another world (even though this is just across the Rhine) – the *German* thought-version [*Gedankenbild*] of the modern state, on the other hand, which abstracts from *actual man*, was only possible because and in so far as the modern state itself abstracts from *actual man*, or satisfies the whole man only in an imaginary way. In politics the Germans have *thought* what other nations have done.

---

* Marx's reference to the 'practical political party' is unclear, and commentators differ about it. Most probably he means elements of the liberal bourgeoisie and intelligentsia who were demanding constitutional reform of the monarchy or more radically, establishment of a democratic republic.

† Marx refers here to the 'Young Hegelians' or, more specifically, to Bruno Bauer and his circle.

Germany was their *theoretical conscience.* The abstract and presumptive character of its thinking was in step with the partial and stunted character of their actuality. If, then, the status quo of the *German political system* expresses the *perfection of the ancien régime*, the thorn in the flesh of the modern state, the status quo of *German political thought* expresses the *imperfection of the modern state*, the damaged condition of the flesh itself.

As the determined adversary of the prevailing mode of *German* political consciousness, criticism of the speculative philosophy of right does not remain within itself, but proceeds on to *tasks* for whose solution there is only one means – *praxis*.

The question arises: can Germany attain a *praxis à la hauteur des principes*, that is to say, a *revolution* that will raise it not only to the *official level* of modern nations, but to the *human level* which will be the immediate future of these nations?

The weapon of criticism certainly cannot replace the criticism of weapons; material force must be overthrown by material force; but theory, too, becomes a material force once it seizes the masses. Theory is capable of seizing the masses once it demonstrates *ad hominem*, and it demonstrates *ad hominem* once it becomes radical. To be radical is to grasp matters at the root. But for man the root is man himself. The manifest proof of the radicalism of German theory, and thus of its practical energy, is the fact of its issuing from a resolute *positive* supersession [*Aufhebung*] of religion. The critique of religion ends in the doctrine that *man is the supreme being for man*; thus it ends with the *categorical imperative to overthrow all conditions* in which man is a debased, enslaved, neglected, contemptible being – conditions which cannot be better described than by the Frenchman's exclamation about a proposed tax on dogs: 'Poor dogs! They want to treat you like men!'

Even from the historical point of view, theoretical emancipation has a specific practical importance for Germany. Germany's *revolutionary* past is precisely theoretical: it is the *Reformation*. As at that time it was a monk, so now it is the *philosopher* in whose brain the revolution begins.

Luther, to be sure, overcame servitude based on *devotion*, but by replacing it with servitude based on *conviction*. He shattered faith in authority by restoring the authority of faith. He transformed the priests into laymen by changing the laymen into priests. He liberated man from external religiosity by making religiosity that which is inner-most to man. He freed the body of chains by putting the heart in chains.

But if Protestantism was not the real solution, it at least posed the problem correctly. Thereafter it was no longer a question of the laymen's struggle with the *priest outside of him*, but of his struggle with his own *inner priest*, his *priestly nature*. And if the Protestant transformation of the German laity into priests emancipated the lay popes – the *princes* together with their clergy, the privileged and the philistines – so the philosophical transformation of the priestly Ger-mans into men will emancipate the *people*. But just as emancipation is not limited to the princes, so the *secularisation* of property will not be limited to the *confiscation of church property*, which was practised especially by hypocritical Prussia. At that time, the Peasant War, the most radical event in German history, foundered because of theology. Today, when theology itself has foundered, the most unfree thing in German history, our status quo, will be shattered by philosophy. On the eve of the Reformation official Germany was the most abject servant of Rome. On the eve of its revolution Germany is the abject servant of those who are inferior to Rome, of Prussia and Austria, of petty squires and philistines.

However, a major difficulty appears to stand in the way of a *radical* German revolution.

Revolutions require a *passive* element, a *material* basis. Theory will be realised in a people only in so far as it is the realisation of their needs. Will the enormous discrepancy between the demands of German thought and the answers of German actuality be matched by a similar discrepancy between civil society and the state, and within civil society itself? Will theoretical needs be directly practical needs? It is not enough that thought strive to actualise itself; actuality must itself strive toward thought.

But Germany has not passed through the middle state of political emancipation at the same time as the modern nations. The very stages it has surpassed in theory it has not yet reached in practice. How is Germany, with a *salto mortale*, to surmount not only its own limita-tions, but also those of the modern nations, limitations which it must actually experience and strive for as the liberation from its own actual limitations? A radical revolution can only be a revolution of radical needs, whose preconditions and birthplaces appear to be lacking.

But if Germany accompanied the development of modern nations only with the abstract activity of thought, without taking an active part in the actual struggles of development, it has still shared the *pains* of this development without sharing its pleasures or its partial satisfaction. The abstract activity on the one hand corresponds to the abstract pain on the other. One day Germany will find itself at the level of European decadence before it has ever achieved the level of European emancipation. It will be like a *fetishist* suffering from the illnesses of Christianity.

If we examine the *German governments* we find that the circumstances of the time, the situation in Germany, the viewpoint of German culture, and finally their own lucky instinct, all drive them to combine the *civilised deficiencies* of the *modern political world*, whose advantages we do not enjoy, with the *barbaric deficiencies* of the *ancien régime*, which we enjoy in full measure; so that Germany must participate more and more, if not in the rationality, at least in the irrationality of the political forms that transcend its status quo. For example, is there any country in the world which shares as naively as so-called constitutional Germany all the illusions of the constitutional regime without any of its realities? Was it not somehow necessarily a German government brain-wave to combine the torments of censorship with those of the French September Laws [of 1835], which presuppose the freedom of the press! Just as the *gods* of all nations were found in the Roman Pantheon, so the *sins* of all state-forms are to be found in the Holy Roman German Empire. That this eclecticism will attain an unprecedented level is assured by the *politico-aesthetic gourmanderie* of a German king [Frederick William IV], who intends to play all the roles of royalty – the feudal as well as the bureaucratic, absolute as well as constitutional, autocratic as well as democratic – if not in the person of the people at least in his *own* person, if not for the people at least for *himself. Germany, as the deficiency of the political present constituted into an individual system*, will be unable to demolish the specific German limitations without demolishing the general limitations of the political present.

It is not a *radical* revolution, *universal human* emancipation, that is a utopian dream for Germany, but rather a partial, *merely* political revolution, a revolution that leaves the pillars of the edifice standing. What is the basis of a partial, merely political revolution? It is this: a *section of civil society* emancipates itself and achieves *universal* dominance; a determinate class undertakes from its *particular situation* the universal emancipation of society. This class emancipates the whole society, but only on the condition that the whole society shares its situation; for example, that it has or can obtain money and education.

No class of civil society can play this role unless it arouses in itself and in the masses a moment of enthusiasm, a moment in which it associates, fuses, and identifies itself with society in general, and is felt and recognised to be society's *general representative*, a moment in which its demands and rights are truly those of society itself, of which it is the social head and heart. Only in the name of the universal rights of society can a particular class lay claim to universal dominance. To take over this liberating position, and therewith the political exploitation of all the spheres of society in the interest of its own sphere, revolutionary energy and spiritual self-confidence do not suffice. For a *popular revolution* and the *emancipation of a particular class* of civil society to coincide, for *one* class to stand for the whole of society, another class must, on the other hand, concentrate in itself all the defects of society, must be the class of universal offense and the embodiment of universal limits. A particular social sphere must stand for the *notorious crime* of the whole society, so that liberation from this sphere appears to be universal liberation. For one class to be the class *par excellence* of liberation, another class must, on the other hand, be the openly subjugating class. The negative general significance of the French nobility and clergy determined the positive general significance of the bourgeoisie, the class standing alongside of and in opposition to them.

But every class in Germany lacks the consistency, the keenness, the courage, and the ruthlessness which would mark it as the negative representative of society. Moreover, every class lacks that breadth of soul which identifies it, if only for a moment, with the soul of the people; that genius which animates material force into political power; that revolutionary boldness which flings at its adversary the defiant phrase: *I am nothing and I should be everything*. The principal feature of German morality and honour, not only in individuals but in classes as well, is that modest egoism which asserts its narrowness and allows narrowness to be asserted against it. The relationship of the different spheres of German society is, therefore, not dramatic, but epic. Each of them begins to be aware of itself and to establish itself with its particular claims beside the others, not as soon as it is oppressed, but as soon as circumstances independent of its actions create a lower social stratum against which it can in turn exert pressure. Even the *moral self-esteem of the German middle class* is based merely on the consciousness of being the general representative of the philistine mediocrity of all the other classes. It is, therefore, not only the German kings who ascend the throne *mal a propos*. Each sphere of civil society suffers its defeat before it celebrates its victory, erects its own barrier before it overthrows its opposing barrier, asserts its narrow-minded nature before it can assert its generosity, so that the opportunity of playing a great role has passed before it ever actually existed, and each class, at the moment it begins to struggle with the class above it, is involved in the struggle with the class beneath. Hence, the princes are in conflict with the king, the bureaucracy with the nobility, the bourgeoisie with all of them, while the proletariat is already beginning its struggle against the bourgeoisie. The middle class hardly dares to conceive of the idea of emancipation from its own point of view, and already the development of social conditions and the progress of political theory show that this point of view itself is antiquated, or at least questionable.

In France it is enough to be something in order to desire to be everything. In Germany no one may be anything unless he renounces everything. In France partial emancipation is the basis of universal emancipation. In Germany universal emancipation is the *conditio sine qua non* for any partial emancipation. In France it is the actuality, in Germany the impossibility, of gradual emancipation which must give birth to full freedom. In France every national class is *politically idealistic* and considers itself above all to be not a particular class but the representative of the needs of society overall. The role of the *emancipator* thus passes in a dramatic movement to the different classes of the French nation, until it finally reaches the class which actualises social freedom no longer on the basis of presupposed conditions which are at once external to man yet created by human society, but rather organises all the conditions of human existence on the basis of social freedom. In Germany, on the other hand, where practical life is as little intellectual as intellectual life is practical, no class of civil society has the need and the capacity for universal emancipation until it is forced to it by its *immediate* situation, its *material* necessity, and its *very chains*.

Where, then, is the *positive* possibility of German emancipation? *Our answer:* in the formation of a class with *radical* chains, a class in civil society that is not of civil society, an estate that is the dissolution of all estates, a sphere of society having a universal character because of its universal suffering and claiming no *particular right* because no *particular wrong* but *unqualified wrong* is perpetrated on it; a sphere that can claim no *historical* title but only a *human* title; a sphere that does not stand partially opposed to the consequences, but totally opposed to the premises of the German political system; a sphere, finally, that cannot emancipate itself without emancipating itself from all the other spheres of society, thereby emancipating them; a sphere, in short, that is the *complete loss* of humanity and can only redeem itself through the *total redemption of humanity.* This dissolution of society existing as a particular estate is the *proletariat.*

The proletariat is only beginning to appear in Germany as a result of the *industrial* development taking place. For it is not *naturally existing* poverty but *artificially produced* poverty, not the mass of men mechanically oppressed by the weight of society but the mass of men resulting from society's and especially the middle class' *acute dissolution* that constitutes the proletariat – though at the same time, needless to say, victims of natural poverty and Christian-Germanic serfdom also become members.

When the proletariat announces the *dissolution of the existing world order,* it merely declares the *secret of its own existence,* for it is the *de facto* dissolution of this world order. When the proletariat demands the *negation* of *private property,* it merely elevates into a *principle of society* what society has advanced as the principle *of the proletariat,* and what *the proletariat* already involuntarily embodies as the negative result of society. The proletariat thus has the same right relative to the new world which is coming into being as has the *German king* relative to the existing world, when he calls the people his people and a horse *his* horse. In calling the people his private property, the king merely expresses the fact that the owner of private property is king.

Just as philosophy finds its *material* weapons in the proletariat, so the proletariat finds its *spiritual* weapons in philosophy; and once the lightning of thought has struck deeply into this naive soil of the people the emancipation of the *Germans into men* will be accomplished.

Let us summarise:

The only *practically* possible emancipation of Germany is the emancipation based on the unique theory which holds that man is the supreme being for man. In Germany emancipation from the *Middle Ages* is possible only as the simultaneous emancipation from the *partial* victories over the Middle Ages. In Germany no form of bondage can be broken unless *every* form of bondage is broken. Germany, *enamoured of fundamentals*, can have nothing less than a *fundamental* revolution. The *emancipation of Germany* is the *emancipation of man*. The *head* of this emancipation is *philosophy*, its *heart* is the *proletariat*. Philosophy cannot be actualised without the abolition [*Aufhebung*] of the proletariat; the proletariat cannot be abolished without the actualisation of philosophy.

When all the intrinsic conditions are fulfilled, *the day of German resurrection* will be announced by the *crowing of the Gallic cock*.

From the Paris Notebooks (1844)

[Self-Estrangement]

We begin with a fact of *contemporary* economic life: The more wealth the worker produces, the more his production grows in power and scope, the poorer he becomes. The more commodities he creates, the cheaper a commodity he becomes. The more the world of things increases in value, the more in direct proportion the world of men loses value. The activity of labour does not just produce commodities, but also turns itself and the worker into a *commodity*, and it does this to the same extent that it produces commodities in general.

This fact simply expresses the following: The object that labour produces, labour's own product, confronts it as an *alien thing*, a *power independent* of the producer. The product of labour is labour that has taken the form of an object, labour that has made itself into a thing; it is the transformation of labour into an object. The actualisation of labour is its objectification [*Vergegenständlichung*]. But in present economic conditions, labour's actualisation carries with it the worker's *loss of actualisation*, labour's objectification is the worker's *loss of the object and servitude to it*, and instead of appropriation, there is for the worker estrangement [*Entfremdung*], alienation [*Entausserung*].

So much is labour's actualisation the worker's loss of it that this loss goes even to the point of death by starvation. So much is labour's objectification the worker's loss of the object that the worker is robbed even of the objects he needs for both his life and his work. Indeed, the very exercise of his own labouring activity becomes an object he can get only with the greatest effort and the most irregular interruptions. And so much is the worker's relation to the object one of estrangement instead of appropriation that the more objects he

71

produces the less he can possess and the more he falls under the domination of his product, capital.

All of these consequences result from the fact that the worker relates to the *product of his labour* as to an *alien* object. Given this fact, it is clear that the more the worker expends of himself, the more powerful becomes the alien world of objects he creates over against himself, the poorer he himself – his own inner world – becomes, the less he has to call his own. It is exactly the same as in religion. The more man puts into God, the less he keeps in himself. The worker puts his life into the object, but then it no longer belongs to him but to the object. The greater this activity, the more the worker is bereft of objects. What the product of his labour is, that he is not. So the greater this product, the less he is himself. The alienation of the worker in his product means not only that his labour becomes an object, an *external* existence, but that it becomes *external to him*, independent, alien to him, an independent power that confronts him; the life he gave to the object confronts him, hostile and alien.

Let us look more closely at *objectification*, at the worker's production, and within that at the *estrangement*, the loss of the object, his product.

The worker can create nothing without *nature*, without the *sensuous external world*. This world is the matter in which his labour is actualised, within which it is active, out of and by means of which it produces.

But just as nature provides labour its *means of life*, in the sense that labour cannot exist without objects on which to exercise itself, so too it furnishes the *means of life* in the more particular sense of the means of physical subsistence of the *worker* himself.

So the more the worker by his labour *appropriates* the external world of sensuous nature, the more he deprives himself of the *means of life* in two respects: First, the sensuous external world increasingly ceases to be an object belonging to his labour, ceases to be his labour's *means of life*; and second, it increasingly ceases to be a means of life in the direct sense, i.e. it ceases to be the worker's means of physical subsistence.

In these two respects, therefore, the worker becomes enslaved to his object: first, in getting an *object of labour*, i.e. in getting *work*; and second, in receiving his *means of subsistence*. In the first respect he can be a *worker*, and in the second he can exist as a *physical subject*.

The peak of this slavery is this: It is only as a *worker* that he can maintain himself as a *physical subject*, while as a worker he is only a *physical subject*.

(According to the laws of political economy, the worker's estrangement in his object is expressed thus: the more the worker produces the less he has to consume, the more values he creates the more devoid of value and worthless he becomes, the more formed his product the more deformed the worker, the more civilised his object the more barbaric the worker, the more powerful labour becomes the more powerless becomes the worker, the more intelligent labour becomes the more the worker becomes unintelligent and a slave to nature.) [...]

The direct relationship of labour to its products is the relationship of the worker to the objects of his production.

[...]

So far we have considered only one aspect of the estrangement or alienation of the worker, i.e. his *relationship to the products of his labour*. But the estrangement appears not only in the result but in the *act or production*, within the producing activity itself. How could the worker come to confront the product of his activity as something strange unless he were becoming estranged from himself in the very act of production? The product, after all, is but the resumé of the activity of production. If the product of labour is alienation, therefore, production itself must be active alienation, the alienation of activity, the activity of alienation. The estrangement of the object of labour is but the resumé of estrangement, the alienation in the activity of labour itself.

Now what does the alienation of labour consist of?

First, that labour is *external* to the worker, i.e. is not part of his very being; that in his work, therefore, he does not affirm himself but denies himself, feels miserable instead of satisfied, does not freely exercise and develop physical and intellectual energy but mortifies his body and ruins his mind. And so the worker only feels himself outside his work, and in his work feels outside himself. He is at home when not working and is not at home in his work. His labour is, therefore, not voluntary but coerced, *forced labour*. It is not the satisfaction of a need but rather just a *means* to satisfy needs outside itself. Its estranged character is clearly evident in the fact that when no physical or other compulsion is present labour is avoided like the plague. External labour, labour in which man alienates himself, is a labour of self-sacrifice, of mortification. Finally, the externality of labour for the worker manifests itself in the fact that it is not his own but someone else's, that it does not belong to him, that in it he belongs not to himself but to someone else. Just as in religion, the activity of man's imagination, of the human head and heart, operates on the individual as something independent of him, i.e. as an alien activity of gods or devils, so the worker's activity is not his self-activity. It belongs to another and is his loss of self. [. . .]

We have considered the estrangement of practical human activity, labour, under two aspects. (1) The labourer's relationship to the *product of labour* as an alien object with power over him. This relationship is at the same time his relationship to the sensuous external world, to natural objects, as an alien and hostile world opposed to him. (2) The relationship of labour to the *act of production* within *labour*. This relationship is that of the worker to his own activity as something alien and not belonging to him; activity as passivity, strength as weakness, procreation as emasculation. The worker's *own* physical and intellectual energy, his personal life – for what is life except activity? – as an activity turned against him, independent of him, not belonging to him. Here, *self-estrangement*, whereas under the first aspect, estrangement of the *thing*.

Now we have to derive a third aspect of *estranged labour* from the two just considered.

Man is a species-being [*Gattungswesen*], which means two things: first, that he has his own species, or specific nature, and the species of all other things as the object both of his practical action and of his theorising; and second (another way of saying the same thing), that he regards and comports himself as the actuality of the living species, i.e. as a *universal* and therefore free being.

Both in man and in animals, the life of the species consists first of all, from the physical point of view, in the fact that man (like the animal) lives on inorganic nature; and the more universal man is, compared to the animal, the more universal is the sphere of inorganic nature on which he lives. Just as plants, animals, stones, air, light, etc. form part of human consciousness at the level of theory, as objects of natural science or as objects of art – his inorganic nature as spiritual or intellectual, his spiritual nourishment which he has first to prepare before he can enjoy and assimilate it – so too at the practical level they form part of human life and human activity. It is from these natural products alone that man lives physically, whether they take the form of food, heating, clothing, habitation, etc. In this practical order, man's universality is seen in the fact that he makes the whole of nature his *inorganic* body in that it is both (1) his direct means of life, and (2) the material object and the instrument of his life-activity. Nature, insofar as it is not itself a human body, is man's *inorganic* body. Man lives from nature, which means that nature is his body with which he must maintain a constant interchange so as not to die. That man's physical and mental life is connected to nature means simply that nature is connected to itself, for man is a part of nature.

In estranging nature from man and man from himself, from his own active function, his life-activity, estranged labour estranges the *species* from man; for him it turns his *species-life* into a means to his individual life. First it estranges species-life and individual life, and then it makes the latter in its abstract form into the aim of the former, likewise in its abstract and estranged form.

For labour, *life-activity, productive life* itself, seems to man from the outset to be merely a *means* to satisfy a need, the need to maintain his physical existence. But productive life is species-life. It is life-generating life. The whole character of a species, its species-character, lies in the form of its life-activity, and free conscious activity is the species-character of man. [Yet] this life itself seems a mere *means to life.*

The animal and its life-activity are one and the same. The animal does not distinguish itself from its activity. It is *that activity* and nothing more. But man makes his life-activity an object of his will and consciousness. His is conscious life-activity and so is not a determinate thing in which he is wholly immersed. Conscious life-activity is what directly differentiates man from animal life-activity. Precisely by reason of that is he a species-being. Or, he is a conscious being, i.e. his own life is an object for him, precisely because he is a species-being. Only because of that is his activity free activity. Estranged labour reverses the relationship such that man, precisely because he is a conscious being, reduces his life-activity, his very *being*, to a mere means to his *existence.*

Man's creation of a *world of objects* through his practical action, his *fashioning* of inorganic nature, verifies his character as a conscious species-being, i.e. a being that relates to the species as to his own being or to himself as a species-being. True, the animal also produces. It builds itself a nest, dwellings, like bees, the beaver, ants, etc. But it produces only what is directly needed for itself or its young; it produces only under the pressure of immediate physical need, whereas man produces when free of physical need and in fact truly produces only when free of such need; the animal produces only itself, while man reproduces the whole of nature; its product belongs directly to its physical body, whereas man freely confronts his product. The animal fashions things only in accord with the standard and need of its species, whereas man knows how to produce in accord with the standard of every species and to apply everywhere the inherent standard of the object; thus man fashions things also in accord with the laws of beauty.

It is, therefore, in his fashioning of the world of objects that man actually begins to affirm himself as a *species-being*. This production is his working, practical species-life. Through it nature appears as *his work* and his actuality. The object of labour is therefore the *objectification of man's species-life*, an objectification in which he duplicates himself not only in consciousness, intellectually, but also in working, practical fashion, in actuality, and thus he contemplates himself in a world he has created. By tearing from man the object of his production, estranged labour tears from him his *species-life*, his actual species-objectivity, and turns his advantage over animals into the disadvantage that his inorganic body, nature, is torn away from him. [...]

Man's species-being includes both nature, on which man's labour operates, and man's spiritual faculties. Where man's labour is estranged, this complex species-being is reduced to a mere means to his existence as an abstract individual. It estranges from man his own body, as well as external nature and his spiritual being, his *human* nature.

An immediate consequence of man's estrangement from the product of his labour, from his life-activity, and from his species-being, is the *estrangement of man from man*. When man is opposed to himself, the *other* man opposes him. What obtains in man's relationship to his labour, to the product of his labour, and to himself obtains in man's relationship to the other man and to his work and object of work.

In general, the statement that man is estranged from his species-being means that one man is estranged from the other and that each of them is estranged from their common human nature.

[...]

Every self-estrangement of man from himself and from nature appears in the relationship he gives to himself and nature *vis-à-vis* other men different than himself. Thus, religious self-estrangement necessarily manifests itself in the relationship of the layman to the priest, or, because here we are dealing with the intellectual world, to a mediator etc. In the actual, practical world, self-estrangement can become evident only through the actual, practical relationship to other men. The means through which estrangement proceeds are themselves *practical*. It is by means of estranged labour, therefore, that man engenders not only his relationship to the object and to the act of production as things alien and hostile, but also the relationship in which other men stand to his production and product, and the relationship in which he stands to these other men. Just as he engenders his own product as his loss, as a product that does not belong to him, so too he engenders the mastery over the production and the product that is exercised by one who does not produce. As he estranges his activity from himself he engenders a stranger's appropriation of activity that is not the stranger's own.

[...]

Thus, through his *estranged, alienated labour*, the worker engenders the relationship to this labour of a man who is alien and external to it. The relationship of the labourer to labour engenders the relationship to it of the capitalist (or whatever else those having mastery over labour might be called).

Private property is thus the product, the result, the necessary consequence of *alienated labour*, of the labourer's externality relative to nature and himself.

Thus does *private property* derive from analysis of the concept of *alienated* labour, i.e. of *alienated man*, of estranged labour, estranged life, *estranged man*.

To be sure, we obtained the concept of *alienated labour* (of *alienated life*) from political economy as the result of the movement of *private property*. But the analysis of this concept shows that although private property seems to be the ground, the origin of alienated labour, it is rather a consequence of it, just as the gods are not *originally* the source but rather the result of human mental aberration. Later, of course, the relationship between alienated labour and private property becomes one of reciprocal action.

Only at the culmination of private property's development does this, its secret, become once again evident, namely, that on one hand it is the *product* of alienated labour, and on the other, it is the *means* by which labour alienates itself, the *realisation of this alienation*. [...]

What additionally follows from the relationship of estranged labour to private property is this: the emancipation of society from private property etc. from servitude, has as its *political* form the *emancipation of the workers*; but not just their emancipation, because their emancipation implies what is included in it, universal human emancipation. For all human servitude is bound up in the relationship of the worker to production, and all relationships of servitude are but modifications and consequences of this relationship.

[Communism: the superseding of self-estrangement]

In its first form, communism is just a *universalisation* and *fulfillment* of [private property].

[...]

Because it systematically negates human *personality*, this communism is just a consistent expression of private property, which is this negation. *Envy*, universal and constituting itself as *power*, is the hidden form in which *greed* asserts itself and satisfies itself in merely *another* way. The thought of every private property owner as such is turned *at least* against the *wealthier* as envy and desire to level down. Crude communism is just the fulfillment of envy and of a levelling down according to an *imagined* minimum. It has a *fixed* and *restricted* standard. How little this abolition of private property is an appropriation is seen precisely in its abstract negation of the entire world of culture and civilisation; the return to the *unnatural* simplicity of the *poor* man, bereft of needs, who has not yet even achieved private property, let alone gotten beyond it.

The community [in this communism] is only a community of *labour* and of *equality* of wages paid by the communal capital, the *community* as universal capitalist. Both sides of the relation are raised to an *imaginary* universality, *labour* as the defined place of everyone, *capital* as the recognised universality and power of the community.

[...]

The *crude* form of communism, the first positive superseding [*Aufhebung*] of private property, is therefore just a manifestation of the ignominy of private property presenting itself as the *positive community*.

The second form of communism can have either a political nature, democratic or despotic, or involve abolition of the state, but in either case it remains incomplete, afflicted with private property, i.e. with man's estrangement. Still, whether political or stateless, this communism already knows itself to be man's reintegration or return to himself, the superseding of human self-estrangement; but because it has not yet grasped the positive nature of private property or understood the *human* nature of need, it remains captured and infected by private property, whose concept it has certainly grasped, but whose essence still escapes it.

Third, there is communism which is the full *positive* superseding of *private property*, of *human self-estrangement*, and consequently the actual *appropriating* of the *human* essence by and for man; the complete and conscious return of man to himself as a *social*, i.e. human being, accomplished within the entire wealth of previous development. This communism, as fulfilled naturalism, equals humanism, and as fulfilled humanism equals naturalism; it is the *genuine* resolution of the conflict of man with nature and of man with man, the true resolution of the conflict between existence and essence, objectification and self-affirmation, freedom and necessity, individual and species. It is the solution of the enigma of history and knows itself to be that.

The entire movement of history, as communism's *actual* act of genesis, the birth act of its empirical existence, is also, for thinking consciousness, the *comprehended* and *known* process of its *becoming*.

[...]

Material, directly *sensible* private property is the material, sensible expression of *estranged human* life. Its movement – production and consumption – is the *perceptible* revelation of the movement of all past production as actualisation or actuality of man. Religion, state, law, morality, science, art, etc. are but *particular* modes of production and fall under its general law. The positive superseding of *private property* as the appropriating of *human* life is therefore the positive superseding of all estrangement, and thus man's return from religion, family, state, etc. to his *human*, i.e. *social* existence. Religious estrangement as such occurs only in the realm of *consciousness*, of man's inner life; but economic estrangement is that of *actual life*, and so its supersession brings supersession in both spheres. [...]

To recapitulate, assuming the positive superseding of private property, man produces man, himself, and the other man; the object, which then directly affirms his own individuality, is at the same time his own existence for the other, the existence of the other, and the existence of the other for him. At the same time, however, both the material of labour and man as the subject of labour are not only the outcome but also the starting point of this movement (and in this fact lies the historical *necessity* of private property). Thus the universal character of the entire movement is *social; just as* society itself produces *man* as *man*, so too he *produces* it. Man's activity and enjoyment, in their content and their mode of existence, are *social* activity and *social* enjoyment. The *human* essence of nature is there only for *social* man, because only for him is nature a *bond* with man, his existence for the other and the other's for him, and the *foundation* of his own *human* existence, the life-element of human actuality. Only in social man have *natural* and *human* existence come to coincide, only in him has nature become man. Thus *society* is the fulfilled essential unity of man and nature, the true resurrection of nature, the accomplished naturalism of man and the accomplished humanism of nature.

By no means, however, do social activity and social enjoyment exist *only* in the form of a *directly* communal activity and directly communal enjoyment. It is true that *communal* activity and *communal* enjoyment – i.e. activity and enjoyment expressed directly in actual association with other men – will in general occur whenever the direct expression of sociability stems from the essential content of the activity and fits the nature of the enjoyment. But even in my *scientific* activity, and in others like that, which I can seldom perform in immediate community with others, I am also *socially* active, because I am active as a *man*. Not only is the material of my activity – in the case of a thinker, the very language in which he expresses himself – given to me as a social product, but my *own* existence *is* social activity; and so what I make of myself, I make of myself for society and with consciousness of myself as a social being.

My *universal* consciousness is just the *theoretical* form of that totality whose *living* form is the *real* community, the social being – although at present, universal consciousness is abstracted from actual life and as such confronts it with hostility. That is why the *activity* of my universal consciousness, as the kind of activity it is, is also my *theoretical* existence as a social being.

But above all we must avoid conceiving of society once again as a fixed, abstract thing opposed to the individual. The individual *is the social being*. His life, therefore, even when it is not manifested in a directly communal way or as accomplished in common with others, is a manifestation and confirmation of *social life*. Man's individual life and species-life are not *different*, even though, necessarily, the mode of existence of individual life will be a more *particular* or more *universal* mode of species-life, or the mode of existence of species-life a more *particular* or more *universal* individual life.

In his *species-consciousness* man affirms his actual *social life* and simply repeats in thought his actual existence, just as conversely his species-being is affirmed in his species-consciousness and, in its universality, exists for itself as a thinking being.

Consequently, each individual man, however particular he be – and it is precisely his particularity that makes him an individual and an *actual individual* species-being – is just as much the *totality*: both the *ideal* totality, i.e. the subjective existence of society present to itself in thought and feeling; and in the actual world, in his contemplation and actual enjoyment of social existence, a totality of human manifestations of life. [...]

Private property is but the sensuous expression of the fact that man, in becoming objective to himself, also becomes an object alien and inhuman to himself; that his expression of his life is his alienation of his life; that his actualisation is his loss of actuality, his creation of an *alien* actuality. Because private property expresses all this, the positive superseding of it, i.e. the *sensuous* appropriating by and for man of human nature and life, of objective man and his *works*, must not be understood merely in the sense of some direct, simple *enjoyment*, merely in the sense of *possessing* or *having*. For man appropriates his universal nature in a universal way, i.e. as a whole man. Each of his human relations with the world, seeing, hearing, smelling, tasting, touching, thinking, contemplating, feeling, willing, acting, loving, in short all the organs of his individuality, including those directly communal in form, in their *objective* relation, their *relation to the object*, are an *appropriating* of it, the appropriating and affirming of *human* activity. [...]

Private property has made us so stupid and narrow-minded, that we consider a thing *ours* only when we have it, thus when it exists as capital for us, or when we have directly possessed, eaten, drunk, or worn it on our body, occupied it, etc., in short *used* it. Although private property grasps all of these direct actualisations of possession itself in turn only as *means of life* and the life whose means they count for is the life of *private property*, labour and capitalisation.

All of the physical and spiritual senses have been replaced by the estrangement of *all* of the senses, i.e. by the sense of *having*. Human being had to be reduced to this absolute poverty in order for it to bring forth out of itself its inner wealth. (On the category of *Having*, see Hess in the Twenty-One Folios.)

The superseding of private property is, therefore, the full emancipating of all human senses and qualities [...]

We see [then] how the *wealthy man* and rich *human need* replace political economic [notions of] *wealth* and *poverty*. The *wealthy* man is at the same time the man *in need of* a totality of human manifestations of life. The man in whom his own actualisation exists as inner necessity, as *need*. Not only wealth but also the *poverty* of man takes on in equal measure – presupposing socialism – a *human* and therefore social meaning. It is the passive bond which allows man to feel the greatest wealth, the *other* man, as need. The power of the objective being within me, the sensuous outburst of the very activity of my being, is *passion*, which here therefore becomes the *activity* of my being.

[...]

Because socialist man understands the *whole of what is called world-history* as nothing but man's creation through human labour, as the becoming of nature for man, he has the observable, irrefutable proof of his *birth* through himself, of his *process of genesis*. Because the essential reality of man and nature, man as the existence of nature

82

for man, nature as the existence of man for man, has become evident in a practical, sensuously observable way, the question about the reality of an *alien* being, of a supernatural and superhuman being – a question that implies admitting the unreality of nature and man – becomes impossible in the practical order. *Atheism*, as the denial of the unreality of nature and man, no longer makes any sense, for atheism is a *negating of God* through which *man's existence* is asserted. But socialism as such no longer needs such a mediation, for it begins with the sensuous consciousness, both *theoretical* and *practical*, of man and nature as what is *truly real*. Socialism is man's *positive self-consciousness*, a *self-consciousness* no longer mediated through the negating of religion, just as *actual life* is man's positive actuality, an actuality no longer mediated through the negating of private property, i.e. through *communism*. Communism is affirmation as negation of negation, and is as such both actual and necessary for the next historical development of human emancipation and recuperation. *Communism is the necessary form and dynamic principle of the immediate future, but communism as such is not the goal of human development – the form of human society.* [...]

[Hegel's philosophy: the false superseding of self-estrangement]

Hegel's *Encyclopedia* begins with logic, i.e. with *pure speculative thinking*, and concludes with *absolute knowing*, with self-conscious and self-comprehending philosophic or absolute, i.e. superhuman, abstract spirit; as such the whole of the *Encyclopedia* is nothing but the displayed essence of the philosophic spirit, its self-objectification; but this philosophic spirit is nothing but the estranged spirit of the world thinking within its self-estrangement, i.e. comprehending itself abstractly. *Logic –* the *money* of spirit, the speculative, *purely theoretical value* of man and nature, its essence having now become wholly indifferent to all real determinateness or specificity, and hence having become itself unreal – is *alienated thinking*, abstracting from nature and real man, *abstract* thinking. What is *external to this abstract thinking* [is] *nature*, but nature as an object of abstract thinking. Nature is external to it, is its self-loss; and it grasps nature also in an external way, as abstract thinking, but as external abstract thinking. – Finally, *spirit –* this thinking which returns to its birthplace, and which as anthropological, phenomenological, psychological, ethical, artistic, and religious spirit is considered invalid until it finally finds and affirms itself as *absolute knowing,* and therefore absolute, i.e. abstract, spirit – has its conscious and appropriate mode of existence as abstract spirit: for *abstraction* is what it actually is.

[...]

Hegel's error is two-fold. First (and this is most evident in the *Phenomenology [of Spirit]*, the birthplace of Hegel's philosophy): when for instance Hegel understands wealth, state power etc. as things estranged from the *human* being, it is only their form as thoughts that is in question ... They are thought-entities, and thus merely an estrangement of *pure,* i.e. abstract philosophic thinking. And so the entire movement ends in absolute knowing. What these objects are estranged from, what they confront with their pretention to reality, is precisely abstract thinking. The *philosopher,* himself an abstract form of estranged human being, takes himself to be the standard of the estranged world. The entire *history of alienation* and the whole of its *withdrawal* is therefore nothing but the *history of the production* of abstract, absolute thinking, of logical, speculative thinking. The *estrangement* which is the real object of interest within this alienation and its supersession is the opposition between *in itself* and *for itself,* between *consciousness* and *self-consciousness,* between *object* and *subject,* i.e. the opposition between abstract thought and sensuous reality, or between abstract thought and the actual sensory content of the thought itself. All other oppositions and their movements are merely the *semblance,* the *cloak,* the *exoteric* form of these [speculative philosophic] oppositions, which alone are important and are the *meaning* of the other, profane oppositions. Here, then, what is essential to the estrangement which is posited and which has to be superseded is not that the human being objectifies himself *inhumanly,* in opposition to himself, but that he *objectifies* himself in *distinction* from and in *opposition* to abstract thinking.

The appropriation of man's essential powers, which have become objects, alien objects, is therefore only an appropriation occurring in *consciousness,* in *thinking,* i.e. in abstraction, the appropriation of these objects as *thoughts* and *movements of thought.* Thus, despite its seeming to be thoroughly negative and critical, and despite some real criticism that it also contains and that prefigures later developments, the

Phenomenology already has within it the germ, potency, and secret of the uncritical positivism and equally uncritical idealism of Hegel's later works – the philosophic dissolution and restoration of the existing empirical world.

Secondly: The vindication of the objective world for man – for example, recognising that *sensuous* consciousness is not *abstract* but *human* sensuous consciousness, that religion, wealth, [state power], etc. are simply the estranged actuality of *human* objectification, of the essential creative powers of human beings, and so just the *path* to true *human* actuality – , this appropriation, or the insight into this process is presented by Hegel in such a way that *sensuousness, religion*, state power, etc. seem to be *spiritual* beings; for only *spirit* is the *true* being of man and the true form of spirit is thinking spirit, logical, speculative spirit. The *humanness* of nature, and of historically produced nature comprised of the products of man, appears in the *Phenomenology* to be *produced by* abstract spirit, and so to be *spiritual* moments, *thoughts*. Therefore the criticism in the *Phenomenology* is concealed, mystifying and obscure to itself. Still, insofar as it does grasp man's *estrangement* – even though man appears in the guise of spirit alone – all the elements of criticism lie hidden within it, already *prepared* and *elaborated* in a way that often far surpasses Hegel's own standpoint. 'Unhappy consciousness', 'honest consciousness', the struggle between 'noble and base consciousness', etc. – these individual sections contain elements of criticism, but still in an estranged form, of entire spheres, like that of religion, the state, bourgeois life, etc. Just as the *being*, the *object* appears to be a being of thought, so the *subject* is always *consciousness* or *self-consciousness*; or rather the object appears only in the form of *abstract* consciousness, and man only in the form of *self-consciousness*, and hence the different forms of estrangement that come into view are merely different forms of consciousness and self-consciousness.

How much the solution of theoretical enigmas is both a task and a result of praxis, how much true praxis is the very condition for actual and positive theory, can be seen by reference to *fetishism*. The sensuous consciousness of a fetish-worshipper is different from that of the Greek, because his sensuous existence itself is different. Abstract hostility between sense and spirit exists necessarily so long as man's sensory relationship to nature, man's sense of nature, and thus also *man's natural* sense are not yet produced through man's own labour. – *Equality* is nothing but the German *Ich = Ich* translated into French, i.e. into political terms. Equality as the *ground* of communism is communism's justification in *political* terms; it is the same thing when the German justifies it to himself [philosophically] by conceiving of man as *universal self-consciousness*. Obviously, the transcendence of estrangement always proceeds from the predominant form of estrangement: in Germany, *self-consciousness* [because of the predominance of philosophy]; in France, *equality*, because politics is dominant; in England, actual material need, practical need which is its own measure. This is the standpoint from which Proudhon is to be both criticised and appreciated. – If we continue to characterise *communism* itself – because it is negation of the negation – as the appropriating of the human essence mediated with itself through the negation of private property, and hence not yet as the *true*, self-originating position, but rather as originating out of private property,* [then we continue to treat it] in old German fashion – in the fashion of Hegel's Phenomenology – [and] so to super[sede private property merely] as a *surmounted moment* now completed. And one [...] could be satisfied with that [i.e. with having superseded it] in one's consciousness. [But the actual appropriation] of the human essence [can be achieved] only through the actual [superseding of private property, which survives the mere] superseding of its thought now as before. Therefore with this [mere thought-supersession] the actual estrangement of human life remains, and all the greater an estrangement remains the more one is conscious of it as an estrangement – [The superseding of estrangement] can be truly completed only by bringing communism about. To supersede the *idea* of private property, communism at the level of *thought* alone is sufficient. But to supersede actual private property requires *actual* communist action. History will bring this about, and that movement, which we already know in thought to be a self-transcending one, will in the actual world pass through a very rough and lengthy process. Still, the fact that we have at the outset gained consciousness of both the limitedness and the goal of this historical movement, and indeed a

---

* From this point to the sentence below which begins, 'To supersede the *idea* of private property ... ', a large tear in the MS prevents sure reading of the text. What follows is an effort to give a likely reading. Cf. MEGA² I, 2, p. 289 (and p. 287 which has a photo of the MS page).

consciousness that reaches beyond it, must be considered to be already a great advance.

[...]

The great thing about Hegel's *Phenomenology* and its final result – the dialectic, negativity as the moving and creating principle – is therefore first that Hegel grasps man's self-creation as a process, objectification as loss of objectivity, as alienation and the superseding of this alienation; that he therefore grasps the essence of *labour* and comprehends objective man – true because actual man – as being the result of his *own labour*. The *actual, active* relationship of man to himself as a species-being, or his self-manifestation as an actual species-being, i.e. as a human being, can come about only through his own creative exercise of his emergent *species-power* – which in turn can come about only through the cooperation of men, only as a result of history – making those powers objective to man himself, which at first can only be done in the form of estrangement.

[...]

We note in passing that Hegel's standpoint is that of modern political economy. He grasps *labour* as the essence, the self-confirming essence of man; he sees only the positive side of labour, not its negative side. Labour is the *self-conscious becoming* of *man* within *alienation*, or the self-conscious becoming of *alienated man*. Hegel knows and acknowledges only labour of the abstractly spiritual kind. Thus, what constitutes the essence of philosophy in general, namely the *alienation of self-knowing man*, or *self-thinking alienated* science [*Wissenschaft*], Hegel indeed grasps as its essence, and hence he can synthetically combine the individual moments of philosophy prior to his own and present his own as *the* philosophy. What the other philosophers did – that they grasped the individual moments of nature and of human life as moments of self-consciousness, and indeed of abstract self-consciousness – that Hegel *knows* to be the *doing* of philosophy. Hence his science is absolute.

[...]

Hegel equates the *human being, man*, with *self-consciousness*. All estrangement of the human being is therefore for him *nothing* but *estrangement of self-consciousness.* He does not consider the estrangement of self-consciousness to be an expression, a reflecting in knowledge and thought, of the *actual* estrangement of the human being. Instead, the *actual* estrangement, the one that seems real, is in its *innermost* hidden reality – a reality which only philosophy brings to light – nothing but the *appearance* of the estrangement of the actual human being, i.e. of *self-consciousness.* Hence, the science that comprehends this is called *phenomenology.* All reappropriating of estranged objective being appears therefore to be an incorporation into self-consciousness; man achieving power over his own being is here *merely* self-consciousness achieving control over objective beings.

[...]

Because Hegel equates man with self-consciousness, man's alienated objective being, the world of *things*, equals *alienated self-consciousness*, and *thinghood* is constituted by this alienation. *Things* are *objects for man,* and the only true object for him is what is essentially objective to him, his own *objectified* being. Because it is not *actual man*, and therefore also not *nature* – for man is *human nature* – which as such is made the subject, but rather the abstract version of man, self-consciousness, *things* can only be alienated self-consciousness. It is completely natural that a living being, a being that is a part of nature, equipped and endowed with essential powers of an objective, i.e. material, kind also has truly *actual* natural *objects* corresponding to what it is, and that its alienation of itself is its creation of an *actually* objective world, but a world having the character of *externality*, of not belonging to itself, of being overwhelming. There is nothing incomprehensible or puzzling in this. Rather the opposite would be puzzling. But it is just as clear that a *self-consciousness*, by its alienation, can posit only *thinghood*, i.e. only an abstract thing, a thing of abstraction, and no *actual* thing. It is further clear that thinghood is therefore utterly devoid of *independence, essentiality*, in relation to self-consciousness; and what is constituted, instead of confirming itself is merely a confirmation of the activity of constituting, which for a moment focuses its energy into the form of the product and gives it the *semblance* – but only for a moment – of an actual, independent being.

[...]

The object is therefore something negative, something that cancels itself out, a *nullity*. This nullity of the object has not only a negative but a *positive* meaning for consciousness, for this *nullity* of the object is precisely the self-confirmation of what is non-objective, the abstraction, consciousness itself. The nullity of the object has the positive meaning for *consciousness itself*, that it *knows* this nullity, the objective being, to be its *self-alienation*, knows it to be the result of its self-alienation alone [...] The manner of being of consciousness, and of anything that is for consciousness, is *knowing*. Knowing is its only act. Something comes to be for consciousness insofar as consciousness *knows* this *something*. Knowing is its only objective relationship. – It now knows the nothingness of the object, i.e. the non-existence of the distinction between the object and itself, the non-being of the object for it, because it knows the object to be its own *self-alienation*, knows itself, knowing as object, because the object is merely the *semblance* of an object, a self-imposed illusion whose being is nothing other than knowing itself which has confronted itself with itself, and hence with a *nullity*, with something having no objectivity outside of knowing; or knowing knows that in relating itself to an object, it is only *outside* itself, alienates itself, that it itself *appears* to itself as object, or that what appears to it as object is only itself.

On the other hand, says Hegel, another moment is also present here, namely that consciousness has in equal measure superseded this alienation and objectivity and taken it back into itself, and so is *at home* in its *other-being as such*.

[...]

If we here abstract from Hegel's abstraction and put the self-consciousness of man back in the place of abstract self-consciousness, then the self-consciousness of man is *at home* in its *other-being as such* [...] This implies that self-conscious man, insofar as he has recognised and superseded the spiritual world, or the spiritual universal existence of his world, as his self-alienation, nevertheless again confirms it in its alienated form and declares it to be his authentic existence, restores it and declares himself to be *at home in his other-being as such*: e.g. after superseding religion, after recognising religion to be a product of self-alienation, nevertheless finding self-confirmation in *religion as religion*. Here *is* the root of Hegel's *false* positivism, or of his mere *semblance* of criticism: what Feuerbach characterised as the positing, negating and restoring of religion or theology, but which we have to apply much more generally. Thus reason is at home in unreason as unreason. The man who has recognised that he leads an alienated life in the sphere of law [*Recht*], politics etc., leads his truly human life in this alienated life as such. Self-affirmation, self-confirmation in *contradiction* with itself as well as with the knowing and being of the object, is thus presented as the true *knowing* and *living*.

There can no longer be any question of Hegel's accommodation to religion, the state, etc., because this falsehood is his very principle.

If I *know* religion to be man's *alienated* self-consciousness, then what I know to be confirmed in it as religion is not my self-consciousness but my alienated self-consciousness. My self-consciousness that is proper to itself, to its own essence, I know to be confirmed therefore not in *religion* but in the *abolishing* and *superseding* of religion.

With Hegel, therefore, the negation of the negation is not the confirming of the true being by negating the mere semblance of being, but rather the confirming of the mere semblance of being, or of the self-estranged being together with its denial; or the denial of this semblance of being as something objective, external to and independent of man, and its transformation into the subject.

The *act of superseding* [*das Aufheben*], therefore, plays a very special role, in which denial and preservation, or affirmation, are combined.

Thus e.g. in Hegel's *Philosophy of Right*, civil law [*Privatrecht*] superseded = *morality*, morality superseded = *family*, family superseded = *civil* [or *bourgeois*] society, civil/bourgeois society superseded equals *state*, state superseded = *world history*. In *actuality*, civil law, morality, family, civil/bourgeois society, state, etc. remain in existence, but they have become *moments*, modes of man's existence and temporal being – which have no validity in isolation from one another, but mutually dissolve and engender one another: moments in a fluid process.

In their actual existence this *fluid* character of theirs is hidden. It becomes manifest and revealed only in thought, in philosophy: Thus my true religious existence is my existence within the *philosophy of religion*; my true political existence is my existence within the *philosophy of right*; my true natural existence is my existence within the *philosophy of nature*; my true artistic existence is my existence within the *philosophy of art*; my true *human* existence is my *philosophic* existence. Likewise, the true existence of religion, state, nature, art is the *philosophy* of religion, nature, state, art. But if the philosophy of religion etc. is the only true existence of religion [etc.], then it is only as *a philosopher of religion* that I am truly religious [etc.]; and so I deny *actual* religiousness and actually *religious* men. Yet, at the same time I affirm them: in part within my own existence, or within the estranged existence that I oppose to them, for this *is* merely their *philosophic* expression; and in part in their particular original form, for they are for me only the *semblance* of other-being, mere allegories, or sensuously cloaked forms of their true existence – i.e. of my *philosophic* existence.

Similarly [in Hegel's *Encyclopedia*], *quality* superseded = *quantity*, quantity superseded = *measure*, measure superseded = *essence*, essence superseded = *appearance*, appearance superseded = *actuality*, actuality superseded = *concept*, concept superseded = *objectivity*, objectivity superseded = *absolute idea*, absolute idea superseded = *nature*, nature superseded = *subjective spirit*, subjective spirit superseded = *ethical* objective spirit, ethical objective spirit superseded = *art*, art superseded = *religion*, religion superseded = *absolute knowing*.

On the one hand this superseding is a superseding of a thought-entity; thus, [in the philosophy of right] the *thought* of private property is superseded in the *thinking* of morality. And because this thinking imagines itself to be immediately its other, i.e. *sensuous actuality*, it takes its action also to be *sensuously* effective action, and so this superseding in thought, which leaves its object existing in the actual world, believes that it has actually overcome it. On the other hand, because the object has now become for thinking a moment or element of itself, of thinking, it is in its actuality a self-confirmation of thought itself, of self-consciousness, of abstraction.

On the one hand, the existence which Hegel *supersedes* in philosophy is, therefore, not *actual* religion, state, nature, but rather religion [etc.] itself already as an object of knowledge, i.e. *dogmatics*, and likewise with *jurisprudence, political science, natural science*. On the one hand, he therefore stands opposed both to the actual being and to immediately unphilosophical *science*, or to the unphilosophic *conceptions* of this being. He contradicts the prevalent conceptions [of jurisprudence, natural science. etc.].

On the other hand, the religious etc. man can find in Hegel his final affirmation.

At this point we should consider the *positive* elements of Hegelian dialectic – within the sphere of estrangement.

(a) The act of superseding, as the objective movement of reabsorbing the alienation back into itself. – This is the insight, expressed within estrangement, of the *appropriation* of the objective being by the superseding of its estrangement; the estranged insight into man's actual objectification in the actual appropriating of his objective being by annihilating the estranged character of the objective world, by superseding it in its estranged existence; just as atheism, as the superseding of God, is the coming-to-be of theoretical humanism, and communism, as the superseding of private property, is the vindication of actual human life as man's own property and thus the coming-to-be of practical humanism; or, atheism and communism – the first through its superseding of religion, the second through its superseding of private property – constitute self-mediated humanism. Only through the superseding of this mediation – which is itself, however, a necessary pre-condition – does positively self-originating humanism, *positive* humanism, come about.

But atheism and communism are no flight, no abstraction from, no loss of the humanly created world, or of the essential powers of man that have issued into that objectivity, no impoverished return to an unnatural, undeveloped simplicity. Rather they are for man the first actual becoming, the true actualisation of his being, or of the becoming of his being as actual being.

Thus, in grasping the *positive* sense of self-referring negation – although in estranged form – Hegel grasps man's self-estrangement, alienation of being, loss of objectivity and actuality as his self-discovery, expression of his being, his objectification and actualisation. In short, in his own abstract way, Hegel grasps labour – as man's act of self-creation, his relation to himself as an estranged being and manifesting of his being as estranged – to be the emergence of *species-consciousness* and *species-life*.

(b) However, in Hegel – apart from, or rather as a consequence of the inversion already described – this act seems at first to be *merely* formal because abstract, because the human being himself has the status only of an abstract thinking being, self-consciousness; and

second, [*sic*] because the conception is *formal* and *abstract*, the superseding of the alienation becomes a confirming of it, or for Hegel this movement of *self-generation* and *self-objectification* as *self-alienation* and *self-estrangement* is the *absolute* and hence final *expression of human life*, having itself as its aim, and at peace with itself having achieved the fullness of its essence. This movement in its abstract form as dialectic is considered to be *truly human life*, and because it is nevertheless an abstraction, an estrangement of human life, it is considered to be a divine *process*, but a divine process of man, a process undergone by man's own essence – abstract, pure, absolute, and separated from him.

Third: This process must have a bearer, a subject; but the subject only comes to be as a result; this result, the subject knowing itself as absolute self-consciousness, is therefore *God, absolute spirit*, the *self-knowing and self-manifesting Idea*. Actual man and actual nature become mere predicates, symbols of this hidden, unreal man and this unreal nature. Subject and predicate have therefore an absolutely reversed relationship to one another – a *mystical subject-object*, or a subjectivity overreaching the object, the *absolute subject* as a *process*, as self-alienation and returning to itself out of its alienation, but at the same time reabsorbing this alienation into itself as *subject*, and as subject of this process: pure, *unceasing* circular movement in itself.

[This is but the mystified] *formal* and *abstract* conception of man's self-creation or self-objectification. [. . .]

Society – in the view of the political economists – is *civil* (*bourgeois*) *society*, in which every individual is a totality of needs and exists for the other, as the other exists for him, only insofar as each becomes a means for the other. For the political economist, as for the political mentality expressed in *The Rights of Man*, everything is reduced to man the individual, stripped of all specific features so as to be treated either as capitalist or labourer. – The *division of labour* is the political economic expression of the *social character* [*Gesellschaftlichkeit*] *of labour* within its estranged condition. Or, because *labour* is but an expression of human activity in its estranged condition, externalisation of life as alienation of life, so too is the *division of labour* just the *estranged, alienated* position of human activity as a *real species-being* or as *activity of man as species-activity*.

[Human relations as complementarity]
(from *Comments on James Mill*)]

The essence or nature of money is not, in the first place, that property is alienated [*entaussert*] in it, but rather that the *mediating activity* or movement, the *human* social act through which the products of men mutually complement each other, is *estranged* and becomes the attribute of a *material thing*, money. Because man alienates this mediating activity itself, he is active only as a man lost to himself, dehumanised; the very *relation* or *connection* to things, the human operation with them, becomes the operation of an entity external to and above man. Because of this *alien mediator*, instead of man himself being the mediator for men, man perceives his will, his activity, his relationship to others as a power independent of both him and them. His slavery thus reaches its peak. That this *mediator* now becomes an *actual god* is clear, for the mediator is the *actual power* over what it mediates to me. Its cult becomes an end in itself. Objects separated from this mediator have lost their value. Thus, only insofar as they *represent it* do they have value, whereas originally it seemed that it had value only insofar as *it* represented *them*. This reversal of the original relationship is necessary. This mediator is therefore the *essence* or *nature* of private property which has become lost to it, the *estranged essence* or *nature* of private property, it is private property external to itself, *alienated* private property, as it is also the *alienated mediation* of human production with human production; the *alienated* species-activity of man. All of the qualities and characteristics of man in the production of this activity are thus transferred to the mediator. And so man as man, i.e. as separated from this mediator, becomes all the poorer as this mediator becomes *richer*.

Christ originally *represents* (1) men before God; (2) God for men; (3) man to man.

So, according to its concept, money originally represents: (1) private property for private property; (2) society for private property; (3) private property for society.

But Christ is the *alienated* God and alienated *man*. God retains value insofar as he represents Christ, and man retains value only insofar as he represents Christ. Likewise with money.

Why must private property advance to the *form of money* [*Geldwesen*]? Because man as a sociable [*geselliges*] being must go on to exchange and because exchange – under the presupposition of private property – must go on to *value*. That is, the mediating movement of man who is exchanging is not a social, not a human movement, not a *human* relationship; it is the *abstract relationship* of private property to private property, and this abstract relationship is *value*, whose actual existence as value is precisely *money*. Because men who are exchanging are not relating to one another as men, the *thing* loses the significance of human, of personal property. The social relationship of private property is estranged from itself. The independent [*für sich seiende*] existence of this relationship, money, is therefore the alienation of the private property, the abstraction of its *specific*, personal nature.

[...]

The *communal being [Gemeinwesen] of man*, or men's self-activating and self-manifesting *human* being, their mutual complementing aimed at species-life, at authentic human being – all of this political economy comprehends only in the form of *exchange* and *trade*. *Society*, says Destutt de Tracy, is a *series of mutual exchanges*. It is exactly this movement of mutual integration. *Society*, says Adam Smith, is a *commercial society*. Each of its members is a *merchant*.

Thus does political economy *fix* on the *estranged* form of sociable interaction and take it to be the form that is *essential, original* and adequate to the nature and destiny of man.

[...]

Just as the mutual exchange of the products of *human activity* takes the appearance of *barter* or *exchange-trade*, of *haggling [Schacher]*, so too the mutual complementing and exchange of activity appear as: *division of labour*, which makes man so far as possible into an abstract being, a machine tool, etc. and transforms him into a spiritual and physical monster.

[...]

Assume that we had produced as men: each of us in his production would have doubly affirmed himself and the other. I would have (1) in my *production* objectified my *individuality* and its *particular characteristics* and thus also enjoyed during the activity an individual *expression of life*, and in contemplating the object had the individual joy of knowing my personality to be *objective, sensibly perceptible* and thus a power raised *beyond all doubt*. (2) In your enjoyment or your use of my product I would *immediately* have had the enjoyment as well as the consciousness of having, in my labour, satisfied a *human* need, and thus of having objectified the *human* essence, and so of having provided an object that meets the need of another *human* being; (3) I would have been for you the *mediator* between you and the species, and so known and felt by you as a complement of your own being, as a necessary part of yourself, and so would know myself to be confirmed in your thought and in your love; (4) I would in my individual life-expression have directly provided your life-expression, and thus in my individual activity, have directly *affirmed* and *objectified* my true being, my *human*, my *communal being*.

Our productions would be just so many mirrors reflecting our being.

This relationship would be reciprocal: what occurs on my side would occur on yours.

To summarise the points under our assumption:

My labour would be a *free manifestation of life*, hence *enjoyment of life*; whereas under private property it is *alienation of life*, for labour is *in order to live*, in order to provide a *means* of life. My labour *is not* life.

Secondly, in labour it is the *particular characteristic* of my individuality that is affirmed, because it is my *individual* life that is affirmed. Labour here, therefore, would be *true, active property*.

'Critical Marginal Notes on the Article "The King of Prussia and Social Reform. By a Prussian"'

Vorwärts!, no. 63 (7 Aug. 1844)
& no. 64 (10 Aug. 1844):

I

(Special reasons lead me to state that the following article is the first that I have submitted to *Vorwärts!* K.M.)

Issue no. 60 of *'Vorwärts!'* contains an article entitled 'The King of Prussia and Social Reform' and signed *'A Prussian'*.

The alleged Prussian begins by reporting the contents of the royal Prussian Cabinet order concerning the *Silesian workers' revolt* and the opinion of the French journal *La Réforme* about the Prussian Cabinet order. According to the *Réforme*, the Cabinet order had its source in the *'terror* and the *religious sentiment'* of the King. It even finds in this document the *presentiment* of the great reforms that await bourgeois society. The 'Prussian' instructs the *Réforme* as follows:

'The King and German society has [*sic*] not yet arrived at the "presentiment of their reform" (Note the stylistic and grammatical nonsense: 'The King of Prussia and society *has* not yet arrived at the presentiment of their (to whom does this "their" refer?) reform'.), and not even the Silesian and Bohemian revolts have generated this sentiment. It is impossible to bring an *unpolitical* country like Germany to regard the *partial* distress of the industrial districts as an affair of general interest, let alone as an injury to the whole civilised world. For the Germans the event had the same character as any *local* flood or famine. Thus the King considers it to be a *failure of administration or of charity*. For this reason, and because a few troops dealt with the feeble weavers, the demolition of the factories and machines also inspired no "terror" in the King or in his authorities. Neither, in fact, did *religious sentiment* dictate the Cabinet order: it is a very sober expression of Christian statecraft and of a doctrine which

97

admits no difficulties that can withstand its sole remedy, the "good-natured disposition of Christian hearts". Poverty and crime are two great evils; who can cure them? The state and the authorities? No, the union of all Christian hearts.'

Among the reasons cited by the so-called 'Prussian' to deny the 'terror' of the King was the few soldiers needed to handle the feeble weavers.

Thus in a country where banquets replete with liberal toasts and liberal champagne – we recall the banquet in Dusseldorf – provoke a royal Cabinet order;* where *not a single soldier* is needed to stifle the aspirations of the *entire* liberal bourgeoisie for freedom of the press and for a constitution; in a country where passive obedience is the order of the day; in that country the need to use armed force against feeble weavers would not be *an event*, a *terrifying* event? And the feeble weavers won the first confrontation. They were suppressed later by an increased number of troops. Is the revolt of a bunch of workers less dangerous because no army is needed to put it down? Let our clever Prussian compare the revolt of the Silesian weavers with the revolts of the English workers, and the Silesian weavers will look like *powerful* weavers to him.

It is on the basis of the *general* relationship of *politics* to *social ills* that we shall explain why the weavers' revolt could instill no special 'terror' in the King. For the moment suffice it to say that the revolt was not immediately directed against the King of Prussia, but against the bourgeoisie. As an aristocrat and absolute monarch the King of Prussia can have no love for the bourgeoisie; and even less can he be frightened if their subservience and their impotence are increased because of their tense and difficult relationship to the proletariat. Moreover: the orthodox Catholic is more opposed to the orthodox Protestant than to the atheist, just as legitimists are more opposed to liberals than to communists. Not that atheists and communists are closer to Catholics and legitimists, but rather because they are more distant from them than are the Protestants and liberals, because they are *outside* their circle. In his political quality the King of Prussia is immediately opposed within politics to liberalism. The opposition of

---

* Frederick William IV's Cabinet order of 18 July 1843 prohibiting government officials from participating in events organised by the liberals, as they had in a banquet in Düsseldorf marking the opening of the seventh Rhenish Diet.

the proletariat exists for the King just as little as the King exists for the proletariat. The proletariat would have to have already attained decisive power for it to smother the existing antipathies and political antagonisms and turn all of the hostility of politics against itself. Finally, given the well-known character of this King, avid for things *interesting* and *important*, it must have been surprising, agreeable, exciting to find on his own soil that *'interesting'* and *'much discussed' pauperism*, and with that a new occasion to have people talk about him. How content he must have been to learn that he possessed his *'own'* royal Prussian *pauperism*.

Our *'Prussian'* is still more unfortunate when he *denies* that *'religious sentiment'* is the source of the royal Cabinet order. Why is religious sentiment not the source of this Cabinet order? Because it is a 'very *sober* expression of Christian statecraft', a *'sober'* expression of the doctrine which 'admits no difficulties that can withstand its sole remedy, the good-natured disposition of Christian hearts'.

Is not *religious sentiment* the source of *Christian* statecraft? Is not a doctrine which has its universal panacea in the good-natured disposition of *Christian hearts* based on religious feeling? Does a *sober* expression of religious sentiment cease to be an expression of religious sentiment? And there is more! I maintain that it is a very *intoxicated* religious sentiment, one very taken with itself, which seeks the *'healing of great evils'*, which it denies to the *'state and its authorities'*, in the *'union of Christian hearts'*. It is a very *intoxicated* religious sentiment that – as our *'Prussian'* admits – locates all evil in the lack of Christian sentiment, and for that reason refers the authorities to the sole means to strengthen this sentiment, to *'exhortation'*. Here, according to the *'Prussian'*, is the purpose of the Cabinet order: *Christian disposition*. Religious sentiment, that is if it is not sober, if it is intoxicated, considers itself the sole good. Wherever it sees evil, it blames it on its own *absence*, for being the sole good, only it can bring forth good. The Cabinet order that was dictated by religious sentiment therefore itself dictates religious sentiment. A politician of *sober* religious sentiment would not in his 'perplexity' seek his 'help' in the 'exhortation of the pious preacher to a Christian disposition'.

How then does the alleged Prussian prove to *La Réforme* that the Cabinet order does not emanate from religious sentiment? By portraying it throughout as an emanation of religious sentiment. Is any insight into social movements to be expected from such an *illogical* mind? Let us listen to his *chatter* about the relationship of *German society* to the labour movement and to social reform in general.

Let us *distinguish* what the 'Prussian' has ignored, namely the various categories which are included in the expression *'German society'*: government, bourgeoisie, the press, and finally the workers themselves. These are the *various* masses at issue here. The 'Prussian' draws these masses together and condemns them *en masse* from his lofty standpoint. *German society* according to him has 'not yet arrived at the presentiment of its "reform" '.

Why is it lacking this instinct?

Our Prussian answers: 'It is impossible to bring an *unpolitical* country like Germany to regard the *partial* distress of the industrial districts as an *affair of general interest*, let alone as an injury to the whole civilised world. For the Germans the event has the same character as any *local* flood or famine. Thus the king considers it to be a *failure of administration or of charity*.'

The 'Prussian' thus explains this *misunderstanding* of the workers' distress by the peculiarity of an unpolitical country.

Admittedly: England is a *political* country. In addition it will be admitted that England is the *land of pauperism*; indeed, the very word is of English origin. Consideration of England, therefore, is the surest way to learn the *relationship* of a *political* country to *pauperism*. In England, distress of the workers is not *partial* but universal; it is not restricted to the industrial districts, but extends to the rural districts. There the movements are not just beginning, but have returned periodically for practically a century.

Now, how does the *English* bourgeoisie and the government and press that are connected with it understand *pauperism*?

In so far as the English bourgeoisie admits pauperism to be a *fault of politics*, the *Whig* considers the *Tory* and the *Tory* considers the *Whig* to be the cause of pauperism. According to the *Whig* the principal source of pauperism is the monopoly of large-scale land-ownership and the prohibitive legislation against the import of corn. According to the Tory, the entire evil lies in liberalism, in competition, in a factory system that has been carried too far. Neither of the parties locates the source in politics in general, but rather only in the politics of the other party; and neither party dreams of any reform of society.

The most rigorous expression of English insight into pauperism – we are still speaking of the insight of the English bourgeoisie and government – is English *political economy*, i.e. the scientific reflection of English political economic conditions.

One of the best and most renowned English political economists, MacCulloch, who is acquainted with contemporary conditions and must have a comprehensive view of the movement of bourgeois society, and who is a pupil of the cynical Ricardo, in a public lecture and with the applause of his audience, even dares to apply to political economy what *Bacon* says of philosophy: 'The man who with true and untiring wisdom suspends his judgement and advances step by step, overcoming one obstacle after another which, like mountains, impede the process of study, will finally reach the peak of science where he can enjoy the calm and the pure air, where nature offers herself to the eye in all her beauty, and from where by a gently sloping path he can descend to the last details of practice'.* The good *pure air* of the pestilential atmosphere of the English cellar dwellings! The *grand natural beauty* of the ragged clothing of the English poor and the wilted, stunted flesh of the women consumed by work and misery; the children crawling in excrement; the deformities caused by overwork in the monotonous mechanism of the factories! The charming *last details of practice*: prostitution, murder, and the gallows!

Even that part of the English bourgeoisie which is penetrated by the danger of pauperism comprehends both this danger as well as the means to its melioration in a way that is not only *peculiar*, but – to speak bluntly – *childish* and *silly*.

Thus, for example, Dr *Kay*, in his brochure 'Recent Measures for the Promotion of Education in England', reduces everything to *neglected education*. Guess why! Because of a lack of education the worker does not grasp the *'natural laws of commerce'*, laws which *necessarily* plunge him into pauperism. For that reason he rebels. That could *'inconvenience* the *prosperity* of the English manufacturers and of English commerce, disturb the mutual trust of business men, *lessen* the *stability* of the political and social institutions'.†

---

* Francis Bacon, *De dignitate et augmentis scientiarum* (1779); quoted in MacCulloch's *A Discourse on the Rise, Progress, Peculiar Objects, and Importance of Political Economy*, which Marx, in summer 1844, read in Prévost's French translation.
† Marx's source on Kay, and his principal source on conditions in England, was Eugène Buret, *De la misère des classes laborieuses en Angleterre et en France* (1840).

So great is the thoughtlessness of the English bourgeoisie and its press regarding pauperism, this national epidemic of England.

Let us suppose then that the accusations of our 'Prussian' against *German* society are justified. Does the reason lie in the *unpolitical* condition of Germany? But if the bourgeoisie of this *unpolitical* Germany is unable to see the general significance of a *partial* distress, the bourgeoisie of a *political* England, on the other hand, is able to misconstrue the general significance of universal distress, a distress whose general significance is shown partly through its periodic recurrence, partly through its geographic extension, and partly through the frustration of all attempts at its alleviation.

Further, the 'Prussian' blames the *unpolitical* condition of Germany when the *King* of Prussia finds the basis of pauperism in a *failure of administration and charity* and therefore seeks the means to combat pauperism in *administrative and charitable measures*.

Is this attitude peculiar to the King of Prussia? One might take a quick look at England, the only country where one can speak of large-scale *political* measures against pauperism.

The present English Poor Laws date from the law in the 43rd act of the reign of Elizabeth. (For our purposes it is not necessary to go back to the statute of labourers under Edward III.) In what do the measures of this legislation consist? In the obligations of the parishes to support their impoverished labourers, in the poor tax, in the legal charities. This legislation – charity via legal administration – has lasted for two centuries. After long and painful experience, what position did Parliament adopt in its Amendment Bill of 1834?

To begin with, it declares the terrible increase of pauperism as being due to a *'failure of administration'*.

The administration of the poor tax, which consisted of officials of the respective parishes, is therefore to be reformed. *Unions* of approximately 20 parishes will be formed, under a single administration. A bureau of officials – a *Board of Guardians* – to be elected by those obliged to pay taxes, will meet on a certain day in the office of the Union and will decide on the admissibility of support. These bureaus will be directed and overseen by delegates of the government, the central commission of Somerset House, the 'Ministry of Poverty', as one Frenchman [i.e. E. Buret] has aptly characterised it. The capital which this administration oversees is almost equivalent to the sum that the military administration costs in France. The number of local administrations employed in this will run to 500, and each of these local administrations will have at least twelve officials so occupied.

The English Parliament did not stop with just the formal reform of the administration. It found the principal source of the *acute* condition of English pauperism in the *Poor Laws* themselves. Charity, the legal remedy for this social malady, encourages the social malady. As far as pauperism in *general* is concerned, it is an *eternal law of nature*, according to the theory of *Malthus*: 'Because the population incessantly tends to outstrip the means of subsistence, charity is foolishness, an official encouragement to poverty. The state therefore can do nothing but allow poverty to run its course and at most ease the death of those in poverty'. The English Parliament combines this philanthropic theory with the view that pauperism is a *misfortune which is the workers' own fault*, and which for that reason is not to be prevented, as a calamity, but is rather to be suppressed, to be punished, as a crime.

Thus arose the regime of the Workhouses, i.e. houses for the poor, whose internal arrangement *frightens* the impoverished away from seeking refuge from starvation. In the Workhouses charity is ingeniously interwoven with the *revenge* of the bourgeoisie on the impoverished who have appealed to their charity.

England has thus attempted first of all to destroy pauperism by means of *charity* and *administrative measures*. It did not then see the progressive increase of pauperism to be the necessary consequence of modern *industry*, but rather a consequence of the *English Poor Tax*. It conceived of universal distress only as *something specific* to English legislation. What was earlier attributed to a *lack of charity* was later attributed to an *excess of charity*. Finally, poverty was considered to be the fault of the impoverished and, as such, to warrant their personal punishment.

The general significance that *political* England has derived from pauperism is limited to this, that in the course of its development and in spite of administrative measures, pauperism has raised itself to the status of a *national institution*, thereby inevitably becoming the object of a wide-spread administration, with many branches to it, an administration which, however, is no longer charged with suppressing pauperism, but rather with *disciplining* it, perpetuating it. This administration has given up trying to stifle the source of pauperism by means of *positive* measures; it is satisfied with digging a grave for it, with police-like charity, whenever it bubbles to the surface of public life. The English state, far from going beyond administrative and charitable measures, has lowered itself far below them. It administers only *that* pauperism which is desperate enough to allow itself to be captured and locked up.

So up to now the 'Prussian' has established nothing *original* in the procedure of the King of Prussia. But why, this great man exclaims with *rare naivety,* 'Why does not the King of Prussia *immediately order the education of all impoverished children?*' Why does he first turn to the authorities and await their plans and suggestions?

Our super-clever 'Prussian' will calm down if he learns that the King of Prussia is just as unoriginal in this as in his other actions; that he has even taken the only path that a head of state *can* take.

Napoleon wanted to eliminate begging with one blow. He commissioned his authorities to prepare plans for the *extermination of begging* in all of France. The project hung in abeyance; Napoleon lost his patience and wrote to his Interior Minister, Crétet, commanding him to put an end to begging within *one* month. He said: 'One must not pass from this earth without leaving some trace behind that recommends our memory to posterity. Do not ask me for three or four more months to gather information: you have young auditors, clever prefects, engineers well-schooled in bridge and road building; put all of them into action and do not doze along with the usual office-work'.* In a few months everything was accomplished. On 5 July 1808, the law was promulgated which suppressed begging. By what means? By means of the *Dépôts* which were so quickly transformed into penitentiaries that soon the indigent wound up in these institutions more by order of the *police court*. And yet at that time M. Noailles du Gard, a member of the Legislative Corps, proclaimed 'Eternal gratitude to the heroes who have secured a place of refuge for the indigent and food for the poor: childhood will no longer be destitute, poor families will no longer do without resources, nor workers be without encouragement and occupation. Our steps will no longer be dogged by the disgusting image of infirmities and shameful poverty.'† This last cynical passage is the single truth in this panegyric.

* Quoted from Buret, *De la misère* I, pp. 225–7
† Quoted from Buret, *De la misère*, I, p. 227.

If Napoleon addresses himself to the intelligence of his auditors, prefects, and engineers, why should not the King of Prussia do the same with his officials?

Why did not Napoleon *immediately* order the abolition of begging? The question of the 'Prussian' is of the same value: 'Why does not the King of Prussia immediately order the education of impoverished children?' Does the 'Prussian' know what the King would have to order? Nothing other than the *annihilation of the proletariat*. In order to educate children, they have to be *nourished* and freed from *wage labour*. Nourishing and educating impoverished children, i.e. nourishing and educating the *entire growing* proletariat, would be the *annihilation* of the proletariat and of pauperism.

For a moment the *Convention* had the courage *to order* the repeal of pauperism, though to be sure not '*immediately*', as the 'Prussian' demands of his King, but only after having charged the Committee of Public Safety with working out the necessary plans and proposals, and after this Committee had used the wide-ranging investigations of the Constituent Assembly regarding the situation of the French poor and had suggested through Barère the foundation of the *Livre de la bienfaisance nationale*, etc. And what was the result of the directive of the Convention? That yet another directive had been promulgated and one year later starving women besieged the Convention.

But the Convention was the *maximum* of *political energy*, of *political power*, and of *political understanding*.

No government in the world has given orders regarding pauperism *immediately*, without consulting with officials. The English Parliament even dispatched commissioners to all the countries of Europe to learn what various administrative remedies had been used against pauperism. But insofar as states have concerned themselves with pauperism, they have not gone beyond administrative and charitable measures or they have descended beneath administration and charity.

Can the *state* proceed any differently?

The *state* will *never* find the basis of *social defects in the 'state* and the *structure of society*', as the Prussian demands of his King. Wherever there are political parties, they all find the basis of every evil in the fact that instead of them, the opposition is *at the controls*. Even radical and revolutionary politicians seek the basis of evil not in the *essence* of the state, but rather in a certain *form of state*, which they want to replace with *another* form of state.

From the *political* standpoint, the *state* and the *structure of society* are not *two* different things. The state is the structure of society. Insofar as the state admits the existence of *social* defects, it seeks their causes either in *natural laws*, which no human power can command, or in *private life*, which is independent of the state, or in the *unsuitableness of the administration*, which is dependent on it. Thus England finds poverty grounded in the *natural law*, according to which the populace always exceeds the means of subsistence. From another point of view it explains *pauperism* as being due to the *bad will of the poor*, just as the King of Prussia explains it as due to the *unchristian disposition of the rich*, and as the Convention explained it as due to the *counterrevolutionary, suspicious sentiments of the property owners*. Hence England punishes the poor, the King of Prussia admonishes the rich, and the Convention beheads the property owners.

Finally, *all* states seek the cause in *accidental* or *intentional failings of the administration*, and therefore resort to administrative *measures* to alleviate the administrative defects. Why? Precisely because the *administration* is the *organising* activity of the state.

Short of abolishing itself, the state cannot abolish the *contradiction* between the role and good will of the administration on the one hand, and its means and power on the other. The state is *based* on this contradiction. It is based on the contradiction between *public* and *private life*, on the contradiction between *universal interests* and *particular interests*. The *administration* therefore must limit itself to a *formal* and *negative* activity, for precisely where civil life and its work begin, there the power of the administration ends. In fact, in the face of the consequences which arise out of the unsocial nature of this civil life, this private property, this commerce, this industry, this mutual plundering of the various civil circles – in the face of these consequences *impotence* is the *natural law* of the administration. For this disunion, this baseness, this *slavery of civil society* is the natural basis on which the *modern* state rests, just as the *civil society* of *slavery* was the natural foundation on which the *ancient* state rested. The existence of the state and the existence of slavery are inseparable. The state of classical antiquity and the slavery of that era – sincere, *classical* antitheses – were not more intimately fused together than the modern state and the modern business world – hypocritical *Christian* antitheses. If the modern state wanted to overcome the powerlessness of its administration, it would have to do away with present *private life*. If it wanted to abolish private life, it would have to abolish itself, for it exists *only* in contrast to private life. No *living thing*, however, believes the deficiencies of its existence are grounded in the *principle* of its life, in the essence of its life, but rather in circumstances *external to* its life. *Suicide* is contrary to nature. So the state cannot believe in the *intrinsic* impotence of its administration, that is, of itself. It can recognise *only* its formal, contingent deficiencies and seek to remedy them. If these modifications are fruitless, then the social defect is judged a natural imperfection, independent of human involvement, a *law of God*, or else the will of the private populace is judged too depraved to meet halfway the good intentions of the administration. And how perverse these private people are! They grumble about the government whenever it limits freedom, while demanding of the government that it prevent the inevitable consequences of this freedom!

The more powerful the state, and therefore the more *political* a country is, the less inclined it is to seek the basis of *social* ills and to grasp their *general* principle in the *principle of the state*, and thus in the *present structure of society*, the active, self-conscious and official expression of which is the state. *Political* understanding is *political* understanding precisely because it thinks *within* the confines of politics. The keener, the more active it is, the *less capable* it is of understanding social ills. The *classical* period of political understanding is the *French Revolution*. Far from seeing the source of social deficiencies in the principle of the state, the heroes of the French Revolution were much more inclined to see social deficiencies as the source of political ills. Thus *Robespierre* sees in great poverty and great wealth only an obstacle to *pure democracy*. For that reason he wants to establish a general *Spartan* frugality. The principle of politics is the *will*. The more one-sided, that is, the more complete *political* understanding is, the more it believes in the *omnipotence* of the will, the more blind it is to the *natural* and spiritual *limits* of the will, and therefore the more incapable it is of discovering the source of social ills. No further argument is needed against the silly hope of the 'Prussian', according to which '*political understanding*' is called on '*to discover the root of social need*' for Germany.

It was foolish not only to expect of the King of Prussia a power such as the Convention and Napoleon together did not possess; it was foolish to expect of him a point of view that goes beyond the boundaries of *all* politics, a point of view which is every bit as foreign to our clever 'Prussian' himself as it is to his King. This entire declaration was all the more foolish in that the 'Prussian' confesses:

'Good words and good intentions are *cheap*, insight and successful deeds are *costly*; in this case they are *more than costly*, they *are not even available*.'

If they are not even available, then anyone who tries to do what he can from the place he occupies should be recognised for that. In any event I leave it to the tact of the reader whether in this connection the mercantile gypsy language – 'cheap', 'costly', 'more than costly', 'not even available' – belongs to the category of '*good* words' and '*good* intentions'.

Let us suppose then that the 'Prussian's' remarks about the German government and the German bourgeoisie – the latter certainly is included in 'German society' – are completely justified. Is this section of society more at a loss in Germany than in England and France? Can one be more helpless than, for example, in England, where *helplessness* has been elevated to a system? If workers' revolts break out today in all of England, the bourgeoisie and government there are no better informed than in the last third of the eighteenth century. Their sole remedy is material force, and since material force declines in the same degree as the spread of pauperism and the insight of the proletariat increase, English helplessness necessarily grows in geometric proportion.

Finally it is *untrue, factually untrue*, that the German bourgeoisie completely misinterprets the general significance of the Silesian revolt. In many cities masters are trying to associate with the journeymen. All *liberal* German newspapers, the organs of the liberal bourgeoisie, are overflowing with organisation of labour, reform of society, criticism of monopoly and of competition, etc. All this as a result of the workers' movements. The newspapers of Trier, Aachen, Cologne, Wesel, Mannheim, Breslau, and even Berlin, often publish very intelligent articles on social questions from which the 'Prussian' can learn. Indeed, in letters from Germany there are constant expressions of amazement at how little opposed the bourgeoisie has been to *social* tendencies and ideas.

The 'Prussian' – had he been better acquainted with the history of the social movement – would have put his question the other way around. Why does even the German bourgeoisie itself attribute to the partial distress such relative universality? Whence come the *animosity* and the *cynicism* of the *political* bourgeoisie, and whence come the lack of *opposition* and the *sympathies* of the *unpolitical* bourgeoisie toward the proletariat?

II

Now for the oracular pronouncements of the 'Prussian' about the *German workers*.

'*The German poor*', he jokes, '*are no cleverer than the poor Germans*, i.e. *nowhere* do they look past their hearths, their factories, their district: the whole question *up to the present* has been left untouched by the all-pervasive *political soul*'.

To be able to compare the condition of the German workers with that of the French and English workers, the 'Prussian' would have had to compare the *initial form*, the *beginning* of the English and French workers' movement with the *incipient German* movement. This he fails to do. For that reason his reasoning runs to trivialities, as, for example, that *industry* in Germany is less developed than in England, or that a movement looks different in its beginning than it does in an advanced stage. He wants to speak about the *peculiarity* of the German worker-movement. About this, his theme, he says not a word.

But let the 'Prussian' adopt the correct standpoint and he will find that *not one* of the French and English workers' uprisings had as *theoretical* and *conscious* a character as the Silesian weavers' revolt.

First, recall the *weavers' song*, this bold call to struggle, in which hearth, factory, district are never mentioned, but instead the proletariat at once proclaims in impressive, sharp, determined, forceful fashion its opposition to the society of private property. The Silesian revolt *begins* precisely with what the French and English worker revolts *end*, with consciousness of the nature of the proletariat. The action itself carries the mark of this *superiority*. Not only are the machines, these rivals of the worker, destroyed, but also the *ledgers*, the property titles, and while all the other movements turned first only against the *industrial baron*, i.e. the visible enemy, this movement turned also against the banker, the hidden enemy. And finally, not a single English workers' uprising was led with similar bravery, deliberation, and perseverance.

As for the level of learning or the capacity for education of the

German workers in general, I would remind the reader of *Weitling's* genial writings, which often surpass Proudhon's in their theoretical character, despite being inferior in exposition. Where among the bourgeoisie – including their philosophers and literary figures – is there a work similar to Weitling's '*Guarantees of Harmony and Freedom*' with respect to the emancipation of the bourgeoisie – the *political* emancipation? If one compares the dull and faint-hearted mediocrity of German political literature with this *immense* and brilliant literary debut of the German workers; if one compares these gigantic *infant's shoes* of the proletariat with the dwarfishness of the worn-out political shoes of the German bourgeoisie, then an *athletic figure* has to be prophesied for this *German Cinderella*. It must be said that the German proletariat is the *theoretician* of the European proletariat, just as the English proletariat is its *political economist* and the French proletariat its *politician*, and that Germany's *classical* calling to *social* revolution is in direct measure to its incapacity for a *political* one. For just as the impotence of the German bourgeoisie is the *political* impotence of Germany, so also is the capability of the German proletariat – even apart from German theory – the *social* capability of Germany. The disparity between the political and the philosophical development in Germany is no *abnormality*. It is a necessary disparity. Only in socialism can a philosophical people find its corresponding praxis, which is to say, only in the *proletariat* can it find the active element of its liberation.

At the moment, however, I have neither time nor desire to explain to the 'Prussian' the relationship of 'German society' to social upheaval, and on the basis of this relationship to explain on the one hand the weak reaction of the German bourgeoisie to socialism and on the other the remarkable predisposition of the German proletariat for socialism. The initial elements for an understanding of this phenomenon he will find in my Introduction to a Critique of Hegel's Philosophy of Right ('*Deutsch-französische Jahrbücher*').

The wisdom of the *German poor* thus stands in an *inverse* relationship to the wisdom of the *poor Germans*. But people who use every event as a pretext for public display of their style wind up through this exercise in *formalism* with distorted content, while for its part the distorted content impresses on the form the stamp of vulgarity. Thus the 'Prussian's' attempt – occasioned by the Silesian labour unrest – to employ the style of antithesis leads him into the greatest antithesis to the truth. The sole responsibility of a thinking, truth-loving mind in the face of the initial outbreak of the Silesian workers' revolt was not to play *schoolmaster* to this event, but rather to study its *unique* character. Of course for that a certain amount of scientific insight and love of humanity is required, while for the other operation a ready phraseology tinted with shallow self-love is entirely sufficient.

Why does the 'Prussian' condemn the German workers so scornfully? Because he finds 'the entire question' – namely the question of the workers' distress – 'until now still' lacking the 'all-penetrating *political* soul'. He enlarges upon his Platonic love for the *political* soul in this fashion:

'Every uprising that breaks out in this wretched *isolation of men from the community and of their thoughts from the social principles* will be smothered in blood and misunderstanding; but when distress begets understanding, and when the *political* understanding of the Germans discovers the root of social distress, then these events will be perceived in Germany too as symptoms of a great upheaval.'

First let the 'Prussian' allow us a *stylistic* observation. His antithesis is incomplete. The first half states: when *distress* begets *understanding*, and the second: when *political understanding* discovers the *root of social distress*. The simple understanding in the first half of the antithesis becomes in the second half a *political* understanding, just as simple *distress* in the first half of the antithesis becomes *social* distress in the second. Why has this stylistic artist endowed the two halves of the antithesis so unequally? I do not believe that he himself realised why. I want to point out to him his correct *instinct*. If the 'Prussian' had written: 'When social distress begets *political* understanding and when *political understanding* discovers the root of *social* distress', then no unbiased reader could have missed the *nonsense* of this antithesis. Immediately everyone would have asked himself: why did not the anonymous author conjoin social understanding with social distress and political understanding with political distress, as simple logic demands? Now to the matter itself!

It is utterly false to say that *social distress* begets *political* understanding. In fact it is just the opposite: what begets *political* understanding is *social well-being*. *Political* understanding is a spiritualist and is given to him who already has, to him who already is comfortably established. Let our 'Prussian' listen to a French political economist, *Michel Chevalier*, on this matter: 'In 1789, when the bourgeoisie rose up, it lacked only participation in the government of the country in order to be free. Its liberation consisted in seizing the leadership of public affairs, the principal civil, military, and religious functions, from the hands of the privileged who monopolised these functions. Rich and enlightened, in a position to be self-sufficient and to manage its own affairs, it sought to escape the *régime du bon plaisir.*'*

We have already demonstrated to the 'Prussian' how incapable *political* understanding is of discovering the source of social distress. *One* more word, however, concerning this view of his. The more developed and general the *political* understanding of a people is, the more the *proletariat* – at least in the beginning of the movement – wastes its strength in stupid, useless, blood-drenched uprisings. Because it thinks in political forms, it sees the basis of all evils in the *will* and all means to their melioration in *power* and the *overthrow* of a *particular* form of state. Proof: the initial outbursts of the *French* proletariat. The workers in Lyons believed they were following only political goals, that they were only soldiers of the Republic, while in truth they were soldiers of Socialism. Thus their political understanding obscured for them the root of social distress, thus it falsified their insight into their actual purpose, and thus their *political understanding deceived* their *social instinct.*

But if the 'Prussian' expects understanding to be engendered by distress, why does he lump '*smothered in blood*' and '*smothered in misunderstanding*' together? If distress in general is a means, then *bloody* distress is certainly a *very acute* means to engender understanding. The 'Prussian' must therefore say: smothering in blood will smother misunderstanding and secure for understanding the necessary breath of air.

The 'Prussian' prophesies the smothering of those revolts which break out in the ' *wretched isolation of men from the community* and in the *separation of their thoughts from the social principles*'.

We have shown that the Silesian revolt by no means took place in the separation of thoughts from social principles. The only thing we have left to consider is the 'wretched isolation of men from the community'. Community here means the *political community*, the state. It is the old refrain about *unpolitical* Germany.

Do not *all* revolts, without exception, break out *in the wretched isolation of men from the community?* Does not *every* revolt necessarily

* M. Chevalier, *Des intérêts matériels en France* (1838), p. 3.

presuppose this isolation? Would the Revolution of 1789 have occurred without the wretched isolation of the French citizens from the community? It was intended precisely to abolish this isolation.

But the *community* from which the worker is isolated is a community whose reality and scope are completely different from the *political* community. This community, from which *his own labour* separates him, is *life* itself, physical and intellectual life, human morality [*Sittlichkeit*], human activity, human enjoyment, *human nature. Human nature* is the *true community* of man. Because the wretched isolation from this nature is incomparably more universal, more unbearable, more horrible, more contradictory than the isolation from the political community, so the supersession of this isolation – and even a partial reaction, a *revolt* against this isolation – is all the more infinite, as *man* is more infinite than *citizen* and *human* life more infinite than political life. Therefore, however *partial* the *industrial* revolt may be, it hides within itself a *universal* soul: and however universal the *political* revolt may be, it conceals beneath the *most colossal* form a *narrow-minded* spirit.

The 'Prussian' concludes his essay in a dignified manner with the phrase:

'A *social revolution without a political soul* (i.e. without an organising insight from the standpoint of the whole) is impossible.'

As we have seen: A *social* revolution, by reason of its being that, occurs from the standpoint of the *whole*, because – even if it occurred in only *one* factory district – it is the protest of man against a dehumanised life, because it procedes from the *standpoint* of the *single actual individual*, and because the *community* from which the individual refuses to be separated is the *true* community of man, *human* nature. In contrast, the *political soul* of a revolution consists on the other hand in the *tendency* of the classes without political influence to abolish their *isolation from the state* and from ruling power. Their standpoint is that of the state, of an *abstract* whole that subsists *only* through separation from actual life, and that is *inconceivable* without the *organised* contradiction between the universal idea and the individual existence of man. That is why a revolution with a *political soul* also organises, in accord with the *limited* and *hybrid* nature of this soul, a circle that rules in society at the cost of society.

We want to share with the 'Prussian' what a '*social revolution* with a *political soul*' is; at the same time we will also share with him the secret that not even in his phrase-making is he himself able to get past the narrow-minded political standpoint.

A '*social*' revolution with a *political* soul is either a piece of composite nonsense, if the 'Prussian' understands by 'social' revolution a 'social' revolution in *contrast* to a political one and nevertheless attributes to the social revolution a political instead of a social soul; or a 'social revolution with a political soul' is nothing but a *paraphrase* of what is otherwise called a '*political revolution*' or '*revolution simply*'. Every revolution dissolves the *old society*; to that extent it is *social*. Every revolution topples the *former power*; to that extent it is *political*.

Let the 'Prussian' choose between paraphrase and nonsense! But a *social revolution* with a *political soul* is as much paraphrase or nonsense as a *political revolution* with a *social* soul is rational. Revolution in general – the *overthrow* of the existing power and the *dissolution* of the former relationships – is a *political act*. Socialism, however, cannot be realised without revolution. It requires this political act in so far as it needs to *overthrow* and *dissolve*. But where its *organising activity* begins, where its *purpose*, its *soul* becomes apparent, there socialism sheds its *political husk*.

So much argument is required to shred the *tissue* of errors concealed in a single newspaper column! Not every reader can have the background and the time to take full account of such *literary charlatanism*. Has not the anonymous 'Prussian' then the responsibility to the reading public of forswearing for the time being all writing of a political and social nature, such as these declamations about German conditions, and of beginning instead with a conscientious self-clarification about his own condition?

Paris: 31 July 1844   Karl Marx

Points on the State and Bourgeois Society
(Paris, January 1845)

1. *The history of the genesis of the modern state* or the *French Revolution.* Exaggeration of the political – confusion with the ancient state. Relationship of the revolutionaries to bourgeois society. Bifurcation of all elements into bourgeois beings and political beings.
2. The *Proclamation* of the *rights of man* and the *Constitution of the State.* Individual freedom and public power. *Liberty, equality* and unity. The sovereignty of the people.
3. The *State* and *bourgeois society.*
4. The *representative state* and the *charter.* The constitutional representative state, which is the democratic representative state.
5. The *separation of powers.* Legislative and executive power.
6. *Legislative power* and legislative bodies. Political clubs.
7. *Executive power.* Centralisation and hierarchy. Centralisation and political civilisation. Federal system and industrialism. *State administration* and *communal administration.*
8'. *Judicial power* and *law.*
8". *Nationality* and *People.*
9'. *Political parties.*
9". The *right of suffrage*, the struggle for the *abolition [Aufhebung]* of the state and of bourgeois society.

'On Feuerbach'
(Brussels, March 1845)

(1)

The chief defect of all previous materialism (including Feuerbach's) is that the concrete thing, the real, the perceptible is considered to an be *object* or [datum of] *perception only* and not to be *perceptible* human *activity*, or *praxis*, i.e. it is not considered subjectively. That is why this *active* aspect or side has been developed abstractly, in opposition to materialism, by idealism, which of course ignores real sensible activity as such. Feuerbach wants sensible objects that are really distinct from thought objects; but he does not grasp the fact that human activity itself is *objective* activity. Hence in *The Essence of Christianity* he considers only theoretic activity to be truly human, while practical activity is conceived only in its grubby Jewish form of expression and is equated with that. Thus he does not grasp the significance of 'revolutionary' activity, of 'practical-critical' activity.

(2)

The question of whether human thinking attains objective truth is not a question of theory but a *practical* question. It is in practice that man must prove the truth, the actuality and power, the subjective aspect and validity [*Diesseitigkeit*] of his thinking. Argument about the actuality or non-actuality of thinking, where thinking is taken in isolation from practice, is a purely *scholastic* question.

(3)

The materialist doctrine regarding changes [in man] brought about by circumstances and by education forgets that circumstances are changed by men and that the educator must himself be educated. And so this doctrine inevitably considers society to be divided into two parts, one of which it construes as being above society.

The coincidence of the change of circumstances and human activity, or human self-transformation, can be grasped and rationally comprehended only as *revolutionary praxis*.

(4)

Feuerbach's point of departure is the fact of religious self-estrangement, the duplication of the world into a religious and a secular world. His work consists in dissolving the religious world into its secular basis. But the fact that the secular basis becomes detached from itself and established as an independent realm in the clouds can be explained only by diremption and self-contradiction in the secular basis. This basis, therefore, must be understood in itself, in its self-contradiction, and be revolutionised in practice. Thus, for instance, once it is discovered that the earthly family is the secret of the Holy Family, it is the former that must then be nullified both in theory and in practice.

(5)

Feuerbach, not satisfied with *abstract thinking*, wants perception; but he does not comprehend the perceptible as *practical*, human-sensible activity.

(6)

Feuerbach resolves the essence of religion into the essence of man. But the essence of man is not an abstraction inhering in isolated individuals. Rather, in its actuality, it is the ensemble of social relations. Because he does not undertake a criticism of this actual essence, Feuerbach is obliged:

(1) to abstract from the process of history and to set religious disposition off by itself, and to assume an individual who is only abstractly – *in isolation* – human;

(2) to conceive of the human essence merely as 'species' , as an inner, dumb generality which connects the many individuals in a merely *natural* way.

(7)

Consequently, Feuerbach does not see that 'religious disposition' is itself a social product and that the abstract individual he analyses belongs to a specific form of society.

(8)

All social life is essentially *practical*. All mysteries which lead theory in the direction of mysticism find their rational solution in human practice and in the comprehension of this practice.

(9)

The highest point attained by perceptual materialism, i.e. materialism that does not conceive of the sensible as practical activity, is the view of isolated individuals and of bourgeois society.

(10)

The standpoint of the old materialism is bourgeois society; the standpoint of the new is human society or social humanity.

(11)

The philosophers have only *interpreted* the world in different ways; the point is to *change* it.

'The German Ideology'
Chapter One, 'Feuerbach'

Preface

Men have until now always generated false notions about themselves, about what they are or should be. They have organised their relationships according to their notions about God, about the normal man, and so forth. The inventions of their minds have come to dominate them. They, the creators, have bowed down to their creations. Deliver us from the phantoms, the ideas, dogmas, imaginary beings under whose yoke they languish. Let us revolt against the domination of thoughts. Let us teach men, says one, to exchange these illusions for thoughts that conform to the nature of man; let us teach them, says another, to take a critical attitude towards them; teach them to chase them from their heads, says the third, and – existing actuality will crumble.

These innocent and puerile fantasies constitute the core of recent Young Hegelian philosophy, which the public in Germany receives with terror and awe, and to which, moreover, the *philosophical heroes* themselves, solemnly convinced that they threaten the world with ruin, attribute an implacable and criminal character. The first volume of this publication has as its aim to unmask these sheep who take themselves, and are taken, to be wolves; and also to show that their philosophic bleatings are simply echoes of the opinions of the German bourgeois, that the braggings of these philosophic exegetes simply reflect the miserable situation in Germany. It proposes to bring into disrepute and to discredit this philosophic combat against the shadow of reality in which the German people, dreaming and somnolent, take pleasure.

Once upon a time there was a brave man who imagined that the only reason men drowned was because they were possessed by the *thought of gravity*. If they could rid their minds of this idea, for example by branding it superstitious, religious, they would be safe from the danger of drowning. Throughout his life he fought against the illusion of gravity, whose pernicious effects were amply demonstrated to him by every statistic. That brave man was the very type of the new revolutionary German philosopher.

I
Feuerbach
The Materialist Way of Conceiving Things as Opposed to the Idealist Way.

[Introduction]

According to certain German ideologues, Germany has in the past few years undergone an unparalleled upheaval. The process of decay of Hegel's system, which began with Strauss, has developed into a universal fermentation into which all the 'powers of the past' have been drawn. In the general chaos immense empires have arisen and then quickly foundered, momentary heroes have appeared only to be cast back into the shadows by cleverer and stronger rivals. It was a revolution compared to which the French Revolution was child's play, a world struggle that made the struggles of the Diadochi* look minuscule. Principles elbowed one another aside, heroes of the world of thought scrambled over one another with unheard of haste, and in three years, from 1842 to 1845, more was swept aside in Germany than in the previous three centuries.

All this took place in the realm of pure thought.

It is to be sure an interesting event: the putrifaction of the Absolute Spirit. After the last spark of life was extinguished, the various elements of this residue, this *caput mortuum*, began to decompose, allowing for new combinations and the formation of new substances. The industrialists of philosophy who had earlier made their living by exploiting the Absolute Spirit now threw themselves on the new

---

* Alexander the Great's generals who, following his death, fought one another for power, resulting in the fragmentation of his empire.

combinations, and each, with all possible diligence, tried to retail the part that had fallen to him. This could not continue without competition, which at first proceeded in a rather middle-class, respectable fashion. Later, when the German market was saturated and, despite all efforts, the merchandise found no buyers in the world market, the business was ruined in the usual German manner: by fabricated and bogus production, deterioration of quality, adulteration of raw materials, falsification of labels, fictitious purchases, bill-jobbing, finally by a credit system without any real basis. This competition wound up in a bitter struggle which is presented to us and hailed as a world-historical revolution, the generator of utterly prodigious results and achievements.

In order to honour properly this philosophical hullabaloo, which awakens in the breast of even a respectable German citizen a warm feeling of national pride, to make obvious the pettiness, the narrow-minded provincialism of this whole Young Hegelian movement, and particularly the tragi-comic contrast between these heroes' actual achievements and their illusions about them, we must look at the entire spectacle from a standpoint outside Germany's borders.

A. Ideology in general and German ideology specifically

Up to and including its latest efforts, German criticism has not quit the soil of philosophy. Far from questioning its general philosophical presuppositions, it has derived its very problems from the soil of a particular philosophical system, that of Hegel. There was a mystification not only in its answers but in the very questions themselves. This dependence on Hegel is the reason why none of these recent critics has even tried a thorough critique of Hegel's system, no matter how much every one of them has claimed to have gone beyond Hegel. Their polemic against Hegel and against each other has been limited to this, that each has extracted one facet of Hegel's system and turned it against the system as a whole as well as against the facets extracted by the others. In the beginning [, with Strauss,] pure and unadulterated Hegelian categories were taken, such as 'substance' and 'self-consciousness', then later [with Feuerbach and Stirner] these categories were profaned with more secular names like 'Species', 'the Unique', 'Man', etc.

From Strauss to Stirner, the whole of German philosophical criticism has been limited to a criticism of *religious* concepts. The starting point was religion as it is practised and theology properly so-called. As the critics proceeded, religious consciousness and the conceptualisation of religion were diversely defined. Progress consisted in subsuming the supposedly dominant metaphysical, political, legal, moral and other concepts under the sphere of religious or theological concepts; and also in proclaiming the political, legal, moral consciousness to be religious or theological consciousness, and declaring political, legal, moral man – in sum, *'Man'* – to be religious. The supremacy of religion was presupposed. In time every dominant relationship was proclaimed a religious relationship and turned into a cult: the cult of Right, the cult of State, and so forth. Everywhere there were only dogmas and the belief in them to deal with. The world was increasingly canonised until finally the venerable Saint Max [Stirner] was able to sanctify it in its entirety and thus to have done with it once and for all. The Old Hegelians had *grasped* everything, once they could trace it back to a category of Hegel's logic. The Young Hegelians *criticised* everything by attributing religious concepts to it or by declaring it to be theological. The Young and Old Hegelians concur in the belief that religion, concepts, the universal dominate the existing world. It is just that the one party repudiates that dominance as a usurpation, while the other celebrates it as legitimate.

Because these Young Hegelians take ideas, thoughts, concepts, in general the products of consciousness which they have rendered independent, to be the actual shackles of man – whereas for the Old Hegelians they are the true bonds of human society – it is evident that the Young Hegelians also have only these illusions of consciousness to struggle against. Because they imagine that men's relationships, all their activities, their chains and barriers are products of men's consciousness, the Young Hegelians quite logically put to men the moral postulate that they exchange their present consciousness for human, critical or egoistic consciousness, and thereby remove these barriers. This demand to alter consciousness is essentially a demand to reinterpret what already exists, i.e. to recognise or acknowledge it by means of a different interpretation. The Young Hegelian ideologues are, despite their 'earth shaking' phrases, the greatest conservatives. The youngest of them found the exact expression for their activity when they affirmed that they were combatting *'phrases'*. They just forget that all they have to oppose these phrases with is other phrases, and that they by no means combat the actually existing world when they combat only the phrases of this world. The only results this philosophical criticism was able to achieve were a few one-sided clarifications of Christianity within religious history; their various other assertions are just further embellishments of their claim that these insignificant clarifications are world-historical discoveries.

It has not occurred to any of these philosophers to inquire into the connection between German philosophy and German reality, into the connection between their criticism and their own material surroundings.

The presuppositions with which we begin are not arbitrary ones, not dogmas, but are real presuppositions from which one can abstract only in one's imagination. We begin with real individuals, together with their actions and their material conditions of life, those in which they find themselves, as well as those which they have created through their own efforts. These presuppositions can, in other words, be confirmed in a purely empirical way.

The first presupposition of all human history is naturally the existence of living human individuals. The first fact to be established is thus the physical organisation of these individuals and, arising out of this, their relationship to the rest of nature. Naturally we cannot deal here with the physical constitution of the human being nor with the natural conditions in which mankind is placed, the geologic, oro-hydrographic, climatic, and other conditions. All historiography must proceed on the basis of these natural conditions and their modifications through the actions of men in the course of history.

Men can be distinguished from the animals by consciousness, by religion, or by whatever one wants. They begin to distinguish themselves from the animals as soon as they begin to *produce* their means of life, a step which is determined by their physical organisation. In producing their means of life, they indirectly produce their material life itself.

The manner in which men produce their means of life depends in the first instance on the character of these means themselves, as they are found ready at hand and have to be reproduced. This form of production is not to be considered solely as a reproduction of the physical existence of the individuals. Rather it is a distinctive form of activity of these individuals, a distinctive form of expressing their life, a distinctive *form of life* of those very individuals. As individuals express their life, so they are. What they are, therefore, coincides with their production, both with *what* they produce and with *how* they produce. Thus, what individuals are depends on the material conditions of their production.

This production first appears along with an *increase in population*. It itself presupposes a commerce, a communication among individuals. The form of this commerce is in turn determined by production.

The facts are as follows: determinate individuals who are productive in determinate ways enter into determinate social and political relationships. In each case empirical observation has to demonstrate, empirically and without any mystification and speculation, the connection of the social and political structure with production. The social structure and the state continuously issue forth out of the life process of given individuals – not as they may appear in their own or in others' imagination, but as they *really* are, i.e. as they function, produce materially, in short as they are active within certain limits, presupposed circumstances, and determinate material conditions, independent of their will.

The production of ideas, of concepts, of consciousness is at first directly interwoven with men's material activity and commerce: it is the language of real life. Here, conceptualising, thinking, the intellectual intercourse of men still appear to emanate directly from their material conduct and relations. The same holds true of intellectual production as it is represented in the language of politics, of the laws, of morality, religion, metaphysics, etc. Men are the producers of their notions and ideas, etc., but they are real, active men, conditioned by a definite development of their productive forces and by the relations that correspond to these forces, up to and including their most extended forms. Consciousness can never be anything other than the conscious being, and the being of men is their real life process. If, in all ideology, men and their relationships appear upside down, as in a *camera obscura*, then this phenomenon stems just as much from their historical life process as the inversion of objects on the retina stems from the process of direct physical life.

In complete contrast to German philosophy, which descends from heaven to earth, the procedure here will be to move from earth to heaven. That is, we will not proceed on the basis of what men say and imagine about themselves, nor on the basis of imagined and conceptualised men, in order to arrive from there at flesh and blood men; we will begin with real, active men, and from their real life process we will expose the development of the ideological reflections and echoes of this life process. The shadowy pictures in the human brain are also necessary sublimations of men's material life process, empirically verifiable and tied to material presuppositions. Consequently, morality, religion, metaphysics, and the other ideological constructs and forms of consciousness that correspond to them no longer retain the appearance of independence. They have no history, they have no development, but rather the men who develop their material production and commerce also alter, with this facet of their reality, their thinking and the products of their thinking. It is not consciousness that determines life, but life that determines consciousness. In the first way of looking at things one begins with consciousness regarded as the living individual; in the second, which corresponds to real life, one begins with the actual living individuals themselves, and regards consciousness only as *their* consciousness.

This way of looking at things is not without presuppositions. It proceeds on the basis of presupposed real circumstances and does not depart from them for one instant. Its presuppositions are human beings, not taken in some sort of imaginary isolation or fixed abstraction, but rather in their real, empirically observable process of development under definite conditions. As soon as this active life process is represented, history ceases to be a collection of dead facts, as it is with abstract empiricists, or an imagined action of imagined subjects, as it is with the idealists.

Where speculation ceases – in real life – there real, positive science begins, the representation of practical activity, of the practical process of development of men. The phrases about consciousness cease, and real knowledge takes their place. With the presentation of reality, independent philosophy loses its medium of existence. At most a recapitulation of the most general results may take its place, results which can be abstracted out of a consideration of the historical development of men. In themselves, apart from real history, these abstractions have no value whatsoever. They can serve only to simplify the ordering of the historical material, to indicate the sequence of its several layers. By no means, however, do they give, as philosophy does, any recipe or scheme for neatly arranging the epochs of history. On the contrary, the difficulty first arises when one begins to study and to classify the material, to really analyse it, whether it has to do with past epochs or the present. Removing these difficulties depends on presuppositions which cannot in any event be indicated here, because they result from a study of the real process of life and the actions of individuals of each epoch. Here we will select several of these abstractions, which we use against ideology, and we will clarify them with historical examples.

Naturally, we will not take the trouble to inform our wise philosophers that when they subsume philosophy, theology, substance, and all that rubbish under 'self-consciousness', and when they have liberated 'Man' from the domination of these phrases under which he was never enslaved, they have not advanced the 'liberation' of man a single step; that it is not possible to effect a genuine liberation apart from the real world and real means; that slavery cannot be eliminated without the steam engine and the mule-jenny, nor indentured service without improved agriculture; that man cannot be liberated at all as long as he is unable to provide himself with food and drink, housing and clothing, sufficient in both quantity and quality. 'Liberation' is an historical act, not an imaginary one, and it is achieved through historical conditions, the level of industry, commerce, agriculture, transportation [. . .]* and subsequently, according to their various levels of development, the nonsense of Substance, Subject, Self-consciousness, and pure Criticism, just like the religious and theological nonsense, which they then eliminate again if they are sufficiently developed. Naturally in a land such as Germany, where only a shabby historical development is under way, these developments in the world of thought, these glorified and sterile trivialities, make up for the lack of historical development, entrench themselves and have to be combatted. But it is a struggle of merely *local* importance.

* MS page is damaged.

A. *Ideology in general and German ideology specifically*

[Division of labour and estrangement]

Dealing as we are with the presuppositionless Germans, we must begin by affirming the first presupposition or premise of all human existence and thus also of all history, the presupposition namely that human beings must be in a position to live in order to be able to 'make history'. But life requires above all food and drink, shelter and clothing, and quite a bit more. The first historical act is therefore the production of the means to satisfy these needs, the production of material life itself; and to be sure, this is an historical act, a basic condition of all history, which still has to be fulfilled today, just as it did centuries ago, daily and hourly, simply to keep human beings alive. Even if material existence is reduced to a minimum, e.g. to a simple stick, as it is with Saint Bruno [Bauer],* still this presupposes the activity of producing this stick. The first rule then for any historical interpretation is to observe this basic fact in all of its breadth and significance and to give it due weight. As is well known, the Germans have never done this, and so have never had an *earthly* basis for history, and in consequence have never had an historian. As for the French and the English, even though they construed the connection of this fact with so-called history in a highly one-sided way, especially when they were captivated by political ideology, they still made the first attempts to give historiography a materialist basis in being the first to write histories of civil society, of trade and industry.

The second preliminary condition is that satisfaction of the first need, the activity of attaining satisfaction, and the already acquired instrument of satisfaction, all lead to new needs – and this production of new needs is the first historical act. In this we can see right away the spiritual ancestry of the great historical wisdom of the Germans, who when short of positive material and when not giving us theological, political, or literary absurdities, admit of no history at all, but rather, of 'prehistorical times', without clarifying for us how actual history is derived out of this nonsense about 'prehistory'; all the same, on the other hand, their historical speculation pays special attention to this 'prehistory' because in their wisdom they believe themselves safe there from the incursions of 'raw facts' and so can let their speculative impulses run unchecked, generating and overthrowing hypotheses by the thousands.

* In an article entitled 'Characteristic of Ludwig Feuerbach' (1845).

The third relationship which appears at the very beginning in historical development is that human beings who daily recreate their own life begin to create other human beings, to reproduce themselves – the relationship between man and woman, parents and children, the *family*. In the beginning the sole social relationship, this family later becomes subordinated (except in Germany) when the increase in population produces new needs and increased needs produce new social relationships. At that point the family has to be treated and analysed on the basis of existing empirical data and not according to the 'concept of the family', as is customarily done in Germany. Moreover these three aspects of social activity are not to be construed as three different stages, but rather only as three aspects or factors – or to make it clear for the Germans, three *'moments'* – which have existed simultaneously from the beginning of history and the appearance of the first humans, and which, still today, play a role in history.

The production of one's own life through labour as well as the life of the other through procreation now appears as simultaneously a double relationship – on the one hand a natural and on the other a social relationship – social in the sense of a cooperative effort of many individuals, regardless of under what conditions, in what manner, or for what purpose. From this it may be concluded that a certain mode of production or stage of industry is always joined to a certain mode of cooperative effort or to a well-defined social level, <and this mode of cooperation is itself a 'productive force',> that the amount of productive forces available to men determines social conditions and thus the 'history of humanity' always has to be studied and treated in conjunction with the history of industry and commerce. But it is also clear how impossible it is in Germany to write such history, because the Germans lack not only the interpretive ability and the material for that, but also the 'sense certainty', and there is no experience of these things on the other side of the Rhine because history no longer occurs there. From the very beginning then, a materialist connection among men is evident that is conditioned by needs and the mode of production and is as old as man himself – a connection that takes on ever new forms and thus offers a 'history', even without the existence of some political or religious nonsense which further binds men together.

Now for the first time, after having already considered four moments, four aspects of the primitive historical relationships, we find that man also has 'consciousness'.* But even so, from the very beginning, not 'pure' consciousness. 'Spirit' is cursed from the very beginning with being 'burdened' with matter, which appears here in the form of agitated layers of air, of sounds – in short, of language. Language is as old as consciousness – language is real, practical consciousness, existing for other men as well as for me, and language, like consciousness, first arises from the need, from the necessity of commerce with other men. Wherever a relationship exists, it exists for me; the animal '*relates*' itself to nothing and has no relationships. <For the animal his relationship to others does not exist as a relationship.> Consciousness is thus from the very beginning a social product and remains so for as long as men exist. At first consciousness naturally is simple consciousness of one's *immediate* sense surroundings and consciousness of the limited connection with other persons and things beyond the individual who is becoming conscious of himself; it is at the same time a consciousness of nature, which at first stands over against men as a thoroughly alien, omnipotent and unassailable power, to which they relate at a purely animal level, as something imposed upon them as it is on cattle; it is thus a purely animal consciousness of nature (natural religion).† On the other hand, it is also a consciousness of the necessity of entering into communication with surrounding individuals: the beginning of man's being conscious at all that he lives in a society. This beginning is as animal-like as social life itself at this stage, it is a mere herd-consciousness, and man only differentiates himself from the sheep in that his consciousness takes the place of instinct, or that his instinct is a conscious instinct. This sheep-like or tribal consciousness is further developed through increased productivity, the multiplication of needs, and the increase in population which is the basis of both these factors. With

* Marginal note by Marx: Man has a history because he must *produce* his life, and, to be sure has to produce it according to a *definite* fashion; this is dictated by his physical organisations, just as is his consciousness.

† Note by Marx: It is easy to see that this natural religion, this restricted behaviour toward nature, depends on the form of society and vice versa. Here as everywhere the identity of nature and men is manifested in the fact that men's limited behaviour toward nature determines their limited behaviour among themselves and, inversely, this determines that. It is precisely because nature is still hardly modified by history.

this the division of labour develops that originally was nothing other than the division of labour in the act of sexual intercourse, and then a division of labour which developed 'spontaneously' on the strength of natural capacities (e.g. physical strength), needs, chance, etc. Division of labour first becomes a genuine division at that instant in which a division of material and intellectual labour appears.* From this moment on consciousness *can* really imagine itself to be something other than the consciousness of existing practice, and that it *really* represents something without representing something real: From this moment on consciousness is able to emancipate itself from the world and proceed to the formation of 'pure' theory, theology, philosophy, morality, etc. But even when this theory, theology, philosophy, morality, etc. come into conflict with existing conditions, this can only occur because the existing social relationships are in conflict with the existing forces of production – which, moreover, can occur within a well-determined national framework when the conflict arises not within this national context but rather between this national consciousness and the practice of other nations, i.e. between the national and the universal consciousness of a nation (as is presently the case in Germany).†

Moreover, what consciousness begins to do on its own is of no importance whatever. From all that muck we derive a single result, namely that these three moments, the productive force, the state of society, and consciousness, can and must come into conflict with one another, because with the *division of labour* it can and in fact does occur that intellectual and material activity, that enjoyment and labour, that production and consumption are distributed to different individuals. The sole possibility of avoiding this conflict lies in superseding the division of labour in its turn. It is moreover self-evident that 'ghosts', 'bonds', the 'higher being', the 'concept', 'scruple', are only idealist, speculative and spiritualist expressions, the representation, apparently, of the <isolated> individual, the representation of very empirical fetters and limitations, within which the mode of production of life and the form of interaction coupled with it move.

---

* Note by Marx: To which corresponds the first type of ideologue, the *priests*.
† Note by Marx: This conflict appears to the German nation as only a conflict within the national consciousness, and so the struggle appears limited to that national impoverishment, precisely because that nation is impoverishment in and for itself, pure and simple crap [*Scheisse*].

Resting on the natural division of labour in the family and on the separation of society in single, mutually opposed families, the division of labour, in which all these contradictions are given, also entails the distribution, and indeed the quantitatively and qualitatively *unequal* distribution, of labour and its products, in short, property, which already has its germ and first form in the family, where the wife and children are slaves of the man. This slavery, still crude and latent within the family, is the first property, which moreover corresponds perfectly to the definition of modern economists, according to whom property is the disposition over others' labour power. Moreover, division of labour and private property are identical expressions – the former describing the activity and the latter the product of the activity.

Further, and simultaneously, the division of labour brings about the contradiction between the interest of each individual or each family and the common interest of all individuals who associate with one another; and this common interest exists to be sure not just in the imagination, as a 'universal', but rather first in reality as the mutual dependence of the individuals among whom the labour is divided.

Precisely because of this conflict of particular and common interests, the common interest takes on as the *state* an independent shape, separate from the genuine individual and collective interests, and simultaneously presents itself as an illusory community, always, however, based on the real ties present in every familial and tribal conglomeration, such as consanguinity, language, division of labour in its larger dimensions and other interests – and, as we shall develop later, especially on the social classes already determined by the division of labour, which separate out in every such human aggregate, and one of which dominates all the others. From this it follows that all struggles within the state, the struggle between democracy, aristocracy and monarchy, the struggle for the right to vote, etc. are nothing but illusory forms – in general the universal [is] the illusory form of the communal – in which the genuine struggles of the various classes among themselves are carried out (and about which the German theoreticians have not the slightest suspicion, although they have been sufficiently informed in the *German-French Yearbooks* and *The Holy Family*); it further follows that every class that seeks to dominate – even if, as is the case with the proletariat, its dominance involves the abolition of the entire old form of society <and of domination in

general> – first must conquer political power in order to represent its interest as the universal interest, as it is forced to do from the very first moment.

<It is precisely because individuals seek *only* their own particular interest, taking these to coincide in no way with their common interest, that this common interest asserts itself as a particular, peculiar 'universal' interest, 'alien' to and 'independent' of them; an alternative is to operate, necessarily, within this discord [of their particular and their genuine common interests], as is the case in democracy. On the other hand, when the *practical* struggle of these particular interests is in constant opposition to both the *genuine* and the illusory common interests, it makes necessary the *practical* intervention and the exercise of restraint by the illusory 'universal' interest, in the form of the state.>

Finally, the division of labour likewise offers us the first example that as long as men find themselves in a natural [*naturwüchigen*] society, as long, that is, as the diremption between particular and common interest exists, as long as activity is not freely [*freiwillig*], but rather naturally [*naturwüchsig*] divided, man's own act acquires an alien character, opposed to and enslaving him, rather than he mastering it. As soon as labour begins to be distributed, everyone has a definite, exclusive sphere of activity which is imposed upon him and from which he cannot escape: he is a hunter, a fisherman, or a herdsman <or 'critical critic',> and must remain so if he does not want to lose his livelihood – while in communistic society, in which no one has an exclusive sphere of activity but can develop himself in any branch [of activity], society regulates the general production and in doing so makes it possible for me to do this today, and that tomorrow, to go hunting in the morning and fishing in the afternoon, to tend the cattle in the evening <and after supper to criticise,> just as I wish, without ever becoming a hunter, fisherman, herdsman <or critic>. This ossification of social activity, this consolidation of our own product into a material power over us, which grows out of our control, cancels our expectations and nullifies our plans, is one of the principal factors in historical development up to now. Social power, i.e. the multiplied forces of production which arise through the cooperative efforts of various individuals as conditioned by the division of labour, appears to these individuals – because their cooperation is not voluntary [*freiwillig*] but natural [*naturwüchsig*] – to be not their own united power, but rather an external power, existing apart from them, whose origin and destination they do not know, and which, therefore, they can no longer control, but rather, on the contrary, is now undergoing a series of phases and levels of development, which is not only independent of but indeed directs the desires and doings of men.

<This '*estrangement*', to use a term understandable to the philosophers, can naturally be superseded only under two *practical* presuppositions. In order that it become an 'intolerable' force, i.e. a force against which revolution is undertaken, it is necessary, on one hand, that it has created a mass of men entirely without property and at the same time in contradiction to them an existing world of wealth and culture, which presupposes an enormous increase in the productive force, a high level of its development. On the other hand this development of productive forces (together with which is given a *world-historical*, instead of merely local, empirical existence of man) is therefore also an absolutely necessary practical presupposition, because without it *scarcity* would just become general, the need-driven struggle over necessities would recommence, and all the old crap would inevitably return. Moreover, only this universal development of the productive forces permits a *universal* commerce of men, whence on one hand the phenomenon of the 'propertyless' masses simultaneously produced ([by] universal competition) within all peoples, each one of them made dependent on the upheavals of the others; and finally, this process replaces local, provincial individuals with empirically universal individuals of *world-historical* character and outlook. Without this, (1) communism could only exist as a local phenomenon; (2) the *forces* of commerce themselves could not have developed as *universal*, and therefore intolerable, forces; they would have remained indigenous-superstitious 'circumstances'; and (3) all further extension of commerce would have abolished local communism. Communism is empirically possible only as the act of ruling peoples, accomplished 'at once' and simultaneously, which presupposes the universal development of the productive forces and of the world commerce connected with it.

Communism is for us not a *state of affairs* to be established, an *ideal* to which reality must conform. We call communism the *real* movement that supersedes the present state of affairs. The conditions of this movement derive from presuppositions that presently exist.

In addition, the multitude of *mere* workers – a massed labour force deprived of capital, or of the least satisfaction – presupposes the *world market*, whose competition creates the completely precarious situation: a no longer temporary loss of its labour precisely as a secured source of life. The proletariat can thus exist only *world-historically*, just as communism, the action of the proletariat, can be present at all only as a 'world-historical' existence; a world-historical existence of individuals, i.e. an existence of individuals who relate directly to world history.>

Without all this, how could property, for example, have had a history, how could it have adopted various forms? How could landed property in France move from parcellisation to centralisation in the hands of a few, as is truly the case today, and vice versa in England, in each case according to different existing preconditions. Or how did commerce, which is really nothing more than the exchange of products of various individuals and countries, come to dominate the entire world through the relationship of supply and demand – a relationship which, as an English economist says, sweeps over the earth like the ancient Fates, distributing with an unseen hand happiness and unhappiness to mankind, founding and destroying empires, making entire peoples appear and disappear? But with the supersession of the basis [of this relationship], the supersession i.e. of private property, with the communist regulation of production and what that regulation implies, namely the destruction of the estrangement with which men relate to their own product, the power of the relationship of supply and demand dissolves into nothing and men regain power over exchange, production, and the way they relate to one another.

The form of commerce that determines and in turn is determined by the existing forces of production in all previous stages of history is *civil society*, which, as is evident in what has been said above, has as its presupposition and basis the simple family and the composite family, the so-called tribal entity [*Stammwesen*], and whose more precise characteristics have been given above. It is already obvious here that this civil society is the true crucible and theatre of all history, and how absurd the traditional concept of history is which neglected real relationships and limited itself to high-sounding activities of princes and states.

Up to now we have for the most part considered only the one aspect of human activity, namely man's *treatment of nature*. The other aspect, man's *treatment of man* – [...]

Origin of the state and relationship of the state to civil society.

Civil society comprises the entire material interaction of individuals within a particular stage of development of the productive forces. It embraces the totality of the commercial and industrial life of that historical stage, and in that it surpasses the framework of the state and the nation, although it must assert itself externally, i.e. in its external relations, as a nationality, and it must organise itself inwardly as state. The expression *'bürgerliche Gesellschaft'*, 'civil society', first appeared in the eighteenth century, when the property relations were already disengaged from the ancient and medieval forms of community. *'Bürgerliche Gesellschaft'* as such, i.e. as bourgeois society, only developed with the bourgeoisie; nevertheless, the social organisation that issues directly from production and commerce, and that in every epoch forms the basis of the state and of every other idealistic super-structure has been continually designated by the same name.

[History and consciousness]

History is nothing but the succession of individual generations, each of which exploits the materials, capital, and forces of production bequeathed to it by all previous generations, and thus on the one hand continues the traditional activity in greatly modified circum-stances, and on the other hand modifies the old conditions by a completely different activity. Speculatively this can be misinterpreted so as to make later history the goal of earlier history. Thus, for example, the discovery of America is alleged to have as its purpose to help the realisation of the French Revolution. Thanks to this, history is assigned particular ends and becomes one 'person among other persons' (as are 'Self-consciousness, Criticism, the Unique', etc.), whereas what is designated by the words 'destiny', 'purpose', 'germ', 'Idea' of earlier history, is nothing more than an abstraction of later history, an abstraction of precisely that active influence which earlier history exercises on later history.

Now the further the individual spheres act upon one another, the further they extend themselves in the course of this development, and the more the original isolation of individual nations is destroyed by the more developed mode of production and commerce, and by the division of labour between various nations (engendered naturally by that production and commerce), the more history becomes world history, so that, for example, if a machine is invented in England that deprives countless workers of their livelihood in India and China and overturns the whole form of existence in these empires, this invention becomes a fact of world-historical importance. In the same way sugar and coffee demonstrate their world-historical importance in the nineteenth century in that their shortage, created by Napoleon's continental system, prompted the Germans to revolt against Napoleon and thus became the real basis of the glorious wars of liberation of 1813. It follows that this transformation of history into world history is not a simple abstract act of 'Self-consciousness', <of the World Spirit> or some other metaphysical phantom, but rather a completely material, empirically verifiable act, an act which every individual exemplifies when he moves about, eats, drinks, and clothes himself.

In previous history, to be sure, it is every bit as much an empirical fact that by the extension of men's activity to world historical dimensions separate individuals have been increasingly subjugated under a power alien to them (whose pressure they then also imagined to be the chicanery of the so-called World Spirit, etc.), a power that has become ever greater and in the end shows itself to be the *world market*. But it is just as empirically grounded that the overthrow of the existing social conditions by the communist revolution (of which more later) and the supersession of private property, which is identical to that revolution, will dissolve this power, so mysterious to the German theoreticians, and then the liberation of each single individual will be achieved in the same measure that history is completely transformed into world history.* <It is clear from the above that the actual spiritual wealth of the individual depends entirely on the wealth of his actual relationships.> Only by these means are single individuals liberated from the various national and local limitations, placed in a practical relation with the production <including that of the spirit> of the entire world, and thus capable of acquiring the ability to enjoy this multiform production of the entire globe <(the creations of men)>. The *all round* dependence, this spontaneously developed [*naturwüchsige*] form of *world-historical* cooperation of individuals is changed through this communist revolution into the control and conscious mastery of these powers, which, generated by the interaction of men, have dominated them and have imposed upon them as utterly alien powers. Here, too, this conception of things can be

---

* Marginal note by Marx: On the production of consciousness.

construed in a speculative-idealistic, i.e. fantastic, fashion as the 'self-generation of the species' ('society as subject') such that the succession of interrelated individuals is represented as a single individual which accomplishes the mystery of generating itself. Here we see that individuals to be sure make *one another*, physically and spiritually, but neither in the (non) sense of Saint Bruno, nor in the sense of [Saint Max's] *'Einzigen'*, the 'Unique', the 'made' man.

This view of history, therefore, has as its object to analyse the actual process of production, starting with the material production of daily life; and to grasp the form of commerce associated with this process and generated by it, i.e. civil society in its various stages, as the basis of all history; to present it in its activity as state, and to explain the various theoretical productions and forms of consciousness, such as religion, philosophy, morality, etc. as deriving from it <and to trace civil society's process of generation out of its various stages and together with these forms and creations, which naturally allows the thing in its entirety (and thus also the reciprocal activity of these various aspects on one another) to be represented.> It does not have to seek a category in each historical period, as does the idealist view of history, but instead remains constantly on the true *ground* of history. Because it does not explain praxis on the basis of the Idea but rather the formation of ideas on the basis of material praxis, it quite logically concludes that all forms and products of consciousness are to be dissolved not by intellectual criticism, resolving them into 'Self-consciousness' or turning them into 'spooks', 'phantoms' and 'whims', but rather only by effectively overthrowing the actual social conditions that spawn these idealist humbugs. In short, not criticism but revolution is the driving force of history and also of religion, philosophy, and other theorising. This view shows that history does not conclude by dissolving itself into 'Self-consciousness' as 'the Spirit of Spirit', but that at every stage of history there is a material result, a sum of productive forces, <an historically created relationship with nature and among individuals>, which every generation receives from its predecessor, a mass of productive forces, of capitals [*Kapitalien*], and of circumstances that are, to be sure, on the one hand modified by the new generation but on the other prescribe its own conditions of life and give it a definite development, a specific character. It shows, in other words, that circumstances make men every bit as much as men make circumstances.

This sum of productive forces, of capitals, and of forms of social commerce that every individual and every generation confronts as something given, is the real foundation of what the philosophers imagine when they speak of 'substance' and 'the essence of man', and which they have apotheosised and fought against, a real foundation whose effects and influence on the development of man are not affected in the least when these philosophers rebel against it behind the mask of 'Self-consciousness' and 'the Unique'.

These given conditions of life of the various generations also decide whether the periodically recurring revolutionary shake-ups are strong enough or not to overthrow the basis of the whole existing order of things, and if these material elements of a total upheaval, <on the one hand, namely, the disposable forces of production, on the other the formation of a revolutionary mass that revolts not only against certain conditions of the previous society but also against the previous 'production of life' itself and the 'entire activity' on which it is based> are not present, then it is of no importance whatever for the practical development whether the *Idea* of this upheaval has been enunciated a hundred times already: the history of communism demonstrates this.

The entire previous view of history has either left this real basis of history completely out of consideration or has regarded it as merely a secondary matter that stands outside the context of the historical course of events. History therefore always has to be written according to an ahistorical measure; the real production of life seems to be unhistorical, while what is historical seems to be separated from common life, to be outside and above the world. With this, the relationship of men to nature is excluded from history, and from this stems the opposition of nature and history. This view has, therefore, been able to see in history only political activities of rulers and states, and religious and, in general, theoretical struggles, and particularly in each historical epoch has *shared the illusion of this epoch.* <For example, if an epoch imagines that it is determined by purely 'political' or 'religious' motives, even though 'religion' and 'politics' are only forms of its real motives, then its historians accept this opinion. The 'imagination', the 'idea' of these particular men concerning their real praxis is transformed into the sole determining and active power>, which rules and determines the praxis of these men. When the crude form of the division of labour with the Indians and

Egyptians engenders within these peoples the caste system in their state and their religion, the historian believes that the caste system is what engendered this crude social form. While the French and English at least maintain the political illusion that most approximates reality, the Germans move in the realm of 'pure spirit' and make the religious illusion the driving force of history. Hegel's philosophy of history is the final consequence of this whole German historiography, brought to its 'purest expression', in which it is a matter neither of real nor even of political interests, but of pure thought. <No wonder this appears to our Saint Bruno as a mere sequence of 'thoughts', in which one devours the other and finally disappears into 'Self-consciousness'; even more> consistent is Saint Max Stirner, who knows nothing at all about real history and to whom the historical course of events appears to be merely a 'history of knights, robbers, and ghosts', from the visions of which he can save himself only by 'unholiness'.* This view is truly religious; it implies that religious man is the original man from whom all history proceeds; and in its imagination it substitutes the religious production of fantasies for the real production of the means of life and of life itself. This entire view of history, together with its dissolution and the scruples and doubts it generates, is purely a *national affair* of the Germans and has only *local* interest for Germany, as, for example, the important and recently much-discussed question of how one really gets 'from the kingdom of God to the kingdom of men', as though this 'kingdom of God' ever existed somewhere other than in the imagination, and the learned gentlemen did not constantly live, and had no doubt about it, in this 'kingdom of men', to which they now seek the way; and as though the scientific amusement – for that is all it is – of explaining the bizarreness of this theoretical cloud-formation, did not consist precisely in proving, on the contrary, that it originates out of the real conditions of the world. In general with these Germans it is always a matter of dissolving the nonsense at hand into some other sort of whimsy, that is, to presuppose that all of this nonsense has a separate *sense* which has to be discovered, when really it is just a matter of explaining these theoretical phrases by showing their basis in actually existing conditions. The real, practical dissolution of these phrases,

---

* Marginal note by Marx: So-called *objective* historiography consists precisely in separating the historical phenomenon from the activity [of men]. Reactionary character [of this].

the elimination of these ideas from the consciousness of men, is, to repeat, accomplished by altered circumstances, not by theoretical arguments. For the mass of humanity, that is, the proletariat, these theoretical notions do not exist and thus do not need to be dissolved, and if this mass ever had any theoretical notions, e.g. religion, these have long since been dissolved by circumstances.

The purely national character of these questions and solutions is also demonstrated by the fact that these theoreticians sincerely believe that chimeras like 'the God-man', 'Man', and so forth have presided over individual epochs of history – Saint Bruno even goes so far as to insist that only 'Criticism and the Critics have made history' – and can be seen too in their own efforts at historical construction, where they jump with utmost haste past all early history and move immediately from 'the Mongol period' to 'substantive' history, i.e. to the history of the Halle and German Yearbooks and of the dissolution of the Hegelian school into a general squabble. All other nations, all real events are forgotten, and the *theatrum mundi* is reduced to the Leipzig Bookfair and the mutual disputes of 'Criticism', 'Man', and the 'Unique'. And if by chance this theory does on occasion attempt to treat actual historical themes, such as the eighteenth century, it limits itself to a history of ideas separated from the facts and practical developments which form their basis, and does this moreover with the intention of portraying this period as an incomplete prelude, as the limited precursor of the truly historical period, i.e. the period of the German philosophical struggles of 1840–1844. Because their goal is to write a history of the past that will allow the reputation of an unhistoric person and his fantasies to shine more brightly, it is to be expected that they leave unmentioned all real historical events, including the really significant intrusions of politics into history, and offer instead a narrative grounded not in studies but on literary constructions and gossip – as was done by Saint Bruno in his now-forgotten history of the eighteenth century. These pompous, haughty idea-peddlers, who believe themselves to be infinitely above all national prejudices, are in practice even more national than the beerhall philistines who dream of Germany's unity. They fail to acknowledge the historical character of other peoples' deeds, they live in Germany, of Germany, and for Germany, they turn the Rhine song into a spiritual hymn, and conquer Alsace and Lorraine by stealing from French philosophy instead of the French state, by germanising French ideas instead of French provinces. Compared with Saints Bruno and Max, who proclaim the world dominance of Germany in the world dominance of theory, Herr Venedey is a cosmopolitan.

In light of these controversies, we can also see how badly Feuerbach deludes himself when (in Wigand's Quarterly of 1845, vol. 2) he uses the qualification ' *Gemeinmensch*', 'communal man', to declare himself a communist, <transforms it into a predicate ' *of*' Man,> and thus believes it possible to make a mere category of the word 'communist', which in the existing world designates an adherent of a definite revolutionary party. Feuerbach's entire deduction about men's relations to one another is designed only to prove that men need one another and *always have*. He wants to establish consciousness of this fact, and thus, like other theoreticians, wants only to bring forth a correct consciousness of an *existing* fact, while for a real communist it is a matter of overthrowing this existing state of affairs. Moreover, we fully recognise that in striving to engender the consciousness of precisely *this* fact, Feuerbach goes as far as any theoretician can go without ceasing to be a theoretician and philosopher. But it is characteristic of Saints Bruno and Max that they immediately put Feuerbach's notion of communism in place of real communism, in part so that they can combat communism as 'Spirit of the Spirit', as a philosophic category, as an opponent of equal rank – and on Saint Bruno's part also for pragmatic reasons. As an example of the recognition and simultaneous misconception of the existing state of affairs, which Feuerbach still shares with our opponents, we recall the place in the 'Philosophy of the Future', where he argues that the being of a thing or of man is at the same time its essence, that the definite conditions of existence, the mode of life and activity of an animal or human individual, is that in which its 'essence' feels itself to be satisfied. Here every exception is expressly taken to be an unfortunate accident, an abnormality that cannot be changed. If, therefore, millions of proletarians feel themselves in no way satisfied with their conditions of life, when their 'being' corresponds not even remotely to their 'essence', this would be, according to the passage cited, an unavoidable misfortune to be borne without complaint. But these millions of proletarians or communists think quite differently and will in good time prove this by bringing their 'being' into harmony with their 'essence' in a practical way, through a revolution. In such cases Feuerbach never speaks of the world of man, but rather each time flees into external nature, and in fact into *that* nature which is not yet under man's domination. But with every new invention, every advance of industry, a new piece is torn from this terrain, and so the ground, in which the examples for similar Feuerbachian propositions grow, becomes ever smaller. The 'essence' of the fish, to stay with the one theme, is its 'being', i.e. the water. The 'essence' of the river fish is the water of a river. But this ceases to be its 'essence' and becomes a medium of existence no longer suitable for the fish, as soon as the river is harnessed by industry, as soon as it is polluted with dyes and other wastes and is used for steamship traffic, as soon as its water is led into irrigation ditches in which the fish's medium of existence can be withdrawn simply by draining it away. To proclaim that all those sorts of contradictions are unavoidable anomalies is basically no different from the consolation that Saint Max Stirner offers to the unsatisfied, when he tells them that this contradiction is their own contradiction, this misfortune is their own misfortune, in which they can either resign themselves, or keep their disgust to themselves, or rebel against it in some fantastic manner. And this differs hardly at all from Saint Bruno's reproach that these unfortunate circumstances arose because those concerned remained stuck in the mire of 'substance', have not advanced to 'absolute self-consciousness' and recognised these miserable circumstances as spirit of their spirit.

[...] in reality, for the *practical* materialists, i.e., the *communists*, the task is to revolutionise the existing world, to seize and transform existing things practically. While such intuitions are sometimes found in Feuerbach, they never go beyond isolated hunches and have much too little influence on his general manner of thinking to be considered anything other than kernels susceptible of development. Feuerbach's 'conception' of the perceptible world is limited on the one hand to the simple contemplation of it, and on the other to pure sensation, <posits '*the* Man' instead of 'real, historical man'. '*The* Man' is in reality 'the German'.> In the first case, that of the *contemplation* of the perceptible world, he necessarily confronts things that contradict his consciousness and his feeling, that disrupt the harmony he presupposes among all the parts of the perceptible world, above all that of man with nature. To remove these things, he has to take refuge in a dual point of view, a secular one, which sees only 'what is before your eyes', and a higher, philosophical one which beholds the 'true essence' of things.* He does not see that the perceptible world around him is not something given from eternity and always the same, but is rather the product of industry and of social conditions, and indeed, in the sense that it is an historical product, the result of the activity of a whole series of generations, each one of which stood on the shoulders of its predecessor, improved further its industry and its commerce, and modified its social order according to altered needs. Even the objects of the most simple 'sense certainty' are given to him only through social development, industry, and commercial trade. The cherry tree, like almost all fruit trees, was planted in our latitude only a few centuries ago, as a result of *commerce*, and thus *through* this action of a certain society in a certain time given to Feuerbach's 'sense certainty'.

Moreover, and as we will show even more clearly below, in this view of things as they actually are and have occurred, every serious philosophical problem dissolves quite simply into an empirical fact. For example, the important question concerning the relationship of man to nature <(or even as Bruno says (p. 110), the 'oppositions within nature and history', as though they were two distinctly separate 'things', as if man did not always have before him an historical nature and a natural history),> a question which has given rise to all of the 'impenetrably sublime works' about 'Substance' and 'Self-consciousness', breaks down of its own accord when one sees that the famous 'unity of man with nature' has existed from time immemorial in industry, while differing in each epoch according to the lesser or greater development of industry, <as will the 'battle' of man with nature, until the development of his productive forces attains a corresponding basis.> Industry and commerce, the production and exchange of the necessities of life for their part condition – while at the same time being conditioned in the way they function by distribution – the arrangement of the various social classes: that is why Feuerbach sees, for example, only factories and machines in Manchester, where a hundred years earlier only spinning wheels and weaver's looms were to be seen, or discovers in the Campagna di

---

* Marginal note: N.B. Feuerbach's error is not that he subordinated the things before his eyes, the perceptible *appearance*, to the sensible reality established and verified by careful examination of concrete facts; rather, his error was that he could deal with it, in the last resort, only with the 'eyes', i.e. through the 'spectacles', of the philosopher.

Roma only cow pastures and marshes, where at the time of Augustus there was nothing but vineyards and villas of Roman capitalists. Feuerbach talks specifically about the view of natural science, mentioning the secrets that are revealed only to the eye of the physicist or the chemist; but where would natural science be without industry and commerce? Even this 'pure' natural science receives its purpose as well as its material, in the first place, from commerce and industry, from the concrete activity of men. This activity, this continuous, sense-involved working and creating, this production, is to such an extent the basis of the entire perceptible world as it presently exists, that were it interrupted for only one year Feuerbach would experience not only an enormous change in the natural world, but would very soon find the entire human world and his own power of observation – his own existence – missing. To be sure, the priority of external nature remains, and what has been said does not apply to the original men, who emerged via *generatio aequivoca*; but this distinction only makes sense insofar as man is considered to be distinct from nature. Moreover, this nature which precedes human history is certainly not the nature in which Feuerbach lives; such a nature no longer exists anywhere today, except perhaps on some recently formed coral islands off the coast of Australia, and so does not exist for Feuerbach either.

Certainly Feuerbach has the great advantage over the 'pure' materialist of recognising that man too is a 'sensible object'; but <apart from that, he views him only as a 'sensible object' and not as 'sensible activity',> [and] thereby holds to that theory which fails to comprehend men in their given social context, in those conditions of life which have made them what they are; thus he never gets to actually existing, active men, but stays with the abstraction 'Man', and recognises 'real, individual, incarnate man' only in his passions, which is to say, he knows no other 'human relationships' 'of man to man' than love and friendship, <and these only in idealised form. He has no criticism of contemporary love relationships.> He thus never gets to an interpretation of the perceptible world as the <entire living> perceptible *activity* of the individuals who comprise this world, and is for that reason compelled – when, for example, instead of healthy human beings he sees a bunch of scrofulous, overworked and consumptive sufferers from hunger – to take refuge in a 'higher way of looking at things' and in an ideal 'compensation in the species', and thus to relapse into idealism at the *precise* point where the communist materialist sees the necessity and at the same time the condition for a restructuring of both industry and the social order.

Insofar as Feuerbach is a materialist, history plays no role with him, and insofar as he considers history, he is no materialist. With him materialism and history are mutually exclusive, which is already obvious from what has been said.

[Classes and dominant ideas]

In every epoch the ideas of the ruling class are the ruling ideas, that is, the class that is the dominant *material* power of society is at the same time its dominant *intellectual* power. The class that has at its disposal the means of material production also for that reason disposes simultaneously of the means of intellectual production, so that in general it exercises its power over the ideas of those who lack the means. The dominant thoughts are, furthermore, nothing but the ideal expression of the dominant material relations; they are the dominant material relations conceived as thoughts, in other words, the expression of the social relations which make one class the dominant one, and thus the ideas of its dominance. The individuals who comprise the dominant class also have, among other things, their consciousness and from this, their thinking. Because they dominate as a class and define the entirety of an historical epoch, it is understandable that this dominance is extensive, i.e. they dominate as thinkers, as producers of thoughts, and regulate the production and distribution of the ideas of their era, such that their ideas are the dominant ideas of the epoch. In that era, for example, and in a country in which the royal power, the aristocracy, and the bourgeoisie struggle for supremacy, and where, consequently, power is divided, the dominant thought is the doctrine of the division of powers, which then is pronounced to be an 'eternal law'.

The division of labour, which we have already found (pp. 130–3) to be one of the principal powers at work in previous history, now also expresses itself in the dominant class as the division of intellectual and material labour, so that within this class one segment steps forth as the thinkers of the class (its active, conceptive ideologues, whose living derives mainly from cultivation of this class's illusion about itself), while the other segment relates more passively and receptively to these ideas and illusions, because in actuality they are the active members of this class and have less time to formulate these illusions and ideas about themselves. This division within the class can even degenerate into a certain antagonism and rivalry between the two parties, which, however, disappears automatically whenever a practical conflict endangers the class itself. At such times what also vanishes is the illusion that the dominant ideas were not the ideas of the dominant class and that they had a strength independent of the power of that class. The existence of revolutionary ideas in a given epoch already presupposes the existence of a revolutionary class, about which all that is necessary has already been said above (p. 138).

If in observing the course of history one detaches the beliefs of a ruling class from the ruling class itself; if one renders them independent; if one is persuaded that in a certain epoch these and those thoughts have dominated, without concerning oneself with the conditions of production and with the producers of these thoughts; if, in short, one leaves out of consideration the individuals and the world conditions that underlie these thoughts, then one can say, e.g. that under the rule of the aristocracy the concepts of honour, loyalty, etc. dominated, while under the rule of the bourgeoisie it is the concepts of freedom, equality, etc. Usually the dominant class persuades itself of this. This view of history, common to all historians especially since the eighteenth century, necessarily confronts the following phenomenon: it is ever more abstract thoughts that dominate, i.e. thoughts that increasingly take on the form of universality. In effect, each new class, which replaces the preceding dominant one, is obliged, even if only to achieve its aims, to represent its interests as the common interests of all members of society; that is to say, in terms of ideas, to give its thoughts the form of universality, to present them as the only reasonable ones, the only ones universally valid. Because it opposes another *class*, the revolutionising class presents itself from the very beginning not as a class, but as representative of the entire society; it appears as the entire body of society opposed to the single, dominating class.* It can do this because in the beginning its interest is in fact closer to the common interest of all the other, nondominant

---

* Marginal note by Marx: The universality corresponds to (1) the class vs. *estate*, (2) competition, world trade, etc., (3) the large plurality of the dominant class, (4) the illusion of the *common* interests. At first this illusion [is] true. (5) The deception of the ideologues and the division of labour.

classes, and because it has not yet been able to develop itself as the special interest of a special class under the pressure of the circumstances inherited from the past. Its victory thus also serves many individuals of the other classes that did not come to power, but only insofar as it now puts these individuals in the position to move up into the dominating class. As the French bourgeoisie toppled the rule of the aristocracy, it made it possible for many proletarians to raise themselves above the proletariat, but only insofar as they became bourgeois. Each new class thus brings its dominance into existence on a broader basis than that of the previously dominant class, while on the other hand the opposition of the nondominant classes toward the dominant one later develops all the more sharply and deeply. Because of these two factors, the struggle to be waged against this new dominant class tends to negate the existing social conditions more decisively and radically than all previous classes that sought dominance were able to achieve.

This whole illusion that the dominance of a particular class is only the dominance of certain ideas, ceases of its own accord as soon as class dominance in general ceases to be the form of social order, as soon, that is, as it is no longer necessary to represent a particular interest as universal or 'the universal' as dominant.

Once the dominant ideas are separated from the dominant individuals <and above all from the social conditions that issue from a given level of the mode of production,> and thus once the notion arises that in history it is always ideas that dominate, it is very easy to abstract from these various thoughts ' *the* Thought', <the Idea,> etc. as what is dominant in history, and to conceive all of these various thoughts and concepts as 'self determinations' of *the* Concept which is developing itself in history. <It is natural then that all human relations can be derived from the concept of man, man represented in thought, the essence of man, *Man*.> This is what speculative philosophy has done. Hegel himself confesses at the end of his Philosophy of History that he had 'considered only the progress of *the Concept*' and had presented in history 'the true *theodicy*'. (p. 446) One can now refer back to the producers 'of the Concept', to the theoreticians, ideologues and philosophers, in order to conclude that at all times the philosophers, the thinkers as such, have dominated in history – a result which, as we have seen, was also pronounced by Hegel. <The whole trick of demonstrating the superiority of Spirit

in history (hierarchy, with Stirner) reduces to the following three efforts.>

No. 1. The ideas of the dominant individuals, who consist of material individuals under empirical conditions and on empirical bases, must be separated from these dominant individuals and the dominance of thoughts or illusions in history be recognised.

No. 2. Order must be brought to this dominance of thought, a mystical connection demonstrated among the dominant thoughts that follow upon one another, which is accomplished by construing them as 'self-determinations of the Concept'. (This is possible because these thoughts are actually connected by the medium of their empirical foundation <and because understood as *pure* thoughts they become self-differentiations, differentiations effected by thinking).>

No. 3. To remove the mystical appearance of this 'self-determining Concept', it is transformed into a person –'Self-consciousness' – or to appear really materialistic, into a series of persons who represent 'the Concept' in history, 'the thinkers', the 'philosophers', <the ideologues,>* who again are to be construed as the fabricators of history, as the 'the Council of Guardians', as the dominant or governing ones. In so doing the various materialist elements are removed from history and the speculative steed can be given free rein.

<This method of history, and the reason why it predominates in Germany, must be analysed in terms of its connection with the illusion of the ideologues in general, e.g. the illusions of the jurists, politicians (including the practical statesmen among them), with the dogmatic dreaming and confusions of these fellows, which is quite simply clarified by reference to their practical station in life, their occupation and the division of labour.>

While in everyday life every shopkeeper can distinguish very well between what someone claims to be and what he really is, our historiography has not yet achieved this trivial insight. It accepts without question what each epoch says and imagines about itself.

[Division of labour and forms of property]

The relations of various nations with one another depend on the extent to which each of them has developed its productive forces, the

---

* Marginal note by Marx: *Man*: the 'thinking human spirit'.

division of labour, and its domestic commerce. This proposition is universally acknowledged. But not only the relations of one nation to another, but also the entire domestic structure of this nation itself depends on the level of development of its production and its domestic and foreign commerce. The extent to which a nation's forces of production are developed shows most visibly the degree to which the division of labour is developed. Each new productive force, insofar as it is not simply a quantitative extension of already known productive forces (e.g. clearing of landed property), results in a new development in the division of labour.

The division of labour within a nation leads first of all to a separation of industrial and commercial labour from agricultural labour, and along with that a separation of *town* and *country* and an opposition of their respective interests. Its further development leads to a separation of commercial labour from industrial labour. Simultaneously, because of the division of labour within these various branches, further subdivisions are developed among the individuals cooperating on certain tasks. The position of these particular subdivisions relative to one another is conditioned by the fashion in which agricultural, industrial, and commercial labour is pursued (patriarchalism, slavery, estates, classes). The same conditions are to be seen in the relations of various nations to one another when commerce is more developed.

The various levels of development in the division of labour are so many various forms of property; i.e. the level attained by the division of labour determines also the relationships of individuals to one another with respect to the materials, instruments, and products of labour.

The first form of property is tribal property. It corresponds to the undeveloped level of production by which a people sustains itself through hunting and fishing, raising livestock, or at best agriculture. In the case of the latter, agriculture, a large amount of uncultivated land is presupposed. The division of labour on this level is still very minimally developed and is restricted to a further extension of that natural division of labour found in the family. The social structure is therefore restricted to an extension of the family: patriarchal clan chiefs, below them the clan members, then the slaves. The slavery latent within the family develops gradually at first with the growth of population and of needs and then with the extension of the clan's external contacts, whether in war or in the trading of goods.

The second form is the ancient communal and state property which arose mainly out of the uniting of several tribes into a *city*, by agreement or conquest, and within which slavery continued to exist. Along with communal property, movable and later immovable private property developed, although as an abnormal form, subordinate to communal property. Only through their community did the citizens possess power over their slaves, and thus they were tied to the communal form of property. It was a communal private property of the active citizens, who in relation to the slaves were forced to remain in this naturally occurring [*naturwüchsigen*] form of association. For that reason the entire structure of society which rests on this form of property, and with it the power of the people, declines to the same degree in which immovable private property especially develops. With the division of labour more advanced we already see the opposition of town and country, and later the opposition between states which represent urban interests and states which represent rural interests, and finally within the cities themselves the opposition between industry and maritime commerce. The class relationship between citizens and slaves is fully developed.

With the development of private property there appear for the first time the same relationships which we will find in modern private property, only to a greater extent. On the one hand we find the concentration of private property, which began very early in Rome (proof – Licinius' agricultural law), developed very quickly following the civil wars and particularly under the emperors; on the other hand, in connection with this, the transformation of the small plebeian peasants into a proletariat, which, however, because of its halfway position between the property-owning citizens and the slaves, did not experience an independent development.

The third form is feudal or estate property. If antiquity was based on the *city* and its small territory, the Middle Ages were based on the *countryside*. The existing sparse population, spread over a vast area of land and not increased by its conquerors, determined this altered point of departure. In contrast to Greece and Rome, feudal development therefore began with a more widespread terrain that was prepared by the Roman conquest and the dispersal of agriculture that initially resulted from it. The decline of the Roman Empire in its last centuries and the conquest by the barbarians themselves destroyed a mass of productive forces; cultivation declined, industry deteriorated from a lack of markets, commerce either languished or was forcefully disrupted, and the rural and urban population had decreased. Out of this state of affairs, together with the mode of organisation of the conquest, which was conditioned by this state of affairs, there developed under the influence of the Germanic military constitution the institution of feudal property. This property, like tribal and communal property, is based on a community, but a community in opposition to which, not slaves as in Antiquity, but an enserfed peasantry comprised the directly producing class. With the full development of feudalism there also arises opposition to the towns. The hierarchical structure of landed property and the armed bands of retainers that went with it gave the nobility power over the serfs. This feudal organisation was, every bit as much as ancient communal property, an association opposed to the dominated producing class; only the form of the association and the relationship to the direct producers were different, due to the different conditions of production.

In the *towns* corporate property, the feudal organisation of the trades, corresponded to the feudal organisation of landed property. Here property consisted mainly in the labour of the individual. The need to unite against the unified plundering nobility, the need for covered communal market places at a time when the one who made the product was also the one who sold it, the growing competition of the runaway serfs who were streaming into the flourishing cities, the feudal structure of the entire country – all of these things together lead to the formation of the *guilds*. The small amounts of capital, gradually saved by individual craftsmen whose number remained relatively stable in a growing population, resulted in the development of the journeyman-apprentice relationship, which brought forth a hierarchy in the cities similar to that in the countryside.

Thus, during the feudal epoch the principal form of property consisted, on the one hand, of landed property together with the serf labour bound to it, and on the other, of individual labour together with small capital dominating the labour of journeymen. In both classes the organisation was determined by the restricted relations of production – the minimal and crude agriculture plus handicraft industry. There was little division of labour while feudalism flourished. Within each land there was opposition of town and countryside; the structure of the estates or social orders was, to be sure, very sharply delineated, but apart from the division into princes, nobility, clergy and peasantry in the countryside, and master, journeyman, apprentice and soon also a rabble working for daily wage in the towns, there was no significant separation. In agriculture such a separation was impeded by the cultivation of small parcels of land, along with which the peasants pursued cottage industries; and in urban industry, labour within the various handicrafts was not divided at all, while between them it was only minimally divided. A separation of industry and commerce could be found in the older cities, but in the newer ones it developed only later, as the cities entered into relations with one another.

The uniting of larger countries into feudal kingdoms was necessary for both the landed nobility and the cities. Therefore the organisation of the ruling class, the nobility, everywhere had a monarch at its head.

This entire conception of history seems to be contradicted by the phenomenon of conquest. Up to the present, violence, war, pillages, murder and robbery etc. have been considered the driving force of history. Because we have to limit ourselves here to the essential points, we will take only the most striking example, the ruin of an old civilisation by a barbaric people and, joined with that, the genesis of a new organisation of society. (Rome and the Barbarians, feudalism and Gaul, the Eastern Empire and the Turks.) For the conquering Barbarians, war itself remains, as we have already indicated, a normal mode of commerce exploited with all the more zeal as the growth of the population, given the traditional and rudimentary mode of production – the only one possible for this people – arouses the need for new means of production. In Italy, on the contrary, the concentration of landed property (concentration provoked not only by buying up and mortgaging, but also by inheritance, given that the old lineages die out slowly, because of their great debauchery and the rarity of marriage, and the fact that their goods fell into a small number of hands), its transformation into pasturage (this transformation had not only the ordinary economic causes, still at work in our own time, but was due also to the importation of grain that had been stolen or exacted as tribute, which diminished the number of consumers for Italian grain), caused the near-total disappearance of the free population; death worked its ravages among the slaves themselves, who had constantly to be replaced by new ones. Slavery remained the foundation of the whole of production. Located between the free men and the slaves, the plebeians never raised themselves above the level of a *Lumpenproletariat*, a sub-proletariat. In general, Rome never exceeded the limits of the city, and its relations with the provinces, which were almost exclusively political, could naturally, in their turn, be interrupted by political events.

There is nothing more common than the notion that, up to now, the only thing that has counted in history is *taking*. The Barbarians took the Roman Empire, and it is the fact of that seizure which is invoked to explain the transition from the Ancient world to feudalism. But what is important in the case of the seizure by the Barbarians is to know whether the conquered nation had deployed industrial productive forces, as is the case with modern peoples, or whether its productive forces rested principally on the association alone and on the community. The taking is further conditioned by the object that is taken. The fortune of a banker, composed of paper, cannot be 'taken' at all without the taker submitting himself to the conditions of production and circulation of the 'taken' country. It is the same with the ensemble of industrial capital of a modern industrial country. And finally, taking in general comes soon to an end, and when there is nothing more to take, one has to begin producing. From this necessity of producing, which manifests itself very early, it follows that the form of community adopted by the conquerors who are establishing themselves must correspond to the level of development of the already existing productive forces; and if such is not the case at first, it will have to be modified as a function of the productive forces. This is the key to the phenomenon which everyone claims to observe in the aftermath of great invasions, namely that the slave was the master and that the conquerors lost no time in adopting the language, the culture and the customs of the conquered peoples.

Feudalism was in no way exported ready-made from Germany, but had its origin, on the side of the conquerors, in the warrior organisation of the army during the conquest itself; and it was not until after the conquest and under the influence of the productive forces of the conquered lands that this organisation became, through a process of self-development, feudalism properly so-called. The vain attempts to impose other forms, issuing from reminiscences of ancient Rome, show the point to which that feudal form depended on productive forces (Charlemagne, etc.).

[B. The genesis of capital and of the modern state]

[...]* From the first case there results the presupposition of a developed division of labour and an expanded commerce, and from the second the locality. In the first case the individuals have to be brought together; in the second they find themselves to be instruments of production alongside the given instruments of production. Here, consequently, appears the difference between the instruments of production that issue from nature and those created by civilisation. The *soil* <(water, etc.)> can be considered a natural [*naturwüchsiges*] instrument of production. In the first case, with the natural instruments of production, the individual is subordinated to nature, in the second, to a product of labour. That is why, in the first case, property (landed property) appears as immediately and naturally predominant; in the second, it is labour that predominates, particularly accumulated labour, capital. The first case presupposes individuals united by some kind of bond, be it family, tribe, the soil itself, etc.; the second case presupposes that they are independent of one another and are held together only by exchange. In the first case, exchange is mainly an exchange between man and nature, an exchange in which the labour of the one is exchanged for the products of the other; in the second case, it is predominately an exchange of men among themselves. In the first case, average human understanding suffices, and physical and mental labour are not yet divided; in the second case, the separation between intellectual and physical labour must already be completed in practice. In the first case, the dominance of the property owner over the non-owner rests on personal relationships, on a form of community; in the second case, this dominance must have taken on the form of a third element, the form of a thing, money. In the first case, small industry exists but depends on the use of natural instruments of production and therefore lacks division of labour among various individuals; in the second case, industry exists only in and through the division of labour.

---

* The first four page sides of this section of text are missing.

Up to this point we have proceeded on the basis of the instruments of production, and we have already shown the necessity of private property for certain industrial levels. In *industrie extractive* private property is still entirely co-extensive with labour; in small-scale industry and in all previous agriculture, property is a necessary consequence of the available instruments of production; in large industry the contradiction between the instruments of production and private property is a product of the system itself, and this industry must be already highly developed to produce this effect. Further, it is only with this development of large industry that the supersession of private property becomes possible.

The greatest division of physical and intellectual labour is the separation of town and country. The contrast between town (or city) and country begins with the transition from barbarism to civilisation, from the tribe to the state, from the locality to the nation, and this continues through the entire history of civilisation right up to the present day (the Anti-Corn Law League). With the city comes the necessity of administration, of law enforcement, of taxes, etc., in short, of communal life and with it politics in general. Here, for the first time, the division of the population into two large classes can be seen, which stems directly from the division of labour and from the instruments of production. Already the city represents the concentration of the population, of the instruments of production, of capital, of pleasures and needs, while the countryside represents the opposite, isolation and segregation. The opposition between city and country can exist only within the context of private property. It is the crassest expression of the subordination of the individual under the division of labour, under a specific enforced activity, a subordination which makes one man into an ignorant urban animal and the next into an ignorant rural animal, and each day engenders anew the opposition of the interests of both. Once again labour is the main thing here, the power *over* individuals, and as long as this exists, private property must exist. Overcoming the opposition between city and country is one of the first conditions of community, a condition which itself depends on a mass of material presuppositions and which the mere will cannot fulfill, as is evident at a glance. (These conditions must still be developed.) The division of city and country can also be understood as the division of capital and landed property, as the beginning of an existence independent of landed property, i.e. a development of capital, of a property that has its basis solely in labour and in exchange.

In the medieval towns which were not rooted in earlier history, but rather were newly formed by freed serfs, the only property each one had was his particular labour, together with whatever small capital he brought with him in the form, almost exclusively, of the most necessary hand tools. Competition from the continuously arriving run-away serfs; the incessant war of the countryside against the city, and with that the necessity of a well-organised urban military force; the bond constituted by the common property of a specific form of labour; the need for communal buildings for the sale of their wares at a time when artisans were also *commerçants*, and with that the need to exclude unauthorised persons from these buildings; the opposition of the interests of the various handicrafts; the need to protect laboriously learned trades, and the feudal organisation of the entire country: such were the underlying causes for the uniting of the workers in each handicraft into guilds. Here we need not go further into the multiple modifications of the guild system which arose through later historical developments. The flight of the serfs into the cities occurred uninterruptedly throughout the entire Middle Ages. Persecuted by their masters in the countryside, these serfs came individually into the cities, where they found themselves powerless in the face of an organised community, in which they had to fit themselves into a position determined by the need of others for their labour and by the interests of their organised urban competitors. Arriving singly, these workers could never achieve any power: either their labour was controlled by a guild and required an apprenticeship, in which case guild masters controlled them and organised them according to their own interests; or their kind of work did not require an apprenticeship, and therefore was not guild labour but rather day labour, in which case they never managed to organise themselves but remained an unorganised rabble [*Pöbel*]. The need for day labour in the cities created the rabble.

These cities were true 'associations', born of immediate need, out of concern to protect property and to multiply the instruments of production and the means of defense of all the members. Because it consisted of individuals unknown to one another, who arrived separately and, themselves unorganised, faced an organised, militarily equipped power that jealously watched them, the rabble of these cities was robbed of all power. The journeymen and apprentices were organised in each trade 'so as to best serve' the interests of the masters; the patriarchal relationship to their masters gave the latter a two-fold power, on the one hand in their direct influence over the entire life of the journeymen, and then in the fact that the relationship created, for the journeymen who worked with the same master, a real bond unifying them over against the journeymen of other masters and also separating them from these other masters; and finally, the journeymen were bound to the existing order by their interest in becoming masters themselves. Hence, whereas the rabble at least managed to rebel against the entire urban order, rebellions which, given the powerlessness of the rabble, were totally ineffectual, the journeymen only managed small-scale insubordinations within individual guilds, a phenomenon inherent in the guild system. The great rebellions of the Middle Ages all originated in the countryside, but they too had no effect due to the fragmentation and the resulting crudeness of the peasantry.

In these cities capital was a natural capital, consisting of the dwelling, the tools of the craft, and the inherited, natural clientele; due to undeveloped trade and insufficient circulation, this capital could not as such be realised and had to be passed from father to son. This capital, unlike modern capital, could not be evaluated in money, which can be indifferently invested in one thing or another, but was rather a capital directly linked to and wholly inseparable from the particular labour of its owner, and to that extent was an *estate* capital [*ständisches Kapital*].

Also in the cities the division of labour was as yet little developed between the individual guilds and not at all between the individual workers within the guilds themselves. Each worker had to be proficient in a whole sphere of tasks, had to be able to make everything that could be made with his tools; the limited trade and the minimal communication between the individual cities, the lack of population and the narrowness of needs impeded further division of labour, and therefore everyone who wished to become a master had to excel at his entire craft. For this reason we find that the medieval craftsmen retained an interest in their particular work and pursued a skill which could grow to a certain artistic sense while remaining restricted. But for that very reason too every medieval craftsman was completely dedicated to his work, had a relation of comfortable servitude with it, and was much more absorbed in it than the modern worker, who is indifferent to his labour.

The next extension of the division of labour was the separation of production and commerce, the formation of a special class of merchants, a separation that was handed down in the older cities (among other things, with the Jews) and very soon occurred in the newer ones. With this arose the possibility of commercial ties which extended beyond the immediate vicinity, a possibility whose realisation depended on the existing means of communication, on the state of public security which was determined by political conditions (throughout the middle ages merchants were known to have travelled about in armed caravans), and on the needs, either basic or developed, according to the particular cultural level of the area accessible to commerce. With commerce constituted in a special class, and with the extension of trade by the merchants beyond the immediate vicinity of the city, an interaction between production and commerce simultaneously occurred. The cities entered into relations *with each other*, new tools were taken from one city to another, and the division between production and commerce soon called forth a new division of production among the individual cities, each of which exploited a dominant branch of industry. The initial restriction of commerce to a given locality gradually began to dissolve.

Whether the productive forces achieved in a particular place, notably inventions, were lost to later development or not depended entirely on the extension of commercial relations. As long as trade did not extend beyond the immediate neighbourhood, every invention had to be specially made in each area, and mere accidents like the invasions of barbaric peoples or even ordinary wars were enough to reduce a country with developed forces of production and needs to the point at which it had to start over again. In early history each invention had to be made anew each day and independently in each locality. Even with a relatively extended commerce, developed forces of production are only minimally secure from complete ruin, as the history of the Phoenicians demonstrates: Their inventions were in large part and for a long time lost, due to their being ousted from commerce by Alexander's conquest, and to the decline that followed it. The same thing happened in the Middle Ages – e.g. the art of glass colouring. Only when commerce becomes world commerce, with large industry as its basis and every nation drawn into the competitive struggle, is the continuance of the acquired productive forces secured.

The division of labour between various cities had as its immediate consequence the rise of manufacture, of a branch of production that outgrew the guild system. The first flowering of manufacturing – in Italy and later in Flanders – had as its historical presupposition commercial relations with foreign nations. In other countries, e.g. England and France, manufacturing was limited at first to the domestic market. Manufacturing also presupposed, in addition to the conditions mentioned, an already advanced concentration of population – particularly in the countryside – and of capital, which began to accumulate in private hands partly in the guilds, despite guild regulations, and partly with the merchants.

The labour which from the very beginning involved use of a machine, even of the crudest sort, quickly proved itself to be the most capable of development. Weaving, which the peasantry previously had carried on in the countryside as a sideline to procure their necessary clothing, was the first occupation stimulated to further development by the extension of trade. Weaving was the first and remained the principal form of manufacturing. The growing demand for materials to clothe the increasing population, the growing accumulation and mobilisation of primitive capital through increased circulation, the demand for luxury called forth by that and further favoured by the gradual expansion of trade, all gave weaving a qualitative and quantitative impetus that lifted it out of the previous form of production. Besides those peasants who wove, and still weave, for themselves, there arose in the cities a class of weavers whose products were intended for the entire domestic market and also, more often, for foreign markets.

Weaving, a form of labour which in most cases demands little skill and is readily subdivided into infinitely many branches, resisted by its very character the bonds of the guild. It was therefore pursued mostly in villages and small market-towns, devoid of guild organisation, that gradually became cities, and indeed soon the most prosperous cities of each country.

With manufacturing freed from the constraints of the guild, property relations also were rapidly altered. Initial advance beyond the primitive guild-capital came with the rise of merchants whose capital was movable from the very beginning: it was capital in the modern sense, insofar as that can be said given the conditions of that epoch. The second advance resulted from manufacturing, which in its turn mobilised a mass of primitive capital and in general increased the amount of movable capital relative to primitive capital. Simultaneously manufacturing became for the peasants a refuge from the guilds which either excluded them or paid them poorly, just as earlier the guild cities had provided the peasants a refuge from the land owners.

With the beginning of manufacturing came a period of vagabondage, stimulated by a cessation of feudal retainers, the disbanding of private armies that had served the kings against their vassals, and by improved agriculture and the transformation of large strips of cultivated land into pasturage. This already explains how this vagabondage coincides precisely with the dissolution of feudalism. As early as the thirteenth century, individual episodes of this sort occur, but as a generalised and enduring phenomenon vagabondage first appears at the end of the fifteenth century and the beginning of the sixteenth. These vagabonds were so numerous that Henry VIII of England alone had 72,000 of them hanged, and it was only with the greatest difficulty and by reason of extreme need, and only after much resistance, that they were put back to work. The rapid flowering of manufacturing, especially in England, gradually absorbed them.

With manufacturing, relations of competition arose among the various nations, and the commercial struggle was carried out by means of wars, protective tariffs and prohibitions, whereas earlier, the nations, insofar as they entered into contact, maintained among themselves only peaceful exchanges. From this moment on, commerce had a political significance.

Simultaneous with the rise of manufacturing there was a new relation of the worker to his employer. In the guilds a patriarchal relationship had continued between journeymen and master; in its place, in manufacturing a monetary relationship between worker and capitalist was now substituted, a relationship which in the countryside and in the small cities, the manufacturing cities, very soon lost almost all its patriarchal colouring.

The expansion of commerce following the discovery of America and the sea route to the East Indies gave enormous impetus to manufacturing, and in general to the movement of production. The new products imported from these lands, especially the amounts of gold and silver thrown into circulation, radically altered the mutual relations of classes and struck a telling blow to feudal landed property and to the labourers; the voyages of adventure, the colonisation, and above all the expansion of markets into a world market that now became increasingly more possible, all called forth a new phase of historical development that in general cannot be treated here. The colonisation of the newly discovered lands helped fuel the struggle for trade between the nations, enlarging and embittering it.

The expansion of commerce and of manufacturing accelerated the accumulation of movable capital, whereas in the guilds, where there was no stimulus to expand production, the primitive capital remained stable or even declined. Commerce and manufacturing created the grand bourgeoisie, while the small-scale citizenry, no longer dominant in the cities as previously, were concentrated in the guilds and had to bend to the power of the large-scale tradespeople and manufacturers.* Whence the decline of the guilds once they encountered manufacturing.

The commercial relations of nations during the epoch we are speaking about took on two different forms. In the beginning the small quantity of gold and silver in circulation resulted in a prohibition on the export of these metals; and industry, which largely was imported from abroad to provide occupations for the growing urban population, could not dispense with the privileges that could naturally be granted not only against domestic competition, but prinicipally against foreign competition. In these primitive prohibitions, local guild privilege extended to the entire nation. Tariffs originated in the duties or tributes which the feudal lords demanded, as an alternative to outright plunder, from merchants who travelled through their territory, duties which later the cities also introduced and which became, with the origin of the modern state, the most convenient way for the treasury to gain money. The appearance of American gold and silver on the European markets, the progressive development of industry, the rapid increase in commerce and as a consequence the prospering of the non-guild bourgeoisie and the increase of money, gave these measures a new significance. The state, day by day more dependent on money, for fiscal reasons maintained the prohibition

* Marginal note by Marx: Petty bourgeois – Middle class – Grand bourgeosie.

on the export of gold and silver; the bourgeois, for whom these newly appearing masses of money were the main object of his hoardings, was entirely satisfied with these arrangements; already acquired privileges became a source of revenue for the government and were sold for money; and customs legislation yielded export duties, which were nothing but a hindrance to industry, and had a purely fiscal purpose.

The second period was introduced toward the middle of the seventeenth century and lasted almost until the end of the eighteenth. Commerce and shipping had expanded faster than manufacturing, which played a secondary role; colonies gradually became large-scale consumers; and individual nations divided up through long struggles the newly opened world market. This period begins with the laws of navigation and the colonial monopolies. Competition among nations was eliminated where possible through tariffs, prohibitions, and treaties; and in extreme cases the competitive struggle was carried on and decided through warfare (especially maritime wars). The most powerful maritime nation, the English, retained dominance in commerce and manufacturing. Here there is already concentration in *one* country.

Manufacturing was constantly protected in the domestic market by protective tariffs, in colonial markets by monopolies, and in foreign markets, to the maximum extent possible, by differential tariffs. The processing of domestically produced materials (wool and linen in England, silk in France) was favoured, the export of raw materials generated at home was prohibited (wool in England) and the [processing] of imported materials was either neglected or suppressed (cotton in England). The dominant nation in maritime commerce and in colonial power was naturally also assured of the largest quantitative and qualitative expansion of manufacturing. In general, manufacturing could not dispense with protection, because the slightest change occurring in other countries can cause it to lose its markets and be ruined. Under halfway favourable conditions it is easily introduced in a country and for precisely that reason it is also easily destroyed. At the same time, because of the way it was pursued in the countryside in the eighteenth century, it is so interwoven with the conditions of life of a large number of people that no country can endanger its manufacturing by permitting unrestricted competition. It therefore depends, insofar as it extends to exports, entirely on the extension or restriction of commerce, and exercises a relatively min-

imal reciprocal effect on commerce. Thus its secondary role during
the eighteenth century compared to the influence of the merchants.
It was the merchants and especially the shipowners who more than
anyone else urged protection of the state and the monopolies; to be
sure, the manufacturers also demanded and received protection, but
they were constantly overshadowed by the merchants in political
importance. The commercial cities, especially the maritime cities,
became passably civilised and the cities of the grand bourgeoisie,
while the petty bourgeoisie maintained itself for the most part in the
factory towns. (Cf. Aikin, etc.) The eighteenth century was the century of commerce. Pinto states expressly: 'Commerce is the rage of
the century'; and 'for some time, all that is talked about is commerce,
navigation and the navy'.*

The movement of capital, although significantly accelerated, still
remained relatively slow. The splintering of the world market into
individual parts, each of which was exploited by a specific nation,
the elimination of competition among nations, the helplessness of
production itself, and the still rudimentary monetary system all
together considerably retarded circulation. The result of this was a
miserable, petty, mercantile spirit that characterised all the merchants
and all the commercial methods and operations. Compared to the
manufacturers and above all the artisans they were certainly
Grossbürger, grand bourgeois; but compared to the merchants and
industrialists of the following period they remained petty bourgeois.
Cf. A. Smith.

This period is also characterised by the lifting of the prohibitions
on the export of gold and silver, the rise of commercial banking,
the banks, paper money, stocks and speculation, national debt, stock
jobbing in goods of all sorts, and the development of a monetary
system in general. Capital itself lost a large part of the primitive
character it still had.

The concentration of commerce and manufacturing in one country, England, which developed continuously throughout the seventeenth century, gradually created for this country something of a
world market and with that a demand for its manufactured products
that could no longer be satisfied by the productive forces of the

* The quote, in French in the MS, is from Isaac Pinto's *Treatise on Circulation and
Credit* (1771).

traditional industry. This demand, which exceeded the capacity of the productive forces, was the driving force that brought about the third period of private property since the Middle Ages: it created large industry founded on the application of elementary forces to industrial ends, machinery, and the most extensive division of labour. The other conditions of this new phase – the freedom of competition within the nation, the development of theoretical mechanics (Newton's mechanics was the most popular science of all in France and England in the eighteenth century), etc. already existed in England. (Free competition within a nation itself had everywhere to be achieved by revolution – 1640 and 1688 in England, 1789 in France.) Competition soon compelled every country jealous of its historical role to protect its manufacturers with renewed customs measures (the old tariffs no longer helped against large industry) and soon thereafter to introduce large industry shielded by protective tariffs. Despite these protective measures large industry universalised competition (which is the practical freedom of commerce, protective tariffs being only a palliative, a countermeasure *within* the freedom of commerce), established the means of communication and the modern world market, subjugated commerce under its domination, changed all capital into industrial capital, and generated the rapid circulation and centralisation of capital (the development of the monetary system). Through universal competition it forced every individual to the utmost exertion of his energies. Wherever possible it destroyed ideology, religion, morality, etc., and where it could not manage this, it turned them into obvious lies. It created world history in that it made every civilised nation and every individual in them dependent on the entire world for the satisfaction of their needs, and destroyed the previous natural isolation of the separate nations. It subordinated natural science to capital and stripped the last semblance of natural spontaneity from the division of labour. In general, and so far as possible, it destroyed the naturalness within labour and dissolved all natural relations into money relations. In place of naturally developed cities it created the modern, large industrial cities that arose over night. Wherever it penetrated it destroyed the handicrafts and in general all previous stages of industry. It completed the victory of the city over the countryside. Its [outcome] is the automatic system. It generated a mass of productive forces for which private property became just as much a fetter as the guild was for manufacturing and the small, rural enterprise was for the developing handicrafts. Under the institution of private property these productive forces received only a one-sided development; they became destructive forces for the majority, and many of them could not even be utilised within the private property system. In general it generated everywhere the same relationships between classes of society, and thereby destroyed the particularity of individual nations. And finally, while the bourgeoisie of each nation retained its separate national interests, large industry created a class that has the same interest in all nations and for whom nationality is already destroyed, a class that is truly rid of the entire old world and simultaneously stands opposed to it. For the labourer it makes not only his relationship to the capitalist, but labour itself unbearable.

It is evident that large industry cannot achieve the same stage of development in every region of a country. But this does not delay the class movement of the proletariat, because the proletarians created by large industry take the lead in this movement and carry the entire mass along with them, and because the workers excluded from large industry are put by that industry in a situation worse still than that of the workers in large industry itself. In the same way, countries in which large industry is developed affect the more or less nonindustrial countries insofar as these latter are drawn by the world commerce into the universal competitive struggle.

These various forms are so many forms of the organisation of labour and therefore of property. In every epoch, there is produced a concentration of existing productive forces in function of the needs that made them necessary.

[Social conflicts and revolution]

This conflict between the forces of production and the form of inter-action, which, as we have seen, has already occurred many times in previous history, but without endangering the basis, each time exploded necessarily in a revolution in which it simultaneously took on various secondary forms, e.g. as a totality of collisions, collisions of various classes, as a conflict of consciousness, a battle of ideas, a political struggle, etc. Considered from a narrow point of view one could take one of these secondary forms out of context and interpret it as the basis of these revolutions, which is all the easier because the individuals who make the revolutions were themselves victims of illusions about their own activity, according to their level of culture and the level of historical development.

According to our view, all historical collisions thus have their origin in the conflict between the forces of production and the form of interaction. Moreover, it is not necessary that this contradiction be carried to an extreme in a country in order to lead to collisions in that country. Competition with industrially more developed countries that stems from expanded international trade suffices to generate a similar contradiction also in countries with a less developed industry (e.g. the latent proletariat in Germany generated through competition with English industry). Despite the fact that it brings them together, competition isolates individuals against one another, not only the bourgeois but even more the proletarians. Therefore it takes a long time before these individuals can unite, not to mention the fact that if it is not to remain merely local, this unity requires the prior creation by large industry of the necessary means, such as large industrial centres and cheap and rapid communications; that is why long struggles are required to conquer each organised power that opposes these individuals who are isolated and live in conditions that daily reproduce isolation. To demand the contrary would be equivalent to demanding that competition not exist in our particular historical epoch or that individuals pay no attention to conditions over which as isolated individuals they have no control.

Housing construction. With primitive peoples it is understandable that each family has its own cave or hut, as with the nomads that every family has a separate tent. This separation of domestic units was only made more necessary by the further development of private property. With agricultural peoples a common domestic arrangement was just as impossible as common working of the soil. The building of cities represented great progress. In all previous periods the supersession of such a divided economic system, which is inseparable from the supersession of private property, was impossible simply because the material conditions for it were lacking. The institution of a common cottage economy presupposes the development of machinery and the use of natural and many other productive forces, e.g. water systems, gas lighting, steam heat, etc. <Ending the opposition between town and country.> Without these conditions the common economy would not itself be a new

---

force of production; it would lack any material basis and would rest on a purely theoretical one; i.e. it would be a mere fancy and would at most develop into a cloister economy. The possibilities appeared when people collected into towns and erected common buildings for various particular purposes (prisons, barracks, etc.). It is obvious that the disappearance of the fragmented economic system and the supersession of the family are inseparable.

[Genesis of the bourgeoisie]

In the Middle Ages, the citizens in every city were forced to protect their own hides by uniting against the landed nobility. The expansion of trade and the development of communications led the individual cities to establish contact with other cities that had advanced the same interests in the struggle against the same adversary. Out of the many *Bürgerschaften*, or local 'bourgeoisies', of the individual cities there arose, very gradually, the *class* of the *Bürger*, of the 'bourgeois'. By reaction against the existing conditions and by the form of labour determined by them, the conditions of life of individual citizens became at the same time conditions common to all and independent of each one taken separately. The *Bürger*, the 'bourgeois', had created these conditions, insofar as they had severed their feudal ties, and were themselves created by them insofar as they were constrained to oppose the feudal system in which they found themselves. With the introduction of a connection among individual cities these common conditions developed into class conditions. The same conditions, the same opposition, the same interests had by and large to call forth the same customs everywhere. The bourgeoisie itself gradually developed along with its conditions, then divided itself into various factions according to the division of labour, and finally absorbed into itself all existing propertied classes (while giving rise to a new class, the proletariat, constituted of the majority of the previously propertyless, and a part of the previously propertied, class) insofar as all previous property was changed into industrial or commercial capital.* The separate individuals form a class only insofar as they have a common struggle to wage against another class; moreover, they remain

---

* Marginal note by Marx: The bourgeoisie first absorbs the branches of labour directly relevant to the state, and then all of the more or less ideological social orders [*Stände*].

opposed to one another in their competition. On the other hand the class becomes autonomous *vis-à-vis* individuals, so that these find their living conditions already preestablished, receiving their position in life and with that their personal development from the class to which they are subordinate. This is the same phenomenon as the subordination of separate individuals under the division of labour, and it can be suppressed only by superseding private property and labour itself. We have already indicated enough how the subordination of individuals to their class becomes a subordination to all sorts of ideas, etc.

If one considers *philosophically* this development of individuals within the general conditions of existence of historically successive estates and classes, and with the general conceptions which were imposed upon them, one can easily imagine that what has evolved in these individuals is the Species, or Man, or that it is they who have constituted Man: an illusion which gives history some sharp blows to the ears. One can then conceive of these various estates and classes as specifications of a universal expression, as subsidiary forms of the Species, as phases of the evolution of Man. (The proposition that occurs often with Saint Max, that each person is what he is thanks to the state, is essentially the same as that which asserts that the bourgeois individual is only an example of the bourgeoisie; the proposition presupposes that the *class* of the bourgeoisie already exists prior to the individuals who constitute it.)*

This subsumption of individuals within certain classes can not be suppressed until a class has formed that no longer has any particular class interest to advance against the ruling class.

[Relation of the state and law to property]

In the ancient world and in the Middle Ages, the first form of property is tribal property; with the Romans it is principally the effect of war; with the Germans it depends on the raising of livestock. With the ancient peoples, several tribes lived together in one city, hence tribal property appeared as state property, and the individual's right to it was merely *possessio*. This 'possession', however, was restricted, as was tribal property in general, to property in land only. Private property properly so-called originates with the ancients, as with

---

* Marginal note by Marx: With the philosophers, preexistence of the class.

modern peoples, in movable property. (Slavery and community, *Dominium ex jure Quiritum*: property in conformity with Roman civil law.) With those peoples who arose during the Middle Ages, tribal property developed through various stages – feudal landed property, corporative movable property, manufacturing capital – to modern capital conditioned by large industry and universal competition: private property in its pure state, which has shed all resemblance of community and has eliminated all influence of the state on the development of property. To this modern form of private property corresponds the modern state, which is gradually purchased through taxes by private property owners and completely falls into their hands through state debt, and whose existence has become entirely dependent, through the rise and fall of state bonds on the stock exchange, on the commercial credit granted the state by private owners, the bourgeois. Because the bourgeoisie is a *class* [*Klasse*], and no longer an *estate* [*Stand*], it is forced to organise itself no longer locally, but nationally, and to give its average interest a universal form. With the emancipation of private property from the community the state achieved a particular existence next to and outside of civil society; but it is nothing more than the form of organisation which the bourgeois are forced to give themselves externally as well as internally, to mutually guarantee their property and their interests. Today the independence of the state exists only in those countries in which the estates that have been eliminated in more progressive countries still have a role to play, and where, consequently, a mixture exists in which no part of the population can assure its dominance over the others. This, in particular, is the case in Germany. The most complete example of the modern state is North America. Recent French, English, and American writers all declare that the state exists only for the sake of private property, so that this thesis has even entered public consciousness.

Because the state is the form in which the individuals of a ruling class assert and validate their common interests, the form in which the entire civil society of an epoch is summarised, it follows that all of the common institutions are mediated by the state and receive a political form. Thus the illusion that the law rests on the will, and indeed on the *free* will, divorced from its real basis. Similarly, right is then reduced to law.

At the same time, private right [or civil law: *Privatrecht*] develops along with private property out of the dissolution of the natural community. With the Romans the development of private property and private right had no industrial and commercial consequences, because their entire mode of production stayed the same. With modern peoples, the dissolution of the feudal community by industry and commerce marked, with the rise of private property and private right, the beginning of a new phase that was capable of further development. Thus Amalfi, the first city in the Middle Ages to pursue an extensive maritime commerce, also formed the code of maritime law. First in Italy and later in other countries, as soon as industry and commerce had given new development to private property, an already perfected Roman civil law was taken up again and elevated to a position of authority. Later, when the bourgeoisie had attained so much power that the princes adopted its interests in order to topple the feudal nobility with the help of the bourgeoisie, there began in all countries – in France in the sixteenth century – the veritable development of law, which proceeded everywhere except England on the basis of the Roman code. Even in England principles of Roman law had to be incorporated into the further development of the civil law (especially with moveable property). – (Not to be forgotten: law does not have a history of its own any more than religion does.)

In civil law the existing property relations are said to be the results of the general will. The *jus utendi et abutendi*, the right of unrestricted use, itself expresses on the one hand the fact that private property has become thoroughly independent from the community, and on the other the illusion that private property itself rests solely on the private will, on the right of utterly free disposition of the thing. In practice, *abuti*, abuse, has very definite economic limits for the private owner, if he does not want to see his property, and with it his *jus abutendi*, his right to abuse, pass into other hands; for in general the thing, considered simply in relation to this will, is no thing at all, but becomes an object, an actual property, only in commerce, and independently of right (a *relation* which the philosophers call an idea). <(*Relation for the philosophers = Idea*. The sole relation they know is '*of* Man' to himself, and therefore all actual relations become, for them, ideas.)> This juridical illusion, which reduces right to the mere will, necessarily leads in the further development of property relations to someone's being able to have a juridical title to a thing without actually having the thing. If, for example, the revenue from a parcel of land is eliminated through competition, its owner certainly retains his juridical title to it, including the *jus utendi et abutendi*. But he can not do anything with it, as a land owner he owns nothing, unless he otherwise has sufficient capital to cultivate his land. This same illusion of the jurists explains the fact that for them and for every juridical code, individuals enter into relations with one another (for example, into contracts) in a purely accidental way, that they are relations of the type that one can enter or not as a matter of choice, and that the content of the relations rests entirely on the individual caprice of the contracting parties. Each time new forms of commerce have arisen through the development of industry and trade, e.g. insurance etc. companies, the law was required to include them among the types of property acquisition.

[Towards the abolition of labour and of the state]

The transformation of personal aptitudes (relations) into material powers through the division of labour cannot be superseded by banishing from the mind the universal conception of this phenomenon, but only by the individuals taking charge of these material powers and superseding the division of labour. This is not possible without the community. Only in the community do the means exist for each individual to develop his abilities in all directions; thus, only in the community does personal freedom become possible. In previous surrogates of the community, in the state, etc., personal freedom existed only for those individuals who had developed within the conditions of the ruling classes and only insofar as they were members of these classes. The semblance of community into which individuals previously united themselves always acquired its own independence over against these individuals; and moreover, being a union of one class against another, it was for the dominated class not only a completely illusory community but also a new fetter. In a real community individuals simultaneously achieve their freedom in and through their association.

Individuals always based their efforts on themselves, but, naturally, within the limits of their given historical conditions and relationships, and not on the 'pure' individual in the ideologues' sense. But in the course of historical development and precisely by reason of the fact, inevitable within the division of labour, that social relations take on fixity and independence, difference emerged between the life of each individual as personal and as subsumed under some branch of labour and the conditions pertaining to it. It is not that wealthy persons or capitalists, for example, cease to be persons, but rather that their personality is entirely conditioned and determined by well-defined class relationships, whose difference appears primarily in the contrast with another class, and is first revealed to themselves when they go bankrupt. Within a feudal estate (and even more in the tribe) this phenomenon is still hidden; a nobleman, for example, remains always a nobleman, a commoner always a commoner, a quality inseparable from his individuality, whatever his other conditions or relationships. The personal individual differentiated from the class individual, the contingency of the conditions of life for the individual, first occurs with the appearance of the class which is itself a product of the bourgeoisie. The competition of individuals who struggle among themselves generates and develops this contingency as such. The reason individuals have the notion that they are freer under the domination of the bourgeoisie than before is because their conditions of life are contingent; in reality they are naturally less free, because they are more subjected to the power of material things. The difference between the feudal order or estate and the class is most manifest in the opposition between the bourgeoisie and the proletariat. When the estate of the urban citizen, of the *Bürger*, corporations, etc. arose in opposition to the landed nobility, their condition of existence – movable property and the handicraft labour that had existed implicitly even before their separation from their feudal associations – appeared as something positive, asserted as valid in opposition to feudal landed property, and for that reason also from the first had its own kind of feudal form. To be sure, the runaway serfs treated their previous servitude as something contingent to their personality. In this, however, they only did the same thing that is done by everyone from a class that is freeing itself from its fetters; and then they freed themselves not as a class, but as individuals. Further, they did not leave the realm of the estate structure but rather merely formed a new estate and retained their previous mode of labour in their new position, developing it further by freeing it from the traditional fetters which no longer corresponded to the development they had already achieved.

With the proletarians, on the other hand, their own condition of life, i.e. labour, and with that all the conditions of existence of today's society, have become for them utterly contingent, over which the individual proletarians have no control <and over which no *social* organisation can give them control.> And the contrast between the personality of the individual proletarian and the condition of life that has been forced upon him, i.e. labour, is evident to the proletarian himself, precisely because he has been sacrificed from his youth onward, and because he lacks all opportunity to achieve within his class those conditions that would raise him to another one.

N.B. [It is] not to be forgotten that the serfs' very need to exist, and the impossibility of large-scale economy due to the distribution of *allotments* to the serfs, very quickly reduced the obligations of the serfs toward their feudal masters to an average of payments in kind and compulsory labour. This made it possible for the serf to accumulate some movable property, thus facilitating his flight from the estate of his master and giving him some prospect of advancement as a *Stadtbürger*, an urban citizen; it also generated a hierarchy among the serfs, such that the serfs who had fled soon were already demi-bourgeois [*halbe Bürger*]. Obviously then, the serfs who knew a trade had a better chance to acquire movable property.

Consequently, while the fugitive serfs wished only to develop and affirm freely their already existing conditions of life, and for this reason in the end achieved only the status of free labourers, the proletarians, to achieve and validate their personal worth, must supersede the condition of existence which has been theirs until now, and which is that of the entire previous society, i.e. labour. Thus they find themselves in direct opposition to the state, the form in which the individuals of society have up to now collectively expressed themselves; and they must overthrow the state to achieve fulfillment of their personality.

From all that has gone before, it follows that the communal relationship into which the individuals of a class entered, and which was conditioned by their common interests in face of a third party, was always a community to which these individuals belonged only as average individuals, only insofar as they lived within the conditions of existence of their class: a relationship in which they participated not as individuals but as members of a class. With the community of revolutionary proletarians, on the other hand, who take under their control their own conditions of existence and those of all members of society, it is the exact opposite: in this community individuals take part as individuals. It is precisely the union of individuals (presupposing, naturally, the presently developed forces of production) that puts the conditions of free development and movement of the individuals under their control, conditions which were previously left to chance and had attained autonomy over against the single individuals precisely because of their separation as individuals and because of the kind of union they had, necessitated by the division of labour; conditions which, because of the individuals' separation, had become an alien bond for them. Until now, the union was in no way a voluntary one – as described, for example, in [Rousseau's] *Contrat social*, but rather an association dictated by necessity (compare, for example, the formation of the state in North America and the republics of South America) aimed at setting the conditions within which individuals may enjoy contingency. It is this right to untroubled enjoyment of contingency, within certain conditions, that has up to now been called 'personal freedom'. – These conditions of existence are, naturally, the forces of production and the forms of interaction proper to each epoch, and nothing more.

[Conclusion: towards the community of complete individuals]

What distinguishes communism from all previous movements is that it overturns the basis of all previous relations of production and commerce, and that, for the first time, it consciously treats all the presuppositions previously considered natural [*naturwüchsigen*] as being in fact creations of earlier generations of men, thus stripping them of their naturality [*Naturwüchsigkeit*] and subordinating them to the power of united individuals. That is why its institution, its establishment, is essentially economic; it is the material establishment of the conditions of union; it turns the existing conditions into conditions of union. The enduring thing that communism creates is precisely the real basis for making it impossible that anything exist independently of the individuals, insofar as this enduring thing, this real basis, is nothing but the product of the previous interaction of the individuals themselves. Consequently, the communists treat in a practical manner, i.e. as inorganic conditions, the conditions generated through previous production and commerce, without however deluding themselves that it was the plan or the destiny of previous generations to furnish material to them, and without believing [that] these conditions had been considered inorganic by the individuals who created them. The difference between a personal individual and a contingent individual is not a matter of conceptual distinction, but an historical fact. This distinction has different meanings at different times, e.g. the estate as something accidental to the individual in the eighteenth century, and more or less the same thing with the family. It is a distinction that we do not have to make for every era, but rather one that each era itself makes among the various elements at hand, and to be sure, not according to the concept, but rather compelled by the material conflicts of life. What appears to be contingent to later periods in contrast to earlier ones, even among the elements inherited from the earlier, is a form of interaction that corresponded to a specific development of the productive forces. The relations of these forces of production to the form of interaction is the relation of the form of interaction to the <activity or active participation> of the individuals. (The basic form of this participation is naturally the material one, upon which all others, intellectual, political, religious, etc. depend. The shape of material life differs, naturally, each time depending on the needs that have already developed, and both the generation as well as the satisfaction of these needs is itself an historical process not found with any sheep or dog (Stirner's perverse main argument *adversus hominem*),* although sheep and dogs in their present form are certainly, but in spite of themselves, products of an historical process.) The conditions under which individuals interact with one another, as long as the conflict has not yet occurred, are conditions that belong to their individuality and are not external for them, conditions under which these definite individuals, living in definite relationships, can alone produce their material life and what goes with it; these are therefore conditions of their self-activity [*Selbstbetätigung*] and are produced by this self-activity.† The definite conditions under which they produce thus correspond, as long as the conflict or antagonism has not yet occurred, to their real restrictedness, their limited existence, whose limitedness is first revealed with the appearance of the antagonism and thus exists for later generations. At that time, i.e. later, this condition looks like a contingent fetter and the consciousness of the fact that it is a fetter is then attributed also to the earlier period.

---

* In *The Ego and its Property (Der Einzige und sein Eigenthum)*, 1845, p. 443.
† Marginal note by Marx: Production of the form of interaction itself.

These various conditions, which at first appear as conditions of self-activity and later as fetters on it, constitute in the entire historical development, a coherent succession of forms of interaction, whose coherence consists in the fact that in the place of earlier forms of interaction that have become fetters, a new one is put, which corresponds to the more developed productive forces and the advanced manner of self-activity of individuals, which in its turn becomes a fetter and is itself replaced by another. Because these conditions at every step correspond to the simultaneous development of the productive forces, their history is at the same time the history of developing productive forces that were taken over by each new generation, and so too the history of the development of the powers of the individuals themselves.

Because this development proceeds naturally [*naturwüchsig*], i.e. is not subordinated to an overall plan of freely united individuals, it goes forward in various localities, tribes, nations, branches of labour, etc., of which each develops at first independently of the others and only gradually enters into ties with them. Further, it proceeds only very slowly; the various stages and interests are never completely overcome, but rather are merely subordinated to the victorious interests and drag themselves along with these interests for centuries. It follows from this that even within a nation individuals, even apart from their conditions of wealth and ability [*Vermogensverhältnissen*], have completely different developments, and that an earlier interest whose characteristic form of interaction has already been pushed aside by a later form characteristic of a subsequent interest, retains traditional power within the illusory community (state, law) that confronts individuals as autonomous: this power, in the final analysis, can be broken only by a revolution. This also explains why with respect to individual points that allow for a more general synthesis, consciousness can sometimes appear to be further advanced than the contemporary empirical conditions, so that in the struggles of a later epoch support can be found by appealing to the authority of earlier theoreticians.

On the other hand, development proceeds very rapidly in countries which, like North America, begin in an already developed period of history. Such countries have no other natural presuppositions except the individuals who settle there and who were prompted to resettle because the forms of interaction in their former lands no longer correspond to their needs. Such countries begin, therefore, with the most advanced individuals of the old countries and thus with the most developed form of interaction corresponding to these individuals, even before this form of interaction can establish itself in the old countries. (Personal energy of the individuals within individual nations – Germans and Americans – Energy through the mixing of races alone – hence the traces of cretinism in the Germans – in France, England, etc. foreign peoples are transported into an already developed terrain, in America into a brand new one, in Germany the native population quietly remained where it is.) This is the case with all colonies which are not simply military or trading stations. Carthage, the Greek colonies, and Iceland in the eleventh and twelfth centuries offer examples of this. A similar phenomenon occurs in conquest, when a form of interaction developed elsewhere is brought ready-made to a conquered country; while in its homeland it was still burdened with interests and relationships of earlier epochs, here, in the conquered land, it can and has to be imposed fully and without hindrance, if only to secure lasting power for the conquerors. (England and Naples after the Norman conquests, when they received the most complete form of feudal organisation.)

In large industry and competition all of the conditions of existence of individuals, all of their limitations and particularisms, are fused together into the two elementary forms: private property and labour. With money each form of interaction and interaction itself is imposed on individuals as contingent, as a matter of chance. Consequently, what the existence of money already signifies is the fact that all interaction up to now was only interaction of individuals under specific conditions, not of individuals as individuals. These conditions are now reduced to two, accumulated labour – or private property – and actual labour. If one or the other ceases, interaction stops. The modern economists themselves, e.g. Sismondi, Cherbuliez, etc. oppose the *association des individus* with the *association des capitaux*. On the other hand the individuals themselves are completely subordinated to the division of labour and so are made completely dependent on one another. Private property insofar as it is opposed to labour within labour itself, develops by the necessity of accumulation; and if in the beginning it still retains the form of the community, in the course of its development it increasingly approaches the modern form of private property. The division of labour brings with it from the very beginning a division also in the *conditions* of labour, the tools and materials, and with that, the dispersion of the accumulated capital to various owners and therefore the division between capital and labour, and the various forms of property itself. The more the division of labour develops and the more accumulation grows, the sharper this division between capital and labour. The existence of labour itself presupposes this division.

Two facts are to be seen here. First of all, the productive forces appear to be completely independent and torn away from individuals, as a separate world alongside of individuals, a phenomenon which is to be explained thus: the individuals whose forces they are, are scattered and opposed to one another, while on the other hand these forces are actual only in the interaction and the connection of these individuals. In other words, on the one hand a totality of productive forces which have taken on, as it were, an objective form and are for the individuals themselves no longer their own forces but rather the forces of private property, and thus of the individuals alone who are property owners. In no previous period have productive forces assumed this form indifferent to the interaction of individuals as individuals, because their interaction itself was still a restricted one. On the other hand, opposed to these productive forces, stands the majority of individuals, from whom the forces have been torn away and who, robbed of any genuine content in their life, have therefore become abstract individuals, but who for that reason are for the first time in a position to enter into association with one another *as individuals*.

The sole connection they still have to their productive forces and to their own existence, i.e. labour, has lost for them all semblance of self-activity and sustains their life only by crippling it. Whereas in earlier periods self-activity and the creation of material life were separated in that they were pursued by different persons and the creation of material life was still considered, because of the restrictedness of the individuals themselves, to be a subordinate form of self-activity, they are now divided such that generally speaking material life appears as the goal, and the creation of this material life, i.e. labour (which is now the sole possible, although – as we have seen – negative form of self-activity) appears as the means.

Consequently, things have gone so far that individuals have to appropriate the existing totality of productive forces, not only to achieve their self-activity, but simply to secure their existence. This appropriation is conditioned in the first place by the object to be appropriated, i.e. the productive forces that are developed to a totality and can exist only within a universal [system of] interaction. From this perspective alone, this appropriation must therefore already have a universal character in keeping with the productive forces and the interaction. The appropriation of these forces is itself nothing but the development of individual capabilities that correspond to the material instruments of production. The appropriation of a totality of instruments of production is therefore the development of a totality of capabilities in the individuals themselves. Further, this appropriation is conditioned by the appropriating individuals. Only the contemporary proletariat, which is completely excluded from all self-activity, is in a position to achieve a complete, and no longer restricted, self-activity that consists in the appropriation of a totality of productive forces together with the development of a totality of capabilities. All previous revolutionary appropriations were restricted; individuals whose self-activity was restricted by a limited instrument of production and a limited interaction, appropriated this limited instrument of production and for this reason brought it only to a new form of limitation. Their instrument of production became their property, but they themselves continued to be subordinated to the division of labour and to their own instrument of production. With all previous appropriations a mass of individuals continued to be subordinated to a single instrument of production; with the proletarians' appropriation a mass of instruments of production must be subordinated to everyone. Modern universal interaction can be subordinated to individuals only by being subordinated to all of them.

Additionally, the appropriation is conditioned by the required manner and means of its achievement. It can be achieved only through an association or union, which itself, because of the very character of the proletariat, must be a universal one, and by a revolution in which, on the one hand, the power of the existing mode of production and interaction and of the existing social structure is toppled, and, on the other hand, the universal character of the proletariat is developed, along with the energy it needs to carry through the appropriation; in sum, by a revolution in which the proletariat divests itself of every remaining vestige of its previous social position.

At this stage self-activity coincides for the first time with material life, which corresponds to the development of individuals into total individuals and to the elimination of all naturality [*Naturwüchsigkeit*].

At this time the transformation of labour into self-activity corresponds to the transformation of previously restrained interaction into an interaction of individuals as such. With the appropriation of the totality of productive forces by individuals united together, private property ceases to exist. Whereas in previous history a particular condition appeared to be accidental, now it is the particularisation of the individuals themselves, the private profession of each in particular, that has become itself accidental.

The philosophers have conceptualised individuals who are no longer subordinated to the division of labour as an ideal, called 'Man', and have conceived the entire process, which we have treated here, as the process of the development 'of Man', such that 'Man' is substituted for the earlier individuals of each historical stage and is portrayed as the driving force of history. The entire process was thus understood as the process of the self-estrangement 'of Man', and this essentially because the average individual of a later stage is attributed to the earlier ones and the later consciousness is attributed to earlier individuals. By means of this inversion, which from the very beginning abstracted from actual conditions, it was possible to turn all of history into a process of the development of consciousness.

[Results]

Finally we get the following results from the conception of history presented here: (1) In the development of the productive forces a stage arises in which productive forces and means of interaction are called forth which, in the existing conditions, cause only harm, i.e. are no longer forces of production but rather forces of destruction (machinery and money). Another consequence, connected with this, is the emergence of a class that must bear all the burdens of society without enjoying its benefits; a class which is forced out of society and into the most resolute opposition to all the other classes; a class which comprises the majority of all members of society and from which emanates the consciousness of the necessity of a thorough revolution, communist consciousness, a consciousness which naturally can also form among the other classes able to appreciate the position of this class;

(2) the conditions on which depends the employment of specific productive forces are those imposed by the rule of a determinate

social class whose social power, derived from its material possessions, finds its expression, at once idealistic and *practical*, in the existing form of state; that is why every revolutionary struggle is directed against a class whose domination has endured too long;

(3) all previous revolutions have left intact the mode of activity; they sought only another distribution of this activity, a new distribution of labour to other persons. In contrast, the communist revolution is directed against the previous form of activity, eliminates [*beseitigt*] *labour*, and abolishes [*aufhebt*] the rule of all classes along with the classes themselves, because it is achieved by the class which does not count as a class in society, is not recognised as a class, is already the expression within contemporary society of the dissolution of all classes, nationalities, etc.;

(4) to produce on a mass scale this communist consciousness, and to attain the goal itself, a transformation touching the mass of men is required, which can take place only in a practical movement, in a *revolution*. Consequently the revolution is necessary not only because the *ruling* class can be overthrown in no other way, but also because only in a revolution can the *overthrowing* class successfully rid itself of all the old muck and become capable of giving society a new foundation.

From *Poverty of Philosophy* (1847)

Big industry brings together in one place a crowd of people who are unknown to one another. Competition divides them in regard to their interests. But maintaining their wages, this common interest which they have against their master, unites them in a single thought of resistance – *coalition*. Thus, the coalition always has a double purpose, that of bringing the competition among them to an end, in order to be able to mount a general competition against the capitalist. If the first aim of the resistance was only to maintain wages, to the extent that the capitalists in their turn unite in the thought of repression, the coalitions, at first isolated, form themselves into groups and, in the face of the always united capital, the maintenance of the association becomes more important for them than the maintenance of wages. So true is this, that the English economists are all astonished to see the workers sacrifice a good part of their wages on behalf of the associations which, in the eyes of the economists, were established only to advance wages. In this struggle – veritable civil war – all the elements necessary for a coming battle are united and developed. At this point, the association assumes a political character.

Economic conditions had first transformed the mass of the country into labourers. The domination of capital has created for this mass a common situation and common interests. Thus this mass is already a class *vis-à-vis* capital, but not yet for itself. In the struggle, only some of whose phases we have indicated, this mass unites itself and it constitutes itself into a class for itself. The interests it defends become class interests. But the struggle of class with class is a political struggle.

In the bourgeoisie, we have two phases to distinguish: that during which it constituted itself into a class under the regime of feudalism and of absolute monarchy, and that where, already constituted as a class, it overthrew feudalism and the monarchy in order to make society into bourgeois society. The first of these phases was the longer and required the greater efforts. It too had begun with partial coalitions against the feudal lords.

Many studies have been done to retrace the different historical phases that the bourgeoisie has gone through from the commune to its constitution as a class. But when it comes to giving an exact account of the strikes and of the coalitions and other forms in which the proletarians effect before our eyes their organisation as a class, some are seized by real fear, while others affect a *transcendental* disdain.

An oppressed class is the vital condition of every society founded on the antagonism of classes. The emancipation of the oppressed class thus necessarily implies the creation of a new society. For the oppressed class to be able to emancipate itself, it is necessary that the already acquired productive powers and the existing social relations can no longer exist side by side. Of all the instruments of production, the greatest productive power is the revolutionary class itself. The organisation of the revolutionary elements as a class presupposes the existence of all the productive forces that can be engendered in the bosom of the old society.

Is this to say that after the fall of the old society, there will be a new class domination culminating in a new political power? No.

The condition of the emancipation of the working class is the abolition of every class, just as the condition of the emancipation of the third estate, of the bourgeois order, was the abolition of all the estates and all the orders.

In the course of its development, the working class will substitute for the old civil society an association that will exclude classes and their antagonism, and there will no longer be political power properly so-called, because political power is precisely the official *resumé* of the antagonisms within civil society.

Meanwhile, the antagonism between the proletariat and the bourgeoisie is a struggle of class with class, a struggle which, carried to its highest expression, is a total revolution. Moreover, why should it be surprising that a society founded on the opposition of classes would culminate in brutal *contradiction*, in the shock of body against body, as its final denouement?

Do not say that the social movement excludes the political movement. There is never any political movement which is not at the same time social.

Only in an order of things where there will no longer be classes and the antagonism of classes, will *social evolutions* cease to be *political revolutions*. Until then, on the eve of every general reordering of society, the last word of social science will always be:

'Combat or death, bloody struggle or annihilation. Thus is the question inexorably put.' (George Sand.)*

* G. Sand, *Jean Ziska. Épisode de la guerre des Hussites. Revue indépendante*. Bk VII (1843), p. 484.

Address on Poland
(given at the international meeting of the 'Fraternal Democrats' on 29 November 1847, on the occasion of the 17th anniversary of the Polish Uprising of 1830)

The unity and brotherhood of nations is a phrase much used today by all parties, as, for example, the middle class advocates of free trade. To be sure, there exists a certain form of brotherhood among the bourgeois classes of all nations. It is the brotherhood of the oppressors against the oppressed, of the exploiters against the exploited. As the bourgeois class of a given country is united and bound by ties of brotherhood against the proletarians of that country, despite competition and the struggle among the members of the bourgeoisie themselves, so also are the bourgeois of all countries bound and united against the proletarians of all countries, despite their mutual antagonism and competition in the world market. Peoples can actually unite only if they have a common interest. They can have a common interest only if present property relations are done away with, for present property relations are the determining cause of the exploitation going on among peoples: To do away with present property relations is the interest of the working class alone. Moreover, only it has the means to this goal. The victory of the proletariat over the bourgeoisie, therefore, is at the same time the victory over the national and industrial conflicts which today place the various peoples in opposition to one another. For that reason, the victory of the proletariat over the bourgeoisie is simultaneously the signal of liberation for all oppressed nations.

To be sure, the old Poland is gone, and we would be the last ones to wish for its restoration. But not only is the old Poland gone. The old Germany, the old France, the old England, the entire old society is gone. But the loss of the old society is no loss for those in the old society who had nothing to lose, and in all contemporary countries this is the case for the vast majority. Much more have they everything to gain by the downfall of the old society, which is the condition for the creation of a new society, one that no longer rests on the opposition of classes.

Of all countries, England is the one in which the antithesis between proletariat and bourgeoisie is the most developed. For that reason the victory of the English proletarians over the English bourgeoisie is decisive for the victory of all oppressed peoples over their oppressors. Thus Poland is not to be freed in Poland, but rather in England. You Chartists, therefore, have no need to proclaim pious wishes about the liberation of nations. Just strike your own enemies here at home and you will know with pride that you have struck a blow at the entire old society.

Index

Index

Index

Index

Cambridge Texts in the History of Political Thought

Titles published in the series thus far

Aristotle *The Politics* (edited by Stephen Everson)
Arnold *Culture and Anarchy and Other Writings* (edited by Stefan
  Collini)
Bakunin *Statism and Anarchy* (edited by Marshall Shatz)
Baxter *A Holy Commonwealth* (edited by William Lamont)
Bentham *A Fragment on Government* (introduction by Ross Harrison)
Bernstein *The Preconditions of Socialism* (edited by Henry Tudor)
Bodin *On Sovereignty* (edited by Julian H. Franklin)
Bossuet *Politics Drawn from the Very Words of Holy Scripture* (edited by
  Patrick Riley)
Burke *Pre-Revolutionary Writings* (edited by Ian Harris)
Cicero *On Duties* (edited by M. T. Griffin and E. M. Atkins)
Constant *Political Writings* (edited by Biancamaria Fontana)
Diderot *Political Writings* (edited by John Hope Mason and Robert
  Wokler)
The Dutch Revolt (edited by Martin van Gelderen)
Filmer *Patriarcha and Other Writings* (edited by Johann P. Sommerville)
Gramsci *Pre-Prison Writings* (edited by Richard Bellamy)
Guicciardini *Dialogue on the Government of Florence* (edited by Alison
  Brown)
Harrington *A Commonwealth of Oceana* and *A System of Politics* (edited
  by J. G. A. Pocock)
Hegel *Elements of the Philosophy of Right* (edited by Allen W. Wood and
  H. B. Nisbet)
Hobbes *Leviathan* (edited by Richard Tuck)
Hobhouse *Liberalism and Other Writings* (edited by James Meadowcroft)
Hooker *Of the Laws of Ecclesiastical Polity* (edited by A. S. McGrade)
John of Salisbury *Policraticus* (edited by Cary Nederman)
Kant *Political Writings* (edited by H. S. Reiss and H. B. Nisbet)
Knox *On Rebellion* (edited by Roger A. Mason)
Lawson *Politica sacra et civilis* (edited by Conal Condren)
Leibniz *Political Writings* (edited by Patrick Riley)
Locke *Two Treatises of Government* (edited by Peter Laslett)
Loyseau *A Treatise of Orders and Plain Dignities* (edited by Howell A.
  Lloyd)
Luther and Calvin on Secular Authority (edited by Harro Höpfl)
Machiavelli *The Prince* (edited by Quentin Skinner and Russell Price)
Malthus *An Essay on the Principle of Population* (edited by Donald
  Winch)